JN144952

Praise for the Life

Works of Architects
Takao Habuka
with mentor Von Jour Caux

生命の讃歌

建築家　梵 寿綱＋羽深隆雄

刊行によせて

　2人の作品集の刊行を構想したのは2006年に作品集『和風モダン建築デザイン術』を六耀社から既刊し、それから2、3年程過ぎた頃であった。今出来ることを最大の効果で残すことが2人の作品集の刊行であった。

　意志が固まり準備に入ってから思いのほか時間がかかった。いつもは方向が決まれば、談論風発に最短距離を走るのが得意なのだが…

　田中さん（梵寿綱）とはお互い10歳ほどの差だが、膠漆の関係で、若い時に仕込んで頂き感謝している。仕事はもちろん生活でも兄弟の様に行動を共にしていた。しかし、この20年ほどは僅かに入ってくる情報のみであった。今ここで2人の作品集をつくることは、フロイトの超自我に類似するように思える。

　それは時代や状況によって変わることではなく、常に内に潜んでいる無意識が甦ることである。

　振り返ることは容易ではあるが、過去を自ら説明することはここではせず、論評をお願いした3氏のそれぞれの視点からの解説に任せることにした。切り口の異なる論評が加わることで、互い手法は似ているようで、全く別のもので似てもいない、複雑怪奇なものだが、それを現すのに3氏の解説に優るものはなく、故に刊行することに意味があると論決した。

羽深隆雄

Forword

The idea of publishing a compilation of our work together came about two or three years after the compilation "Modern Japanese Style Architecture" was published by Rikuyosha in 2006. Publishing the compilation would preserve with maximum effect what we could do now. A lot of time passed after our intentions became firm and preparations began. Ordinarily, once the course was set, I was successful at running the shortest distance with spirited conversation, but … .

Although Tanaka-san (Von Jour Caux) and I are about 10 years apart, our relationship was close. I am grateful for his instruction in my younger years. We worked and spent time together like brothers, although the last 20 years were marked with only minimal notices. Creating a compilation of our work feels similar to Freud's super ego: the restoration of the subconscious that always lies within, without any change over time or circumstances.

The recollecting was easy, but we did not recount the past on our own. Instead, those observations were delegated to three authors, whose reviews we sought. The addition of different views showed their approaches to be seemingly similar, but they were actually entirely different. The subject was difficult and mysterious. I have concluded that their commentary, nevertheless, could not be topped, and has made this publication meaningful.

Takao Habuka

005 刊行によせて
羽深隆雄

008 生命讃歌宣言
梵 寿綱

羽深隆雄

013 「木の狩人」の系譜——羽深隆雄
細野 透

022 湧雲の望楼

048 台付欅の家

058 手業の装飾——羽深隆雄の意匠
細野 透

068 仙寿庵

078 四季彩一力

086 銀座久兵衛

104 会津中央病院

134 **論考1 素材・手仕事・装飾——梵 寿綱と仲間たち**
鈴木博之

梵 寿綱

154 ある寿舞

156 インディアナの家

160 ある美瑠

162 樹下美人図考

166 アート・コンプレックス運動について
梵 寿綱

168 Art Complex Ⅰ　阿維智

174 Art Complex Ⅱ　秘羅樀

180 Art Complex Ⅲ　斐醴祈

186 Art Complex Ⅳ　和世陀

192 Art Complex Ⅴ　無量寿舞

198 Art Complex Ⅵ　精霊の館

206 Art Complex Ⅶ　和泉の扉

210 Art Complex Ⅷ　きらめく器

214 Art Complex Ⅸ　性源寺

220 Art Complex Ⅹ　舞都和亜

224 **論考2 頭と手の邂逅——梵 寿綱・羽深隆雄論**
倉方俊輔

254 掲載建築一覧

256 略歴

258 あとがき
梵 寿綱

もくじ

Contents

005 Forword
Takao Habuka

009 Message for the Praise of Life
Von Jour Caux

Takao Habuka

018 Takao Habuka—Lineage of a Tree Hunter
Dr. Toru Hosono

022 Wakigumo no Boroh

048 House of Zelkova

064 Handcrafted Ornamentation:
Designwork of Takao Habuka **Dr. Toru Hosono**

068 Senjuan Hotel

078 Shikisai Ichiriki Hotel

086 Ginza Kyubey

104 Aidu Chuo Hospital

145 **Essay 1** Material, Handwork, Ornamentation:
Von Jour Caux and his Troupe **Dr. Hiroyuki Suzuki**

Von Jour Caux

154 Family Home of Esotericism

156 Touch of Culture

160 Practice of Mandala

162 Beauty under the Tree

167 Art Complex Movement
Von Jour Caux

168 Art Complex I   Gladiator's Nest

174 Art Complex II   Hiraki

180 Art Complex III   Condo Hiraki

186 Art Complex IV   Waseda el Dorado

192 Art Complex V   Eternal Home

198 Art Complex VI   Mundi Animus

206 Art Complex VII   Door to Fountain

210 Art Complex VIII   Royal Vessel

214 Art Complex IX   Cradle Temple

220 Art Complex X   Trip to Carnival

241 **Essay 2** Happenstance of Head and Hand:
Treatise on Von Jour Caux and Takao Habuka **Dr. Shunsuke Kurakata**

254 Data

256 Biography

259 Epilogue
Von Jour Caux

生命讃歌宣言

人類の歴史の中で、建築は常に日常の社会に深く根を下ろしながらも
さらにそれを超えた次元への架橋の役割を果たし
永遠の実在への人々の理念と信念とを象徴する
文化的装置として創造されてきた。

そして決して便宜的な社会や経済の要求の為にではなく
生きる時代の文化や風土や民衆を讃歌する
記念的構築物として築かれてきたのだ。
今日の如く多様に変化する便宜的な社会の枠組みを
弥縫するためのコンセプトに汲々とする現代建築に
根源的な創造性を期待することは不可能である。
この失われた時代の中で、建築家・梵 寿綱と羽深隆雄は
夢と神話を象徴し芸術と工芸を建築空間に統合する手段を模索し、
ささやかながら実践を通じて営為の成果を社会に問いかけ続けてきた。

機能主義の旗印の下に金融経済や産業構造に
奉仕するビルディング・デザイナーたちは、
狂信的な伝道師として、国際的な表現というコンセプトを旗印に、
人間にとって不可欠な文化や習俗の伝承を否定してきた。
しかし、人間の生命の衝動は、歴史や文化や地域や伝承の形式の
相違を超えて通底しており、人類が存在する限り変わることはないのだ。

いつの時代でも予言的な創造者や革命的な思索家は、
人々に直接働きかけ、日常生活の価値転換という
神秘的経験へ人々を目覚めさせようと努めてきた。
人々の心を彩っているものは、宇宙にあまねく響く生命の鼓動である。
しかしこの彩りや響きは、五感や思考による理解を超えていて、
創作の役割をになう者たちの心の鏡に映し出され、
造形の姿や反映する光芒や共鳴する響きを得てはじめて、
人々の身体に所在する生命の泉・心と響きあう。

現実を超えたものに現実の姿を与えてその彼方にこそ
至福な世界の開示を信じる故に
建築家・梵 寿綱と羽深隆雄は天命に従い天職を全うして
今ここに建築における「生命讃歌」を宣言する。

梵 寿綱

Message for the Praise of Life

In every period throughout history, architecture has been
created as cultural devices, taking root in everyday society,
and deeply symbolizing human faith and belief toward eternal reality.
They have never been produced for economic reasons,
only for cultural, social, and visionary expressions.
Today, it is very rare to find even a fragment of such visions in
architecture throughout the world which is bent on the
concept for carrying out a makeshift framework of an expedient
society which changes constantly. Throughout the past decades,
architects Von Jour Caux and Takao Habuka formed a means of
synthesizing arts and crafts, symbolizing images and myths.
In frame of social and economic and politic structure whole our personal
beings are suppressed and unsettled and kept at distance psychologically
and emotionally. Today, the concept of International Architecture,
which is the symbol of the modern age, is in decline;
and the idea of the Universal Arch-type as an original being of
common sense nourished since ancient times.
It is known that the intense visions of incantation intermediates,
visionary creators, and revelatory philosophers directly act on people and
lead them to a unique experience of different spatial value.
These symbolic fragments drawn from the deep world are not related to
reality but are instead kept within a corner of people's consciousness.
They have the power to potentially revolutionize recognition of
substance by reacting with unconsciousness.
What is coloring people's heart is a beat of life which permeates
throughout the universe. However, this coloring and these sounds
which are beyond understanding through the senses or thinking,
are projected on the mirror of the heart of those who boil and twist the
role of creation, and are echoed within the spring and the heart of the life
which carries out the whereabouts to people's body only after obtaining
the figure and the shaft of light to reflect the modeling,
the resonating sound, and the suit.
Giving an actual figure to the things beyond reality and believing the
indication of extreme happiness in the world of Von Jour Caux and
Takao Habuka who are professed according to Providence Now,
we proudly declare the age of the Praise of Life in Architecture.

Von Jour Caux, 1992

Takao Habuka
羽深隆雄

新潟県上越市（旧東頸城郡牧村）宮口神社の欅と羽深昇。左手に持っているボールドは木のサンプルを抜きとる時に使う道具。
Zelkova and Noboru Habuka at Miyaguchi Shrine in Joetsu City (former Makimura, Higashi-kubiki County) in Niigata Prefecture. The tool that nemed board in Habuka's left hand is used to take core samples.

「木の狩人」の系譜──
羽深隆雄

文=細野 透

　羽深隆雄は、新潟県上越市（旧高田市）で製材所と材木屋を経営していた羽深昇の長男として生まれ、小さいときから父親に連れられて山に入り、木を伐採する現場を数多く回って歩いた。

木の狩人──羽深 昇

　かつて羽深昇という山師がいた。上越市から山に入った東頸城郡一帯で山持ちから山の木を買い、伐採し、製材し、大工や工務店に卸すことを主な仕事としていた。1917年（大正6年）に生まれ、2004年（平成16年）に87歳で没した（figs. 1-3）。

　山師とは、本来は「山で働く人」「山林の売買を業とする人」という意味の言葉なのだが、転じて「投機を好む人」「詐欺師」などとしても使われる。しかし、山に生えている木の側から見ると、さらに別の意味がある。山師とは「木の狩人」でもあるのだ。「木の狩人」に厳しい視線を向けられると、木はただ立ちすくんでしまうしかない。

　山持ちから立木を買い取ると、どの木を伐採するのかを決めるために、山師は山に入る。普通は山持ちと山を管理する山守との3人連れ。大木を見かけると、彼らの足はピタッと止まる。

樹齢は300年の檜
山師は五感で木を感じ取る──。

　この檜は、目通り（目の高さ）の木の周囲が1丈程あろうか

fig.3　1949年（昭和24年）。新潟県上越市（旧三和村）川浦の欅の前で。左端に羽深昇、右端に木挽。
Taken in 1949. In front of a Zelkova in Kawaura, Joetsu City (former Sanwa Village), Niigata Prefecture. Noboru Habuka (left) and a lumberjack (right).

fig.1　1937年（昭和12年）。新潟県上越市（旧東頸城郡牧村）高谷神社の欅。中央が羽深昇の父。
Taken in 1937. Zelkova at Takatani Shrine in Joetsu City (former Makimura, Higashi-kubiki County) in Niigata Prefecture. Noboru Habuka's father stands in the middle.

fig.2　1994年（平成6年）。新潟県上越市（旧高田市）稲田神社の欅。撮影=小林浩志
Taken in 1994. Zelkova at Inada Shrine in Joetsu City (former Takada City) in Niigata Prefecture. Photo by Hiroshi Kobayashi

（1丈とは10尺、1尺約30cm）、樹高が30mを優に超えている。樹齢は推定で300年を超える大木だ。木の足元は幹がごつごつと盛り上がって、大地にしっかりと根を張っている。檜は自ら下方の枝を落とすため、幹はすっくと立ち上がり、高さが15mを超えたあたりから枝が何本も張りだして、頂部にふんわりとした緑の傘を形作っている。実に見事な眺めである。

　木の皮はつやつやとして張りがあり、色もいいし手触りもいい。腰をかがめて、根元の土をほじくって調べると、土がさらさらしている。これなら水はけも良さそうだ。木の皮と土の状態から判断すると、木の肌は薄いピンク色で、年輪の幅が細かい目の詰んだ最上品ではないのか。

　幹に耳を当てる。シューッ、シューッ、シューッ。根から吸い上げた水分を、仮導管を通じて、枝の先端にある葉に送り込んでいる音が聞こえる。リズミカルで心地よい音だ。匂いをかいでみる。匂いもいい。この木は元気だぞ。

　最後に、木にボールトを捻じ込んで、直径5mm、長さ20〜25cm程度のサンプルを取ってみる（figs. 4 & 5）。やはり予想通りの最上品だった。

　「これはいい木だなぁ。伐りましょう」。

山師が心を決めた瞬間に、どうしたことか木の葉がザワザワと音を立て始める。別に風が吹いているわけではないのだが、木全体の葉が確かに小刻みに揺れている。ザワザワッ、ザワザワッ。なんだか異常な気配だ。狩人の標的にされ運命が決まったことが分かって、木が震えているとしか思えない。そのざわめきが静まったのは数分後のことだった。

巨樹の木霊

長い時代を生き抜いてきた威厳のある巨樹の懐に抱かれると、人間は芯から癒された気持ちになる。その理由としていろいろな説がある。

木の葉が光合成で出す酸素が体をリフレッシュさせてくれるため。あるいは、木の幹を流れる水のリズムが耳に優しいため。木をトントンと叩くとごく弱い微電流が流れるのだが、それにより木と心が通じ合えたような気持ちになれるため──。

人間は太古の時代には森に包まれて暮らしていたのだが、脳に刷り込まれていたその記憶が、巨樹に抱かれてよみがえるのだろうか。

fig.5 ボールトにより抜き出された材サンプル。撮影=小林浩志
Wood sample taken by the bold. Photo by Hiroshi Kobayashi

日本は八百万(やおよろず)の神の国だ。古来、山、海、川から恵みを得て生活していく中で、自然そのものを神として崇拝し、巨樹には霊が宿ると信じてきた。その木霊(こだま)の存在を感じとって、心が癒されたのかもしれない。

狩人の視線

山師の羽深昇が「切りましょう」と断を下した檜は、樹齢が300年を超えた程度でまだ名木とも巨樹ともいえないのだが、その檜が確かにザワザワと揺れて震えている。

羽深隆雄が中学生だった頃の忘れられない思い出がある。昇に連れられて神社にお参りに行ったときのことだ。参拝がすんだ後に境内を散歩していて、立派な木があったので立ち止まってなにげなく眺めていると、風もないのにいきなり木がザワザワと音をたて始めたのだ。隣に立っていた昇に「あの音はなにか」と聞くと、「俺が来たから木が震えているんだよ」と答えたそうだ。

神社には参拝に来たのであって、木を切りに来たのではない。しかし、山師の羽深昇が何気なく向けた視線は、やはり狩人の視線だった。木は大いなる脅威を感じとって、敏感に反応したのに違いない。

御神酒で静める

やがて、その日がきた。檜の大木を切り倒すと決めた日に、山師は木挽(こび)きや作業員とともに朝早く山に入る。まず、木の周囲をぐるりと歩きまわって、檜を倒す方向を見定める。木を斜面の下の方に倒すと、木に勢いがついて地面で跳ね返るために木が割れてしまう。よって、木は斜面の上の方に倒すのだが、窪地があると跳ね返る恐れがあるので、慎重に判断する必要がある。また、枝は倒すときのクッション材として調子を見て残す。

「あぁ、やはりその日が来てしまったようだ」。

気配を察した檜はまたザワザワと震え始めるのだが、山師

fig.4 ボールトをネジ込む。撮影=小林浩志
Inserting a bolt. Photo by Hiroshi Kobayashi

と木挽きが整列して頭を下げ、一升瓶から御神酒を木の足元にかけて、「これから切らしてもらいますよ」と声をかけると、観念したかのようにざわめきが静まっていく。

鋭くてもの悲しい泣き声

作業は枝打ちから始まる。高さは30mなのだが、木材がとれるのはそのうち下から5間半（約10m）まで、などと見当をつけて、上部の枝は倒すときのクッション材として残しながら木材をとる部分の枝を払っていく。

木挽きが腰に手斧をかけて、ロープ1本でスルスルと木に登っていく。枝を切るときには、付け根の下側から軽くチョーンと斧を入れ、付け根の上側からスパッときれいに切り落とす。下側から斧を入れるのは、木の皮を傷つけないための配慮だ。枝打ちがすむと、最上部の幹は鋸で切り落としてしまう。

次に、檜を倒すと決めた方向の幹の足元を、楔状（＜型）にカットする。そして、その反対方向から大きな鋸を入れ、シャッシャー、シャッシャーと切り始める。鋸がある程度入ったら、切り口から木の楔を鉞の峰を使って打ち込む。楔を打ち込むにつれて、檜はグーンッと持ち上げられ、メリメリメリッと音

fig.6 「四季彩一力」フロントカウンター。
Shikisai Ichiriki Hotel Main counter.

fig.7 欅玉杢板両脇は杉の桟と絹織物の表装裂地。
A cedar frame and silk fabric mounting on the sides of a Zelkova board with circular burls.

を立てる。木の繊維が引きちぎられているのだ。

このように大きな鋸と楔を使って切り進めていくのだが、木の芯に近づくと、細くて長い芯切り鋸に取り替える。

芯切り鋸が芯を切断すると、ビシーッという音が聞こえる。木が大地から切り離されて、大地と天空の間を結んでいた命が消えてしまったのだ。檜が泣いている。ビシーッ。鋭くてもの悲しい泣き声だ。

武士道では、武士が切腹するに際して、苦しまないように介錯人がついて首を切り落とす。芯切り鋸が使われるのは、木を苦しめないための配慮である。

再び大鋸と楔を使って切り進める。シャッシャー、シャッシャー。メリメリメリッ。そして、最後の瞬間がきた。ドドドーンッ。木が伐り倒された。檜はまた大地に戻ってきたのだ。

名木の条件

木を切るときに鋸を用いていた時代には、山師と木との間に濃密な命のやり取りがあったのだが、チェーンソーが用いられるようになってからは、それがずいぶん希薄になってしまった。

山師、羽深昇が語ったのは、1960年（昭和35年）頃までの記憶である。だとすると、現在とはまったく関係のない、単なる昔話に過ぎないのだろうか。いや、断じてそうではない。その頃切られた木は、銘木に形を変えて現在に残っている。

名木と銘木

山や里に生えているすぐれた木や、いわれのある木は名木と呼ばれる。これに対して、銘木とは、床柱や床框などに使われる、特別な趣のある材木のことだ。名木が伐られて材木になると、その一部が銘木に生まれ変わる。実は、名木が銘木に変化するまでには、20年から30年は寝かせるのだ。木が反ったり割れたりしないように十分に自然乾燥させようと思うと、それぐらいの時間が必要になる。

1965年以降（昭和40年代）には、経済の高度成長に反比例する形で山の産業は衰えていき、さらにはエコロジー意識の浸透とともに巨樹信仰が高まって、名木はそのまま山に残されるようになってきた。結果として、現在残っている銘木の多くは、昭和20年代、30年代に伐り出された名木が生まれ変わったものだ。

「四季彩一力」の銘木

羽深隆雄は代表作の「四季彩一力」でもそのころの銘木を数多く使っている。フロントのカウンターの腰の部分（fig.6）は、樹齢が600年を超える欅で、板目に円環を連ねたような形の玉杢が入った最高級品だ（fig.7）。

宴会場に行く吹き抜け天井に咲く和紙の花びらを支える木骨は樹齢400年の楓材なのだが、その板目の一部には鳥の

fig.8 中央の少し茶に見える部分が杢花。撮影=小林浩志
Burls on the surface of the bark that look like flowers. Photo by Hiroshi Kobayashi

目のような形の模様が入っている。

1階エレベーターホールの組子天井には、樹齢80年の黒柿がはめ込まれている。柿の木には、まれに黒色の縞模様や濃淡が入ることがあり、そうした材は黒柿と呼ばれ古来から珍重されてきた。

これらの銘木は、いずれも羽深昇が山から切り出して、大切に保存していたものばかりだ。

人間に苦労させられる名木

名木はいかにして銘木に育つのだろうか。羽深隆雄は「木が若いときに苦労して育つことが名木の条件」という。その場合に、大きくふたつの分かれ道がある。人間に苦労させられるか、大自然に苦労させられるかだ。苦労とはどういうことだろうか。

普通の植林で、ある面積の中にたとえば檜の苗木を10本植えて、10年から20年後にそのうちの半分を間伐して、5本だけを残すとしよう。残された5本の木は、太陽がよく当たるし、水や栄養分も十分にまわるようになるので、スクスクと成長しやすい。

そして植えてから50年から60年も経つと、高さが20m、目通りの直径が50cmから60cmの木に育つ。

これに対し、人間が木をあえて苦労させる方法に密植がある。密植では苗木の数は6〜7本ぐらいと、普通の植林よりは本数が少ないのだが、間伐しないのでいつまで経っても本数は6〜7本のままだ。したがって、苗木が小さい間は成長しやすいのだが、途中からは木の密度が濃いために、競争が厳しくなってどうしても成長が遅くなる。

その結果、高さが20m、目通りの直径が50cmから60cmの木に育つには、80年くらいはかかる。普通の植林に比べると、20年もの余分な時間が必要なのだ。良材を求めるなら植えた年月が同じなら細い木を買えということだ。

両者の断面を比較してみよう。密植した木は80年分の年輪が詰まっているために、目が細かく詰まっていて美しい。一方、普通に育てた木は、同じ断面の中に60年分の年輪しかないために、目が大雑把であまり美しくはない。要するに、運動不足の子供のように、少し育ちすぎ太りすぎの感じに近い。

人間に苦労させられた木は、生存本能、ハングリー精神が刺激されるからこそ名木になるのだ。ただし、建築家や大工の側の木に対する理解力が低下していて、名木が名木として評価されるとは限らない不安があるし、育てるために20年もの余分な時間がかかるリスクがあるために、密植はあまり普及していない。

大自然に苦労させられる名木

大自然に苦労させられて名木になるとは、どういうことだろうか。

檜の林の中に、自然に生えてきた苗木があり、たまたま檜の林が切り倒されることになったとしよう。林がそのまま残っていると苗木が大きく育つのはむずかしいのだが、林が切られたので苗木にも育つチャンス、幸運が巡ってきたのだ。

しかし、幸運がいつまでも続くとは限らない。その苗木にとっては鹿に新芽を食べられたことが、つまずきの始まりだった。それで大きく出遅れてしまった。他の苗木がスクスク育ったのに比べて、出遅れた苗木は影に覆われて成長がさらに遅れ、差は開く一方だった。

やがて60年が過ぎて、他の檜は立派な成木になったのだが、不運な檜はその半分にも達していなかった。そのとき、山師と木挽きが木を切りに来て、こんな話を交わした。「どうも、この木は細いなぁ。これだけは残しましょう」。

立派な成木がすべて切られたその日から、運命が逆転して、不運なはずだった檜はその林一番の大木に変身してしまったのだ。

さらに60年が過ぎて、山師と木挽きが再びやってきた。林を眺めると、普通の成木とひときわ立派な大木があった。120年前他の木の影にひっそりと隠れ、出遅れた檜は、120年の樹齢に達していたのだ。

山師は木を見上げながら考えた。「120年だと切るにはまだ早すぎる。せっかくここまで育ったのだから、あと150年か200年は待った方がいい。この木だけは残そう」。これでまた、檜の大木は命を長らえることになった。

樹齢900年の欅

羽深隆雄によると、大自然が育てた名木は、林の中ではなく単独にポツンと立っていることが多いそうだ。その名木が自然にどのように苦労させられたのかは分からない。ただ、水はけがよくて、土壌が肥えていることだけは共通している。それ

fig.9 fig.3の木を立木山取りした欅材（幅150、厚18、長300cm）。成長段階で2本の木が1本になったため、中央に辺材の白太が見える。
A piece of Zelkova (150cm wide × 18cm thick × 300cm long) cut by the *tachiki yamadori* method. Two trees had grown into one, which we can see in the white part in the middle of the piece.

さえ整っていれば、いつの日か日当たりに恵まれたとき、大きく育つことが可能になる。

木の種類によって違うのだが、名木と呼ばれるまでには、最低でも400年以上の時間がかかる。檜の大木を切り出すときの一部始終はすでに説明したのだが、名木を切るときの状況はさらにすさまじい。名木は最後まで激しく抵抗し、人間を傷つけることもある。

木が暴れないように

樹齢約900年、目通りの幹周り2丈（約20尺、約6m）、樹高24mの欅の銘木のことを話そう。

この欅は、大相撲の力士の筋肉がもりもり盛り上がるのと同じように、足元の幹がごつごつと力強く盛り上がっていた。ごつごつしているのは、木の繊維が筋肉のように密集して硬くなっている部分なのだが、ここに鋸を入れるとしよう。鋸が筋肉状の繊維を切断すると、木の中の力のバランスが崩れて、木は大きく曲がることがある。これを木が暴れるという。

木が暴れると鋸がはじかれて、バンッと飛ばされてしまう。飛んだ鋸が当たれば人間は大けがをするし、死んでしまうことさえもある。見るからに、手強そうな欅だったのだ。

この欅には杢花（fig.8）が咲いていた。樹皮の表面の白く盛り上がった部分を花にたとえた言葉だが、杢花は玉杢があることの証拠になる。木目には柾目と板目があって、柾目では目がまっすぐに通っていて、板目では目は等高線を連ねたような形になる。玉杢とは円環を連ねたような形の板目のことで、最上級の欅であることを意味する。

鋸を入れるに当たっては、この玉杢をきれいに出すことも絶対的な条件になる。

眠っている間に伐り倒す

広葉樹の大木は、木が眠っている冬の間に切り倒す。樹高24mのうち、最初の股で分れた4～4.5m以上の部分はいい木材が取れないために伐り落として、最後に残った太い幹を立木山取の技法で伐り倒すことになった。

木は普通は、丸太の状態で伐り倒してから、8寸くらいの厚さで挽いて大判の板にする（fig.9）。しかし、地面に倒してしまうと、大木であるために自由がきかず、木性を読めないことがある。木性とは筋肉の通り方や玉杢の入り方のこと。木性を読まないで鋸を入れると木が暴れるので、もちろんやってはいけない。

立木山取とは、立ったままの木にふたりの木挽きが梯子で上部に上がり、互いに向かい合って、前挽大鋸で木を縦に切り下げていくこと。木の上部を処理した後、木の木性を読んで縦方向の両側に木墨で線を引き、ふたりの木挽きが前挽大鋸を両側から交互に挽いていく。

シャッシャー、シャッシャー。

作業の途中で分かったことだが、この欅は元々は2本の木だったが、成長の途中でくっついて1本の木になっていた。だ

から、筋肉のつき方が極めて複雑で、より慎重にならざるを得ない。木と対話をするような気持ちで丁寧に挽いていく。

銘木の心

　この欅は今、銘木となって材木屋の倉庫に眠っている。しかし、時代が変わったといえばそれまでなのだが、昨今は銘木を使いこなせる建築家や大工は少なくなっている。

　名画を飾るためにはそれにふさわしい空間が必要なのだが、銘木でも同じことがいえるのかもしれない。山で働く人が魂を込めて伐り出してきた銘木の心を感じ取れる空間を作って、銘木の命をまっとうさせてあげることもまた、建築家たちの使命なのである。

羽深隆雄の根幹

　父親の羽深昇から教わった「木の命」「木の魂」との接し方が、羽深隆雄を羽深隆雄たらしめている根幹である。彼が使ってきた素材は、体に深く染み込んだ木を中心にした土、紙、鉄など、和の素材であり、彼が創ってきた建築は木をベースにした素材を基に、問いかけ、記憶に残り、そして語りかける新たな和の建築である。

（建築ジャーナリスト）

Takao Habuka — Lineage of a Tree Hunter

Dr. Toru Hosono

Takao Habuka was the first son born to Noboru Habuka, a forester, lumber merchant and mill owner in Joetsu City (former Takada City), Niigata Prefecture. From his boyhood, he accompanied his father on trips to the mountains and watched him fell trees.

Noboru Habuka – Tree hunter

Born in 1917, Noboru Habuka earned his living felling trees and trading in lumber in Higashi-Kubiki County, selling milled lumber to carpenters and builders. He passed away in 2004 at the age of 87 (Figs. 1-3, P.013).

Over the years, the term "forester" has taken on different meanings. In addition to the standard meaning of a man who fells trees and turns them into lumber, it has also been used to mean, a gambler and a swindler. From the perspective of the tree, a forester is also a tree hunter; and when he eyes a tree, they say, the tree becomes petrified with fear.

After negotiating the right to log with the owner of the land, the forester proceeds to look for the right trees to cut down; and a really big one will stop him dead in his tracks.

A 300-year-old cypress
A forester feels a tree with all five senses.

At eye level, the cypress had a diameter of about 3m, and it stood 30 m high. This large tree was thought to be over 300 years old. The base of the tree was rugged and its roots covered the ground. Because the lower branches of cypress trees drop off by themselves, each trunk rises to its full height with many branches growing 15 or more meters from the base to form a round green umbrella on the top. It was a magnificent sight.

The bark was shiny and firm, and the color and texture were very good. He bent down to touch the soil around the roots. The soil was dry and seemed to be well drained. The grain of the wood was slightly pink and the rings were finely layered, showing it to be of the finest quality.

Placing his ear on the trunk of the tree, it was as if he could hear the sound of the water that had been absorbed from the roots running through the xylem and reaching a leaf on the edge of a branch. It was a rhythmic and comforting sound. He took a branch to smell and taste it. It had a fresh taste and scent. He was sure it was a healthy tree.

Then, he took a core sample measuring 5 mm in diameter and 20 to 25 cm long (Figs. 4&5, P.014). It was, as he expected, of the finest quality.

"You're a nice tree," he said, "You're coming home with me."

As soon as he decided upon this tree, its leaves seemed to start rustling, despite the fact that it was a windless day. It was very strange, as if the tree knew that it was going to be cut down. After a few moments, it became quiet.

Spirit of the tree

When we stand under a great tree that has lived long, we feel a deep sense of comfort. There are many thoughts as to why this is so.

Some say that the oxygen produced by the tree refreshes our body. Some say that the rhythm of the water flowing through the trunk is soothing; and some say that the fine current that flows when we tap a tree makes us feel that we can communicate with it.

Humans lived their lives in the forest in ancient times. The memory of this may reside deep in the subconscious of the species and flow through nature.

Japan is a country of myriad gods. Because the ancients were nourished with the bounty of the mountains, seas, and rivers, they worshipped the various aspects of nature as gods and believed that great trees had souls.

Gaze of a tree hunter

The cypress that tree hunter Noboru Habuka decided to bring down was slightly over 300 years old, and the leaves were definitely shaking.

Takao Habuka has an unforgettable memory from his childhood. His father, Noboru, brought him to a shrine. After saying a prayer, they walked around the precincts. Takao stopped in front of a large tree and noticed that the leaves were rustling. Takao asked his father what the sound was. His father said, "The tree is trembling because it knows I am here."

Although they had visited the shrine to pray and not hunt trees, the tree must have felt threatened by Noboru's gaze.

Calming the tree with a libation

The day had come. The tree hunter and his crew headed out early one morning to fell the large cypress tree. He walked around the tree, studying it to determine which direction would be the best for the tree to fall when it was cut. If the tree were to fall toward the downward side of the slope, it could bounce and snap. The tree must be cut so as to fall toward the upward side of the slope. It was also important to ensure that there were no depressions along the direction of fall because they too might cause the tree to snap. In addition, some branches and leaves should be left to cushion the tree's fall.

"We are ready," he announced. "The time has come."

The cypress seemed to tremble, realizing, perhaps, what was about to happen; but when the tree hunter and his crew stood in front of the tree, bowed respectfully, and poured sake onto the roots saying, "It is your time," the tree became calm.

A sharp, sad cry

It was first necessary to prune the tree. Although the tree was 30 meters tall, they could only use the bottom 9 meters. The branches on the upper part were left as a cushion while the branches on the lower part were cut off.

A member of the crew placed a hand axe on his hip, and shimmied up the tree using a rope. To prevent damage to the bark, he made a small cut on the underside of the branches before slicing them off from above. After removing the branches, the top of the trunk was cut off.

Next, they made a wedge-shaped cut at the base of the trunk on the side that they wanted the tree to fall; and then began sawing from the other side. They inserted a wooden wedge into the cut and hammered it in with a broadaxe. With each swing, the wedge was driven in deeper and the cypress creaked as the tree's fibers snapped.

They used a saw and wedge first, and then changed to a fine-toothed long saw to cut the core.

When the saw approached the core, they began to hear a sound. The tree was beginning to tilt. The cypress cried. It was a sharp, sad cry.

When a samurai committed ritual suicide (*seppuku*), another samurai stood by to put him out of his pain. Using a saw to cut the core of the tree is the same. It reduces the tree's pain. They again used a large saw and wooden wedge to cut further. The tree let out a final cry as it toppled to the ground. The cypress had returned to the earth.

Changing but still the same

The relationship between a tree hunter and the tree was closer back when they used hand saws, but that relationship weakened with the coming of the chainsaw.

Although Noboru Habuka's story was related around 1960, it is still quite relevant because the trees cut down at that time are still providing valuable lumber.

Trees with historical significance and trees with special characteristics

Meiboku (valued trees) come in two types. One is a high-quality tree that has some historical significance, and the other is highly-valued wood with special characteristics treasured for use as posts or boards. The two types of *meiboku* are quite similar in one way though: both types take a good twenty to thirty years dry naturally. This is required to prevent them from bowing or cracking.

From 1965, the forestry-related industries waned in inverse proportion to the economic growth of the country. Furthermore, along with an increased awareness of ecology, more trees have been left uncut than before. As a result, much of the high-quality wood material we have now was made from the trees cut down in the 1950s and 1960s.

Fine wood used in the *Shikisai Ichiriki Hotel*

Takao Habuka used valuable wood in the *Shikisai Ichiriki Hotel*, which is a nice example of his work. The panel of the front counter (Fig. 6, P.015) is of the highest quality 600-year-old Zelkova with circular burls known as *tamamoku* in Japanese (Fig. 7, P.015) .

The wooden structure supporting the *washi* (Japanese paper) flower petals that bloom in the open ceiling space connected to a banquet hall is made of 400-year-old maple. The pattern of the wood looks like a bird's eye.

The ceiling in the elevator hall on the 1st floor has muntin of beautiful 80-year-old persimmon. With its rare black stripes and shading, *black persimmon* has been valued since ancient times.

This valuable wood was felled and stored with care by Noboru Habuka.

People helping trees to grow into high-quality wood

How do high-quality trees grow? Takao Habuka points out that the challenges faced by fine trees when they are young make it possible for them to grow into highly valued wood. There are two major types of challenges; one type of challenge is created by people; and the other type of challenge is produced by nature. What are these challenges?

The traditional practice in forestry is to plant 10 cypress seedlings in a certain area, and then remove five of them after ten or twenty years. This gives the five remaining seedlings sufficient water and nutrients to grow well.

In fifty to sixty years, these trees grow to 20 meters high, and measure 50 to 60 centimeters in diameter.

Close planting, on the other hand, creates a challenge for the trees. If we plant six or seven seedlings in a certain area and remove none, the competition among the seedlings increases.

Instead of fifty to sixty years, it takes eighty years for trees growing under such conditions to reach a height of twenty meters and a trunk diameter of fifty to sixty centimeters. By the traditional thinking, then, if you want high-quality trees in a shorter amount of time, you have to thin the competition.

Let's compare the cross sections of trees gown in the two different ways. Trees grown close together have beautiful, close growth rings that develop over eighty years while the rings of trees grown over 60 years in the traditional way are rough and less beautiful. The latter seem to be slightly fatter than they ought to be, like inactive children.

Trees have to face challenges created by people to bolster their spirit and will to survive; and that is what spurs them to grow into high-quality wood. There is concern, however, that architects and carpenters no longer appreciate or value such wood because of their unwillingness to invest the extra twenty years it takes to produce them, and this has made it difficult to spread the practice of close planting.

Nature helping trees to grow into high-quality wood

How do the challenges of nature help increase a tree's quality?

Consider the young cypress seedling growing with others in a natural forest. The foresters thin the area so the seedlings have access to more nourishment.

As fate would have it, though, a deer comes along and nibbles on the seedling's new shoots. Deprived of its shoots, it growth falls behind the other seedlings and it ends up in their shade. As the trees grow the difference in size becomes larger and larger.

Sixty years later, the others have grown into robust adult trees, and the unlucky seedling has grown to only half their size. A wood hunter and his crew came to the mountain to cut down trees, and talked about the tree. "This is very thin. We should leave it here."

On the day that all the other good trees were cut down, this cypress became the largest tree in the forest.

Sixty years later, a tree hunter and his crew came to the area. Looking around the forest, they found a beautiful specimen of a tree. The seedling continued to grow to the age of 120 after the other trees were removed and it was no longer living in their shadow.

The tree hunter looked up the tree and said, "It is 120 years old, but I want it to grow more. We should wait another 150 or 200 years. Let's save this tree." This cypress was once again left to continue growing.

A 900 year old Zelkova

Takao Habuka says that the highest quality trees are often standing alone in the forest. Although they faced severe challenges, all of them were in fertile soil. For this reason, they thrive as the trees around them are cut and they are bathed in sunlight.

Although it differs from tree to tree, it usually takes at least 400 years for a tree to become high-quality wood. Cutting a high-quality tree can be more of a struggle than cutting the large Zelkova that I wrote about above. High-quality trees resist to the last, and can be dangerous foes.

Preventing a tree from bowing

There was a nice tree. A Zelkova. It was about 900 years old. It stood 24 meters high and measured 6 meters around.

The base of the trunk of this Zelkova was rugged like the muscles on a Sumo wrestler. The tree's fibers had grown together like muscles and hardened. When a saw is used to cut the rugged parts, great caution is needed because the tree can lose its balance and bow significantly.

Once a tree loses its balance it can also send the saw flying, creating a serious risk of injury or death. This Zelkova looked tough.

It had white burls (Fig. 8, P.016) on the surface of its bark that looked like flowers, meaning that the wood has circular burls. Grain can be straight or cross. Straight grain has, as the name implies, straight lines, and cross grain forms layers of contour lines. Circular burls look like layers of circles, and these are highly valued.

When a saw is used to cut such a fine tree, it is very important to ensure beautiful circular burls.

Felling a sleeping tree

A large broadleaf Zelkova tree was going to be felled while it slept in the winter. It stood 24 meters high. The upper part from the lowest branch, which was about four, four and a half meters off the ground was going to be cut off, and the remaining thick trunk was going to be cut down using the *tachiki yamadori* method.

A tree is usually felled as a log, and then milled into posts and boards (Fig. 9, P.017) . Once the tree is on the ground, however, its size makes it difficult to read its characteristics, characteristics such as its lines and circular burls. It is a great mistake to fell a tree without understanding its characteristic because doing so might well cause it to bow.

Tachiki yamadori is a method of cutting a tree in which two lumberjacks use ladders to climb to the desired height, face each other, and cut vertically. After processing the upper part of the tree, they read its characteristics, draw lines on both sides, and cut vertically.

During the work, it became clear that the Zelkova had originally been two trees but had joined together and become one. This made the core of the tree extremely complicated, and they had to be more careful when cutting it. They cut the tree gently as if they were communicating with it.

The emotion of a precious tree

This Zelkova is now stored by a lumber dealer. With the passage of time, however, only few architects and carpenters who know how to work with such precious wood.

In order to properly show a masterpiece, there must be suitable space. It is the same for precious wood. It is the architect's goal to create a space in which the value and emotion of each piece of wood that was cut from a precious tree can be felt and appreciated. In this way, the tree can live out its life.

Takao Habuka

Takao Habuka has become who he is by developing an understanding of the spirit and emotion of trees through his experience with his father, Noboru Habuka. Takao used wood combined with soil, paper, and iron, materials used by architects to achieve a Japanese style. What he has developed is a new style of Japanese architecture using wood as a base. His creations call to us, speak to us, and remain in our memory.

(Architecture journalist)

いくつもの思いを込めて創られた
ネクストハウス

　自邸「台付欅の家」（P.048）も竣工後10年を過ぎた頃から、子供の成長リズムに合わせたかのように住まい方に変化が現れ始めた。住居は平均すると10年程で様変わりしていくことをある頃から漠然と捉えてはいたが、意識の変化が見え隠れし始めた頃から、その速度はかなり加速される。

　そこで家族の成長が一区切りついた時を期して追い求めたものは、これから確実に来るであろう身の変化に対応できる住居スタイルであった。そこにはゲストルームはあるが子供部屋はなく、その分ゆったりとした新たな住居が内包された、第二の住まい、即ちネクストハウスを創ること。それは今までの住居と、環境と場所の差が大きいほど良く、それを取り入れるため、内部は大きく開けたフリーの空間とし、外部を積極的に取り込んだ住まいにしようと考えた。

　川越の住まいからの移動は一般道で45〜50分程、約25kmを目安にしていて、自然に囲まれたこの土地を探し求めることは、これまで広く数多くの土地を見てきたので、案外、決定に時間はかからなかった。そこで唯一こだわった条件は、互いの環境が全く異なっていること。故に、必然的に比企の山々に囲まれた檜林、遠方南西方向に幾重に連なる秩父の山々が見渡せるロケーションとなった。

　ネクストハウスは、住まいとしてこれから先を見越し、いくつもの思いを込めて創られている。

　これまで設計で数多くの銘木や大木を使ってきたが、それらの補充はなかなか困難になってきている。そうしたことは今の時代背景による価値観から少し離れているので、難しくなってきているのだ。そこで残された木材の一部を自らの手元で使うと決めたところから設計はスタートしている。

　1階を開放的で周囲の自然を取り込んだギャラリー、サロン、2階をゲストルームとし、各部に無垢の特殊材を用いたディテールによるダイナミズムと、手業による強い緊張感が現れる空間となっている。

　玄関扉は戦後間もない1951年（昭和26年）に伐採された欅の一枚板の大扉。一部建具障子に使っているのは板屋楓の杢板、敷居や手摺に用いたのは硬くてやや赤みがかった塗装仕上がりの良い梨材。戦前に大鋸で板を挽くときに出る鋸目が残っている杉の杢板は、木挽が二分三厘（約7mm）で板取したことがわかり、板幅が450mmと広い。それらは20枚ほど重ねてもビシッと寸分の狂いもなく、その高い技術には驚かされる。この板を壁、天井材として約200枚使用していて、現場で大工が手鉋で1枚1枚仕上げた後、手の脂が染み込まないように追っ掛け塗装をしている。ゲストルームのヘッドボードに飾り板で使用した欅の玉杢は、50年以上も暗い倉庫にガッチリと養生されて眠っていたもので、この木は多分もう手に入らない銘木だと思う。他に銀座久兵衛本店4階花台上部の幕板に1枚使用しているので見ることはできるが、今はもう1枚もない。

　また、1階外壁はコンクリート造に左官黒壁仕上、2階木造外壁は、いつかやらなければと、以前から思いを懐いていた50年程前に廃れた杉柾板割の木羽板葺き（長さ八寸、厚さ一・五分、幅三寸程）で外壁を仕上げている。

P.023　2階和室より組子障子越しに吹抜けを見る。
View toward the void, seen from the Japanese-style room on the 2nd floor.
P.024　和室。欅大テーブルのディテール。撮影＝小林浩志
Detail of the table is made of zelkova. Photo by Hiroshi Kobayashi

外観見上げ。軒裏は秋田杉柾板の本実パネルにシルクスクリーン。外壁は杉の赤身の木羽板葺き。
View of the entrance. The ceiling is cedar which did serigraphy. The exterior wall is wood single using a cedar.

A *Next House* that embodies a variety of dreams

During the 10 years since the *House of Zelkova* (P.048) was built, the family has seen some changes in their lifestyle as the children grew. Although it is natural to expect significant changes over a period of 10 years, the speed of change tends to accelerate after we become conscious of them.

After the children had grown, the family sought a style that could flexibly adjust to the physical changes they would definitely encounter as they aged. This is what I call a "Next House," one that has guestrooms rather than children's rooms, and one that creates a more relaxed space. It is better, I feel, to ensure that the current and *Next* houses differ in terms of environment and locale. To create such differences, I planned a free open design blending outdoor and indoor space.

The family was intent on having a different view, and it didn't take long to find a nice location with a view of a cypress forest and a panoramic view of the Chichibu mountains to the southwest. The distance from the house in Kawagoe is about 25 km, with the drive taking 45 to 50 minutes on ordinary roads.

This *Next* House was created from the desires of a family anticipating a future lifestyle.

I like to use beautiful, large pieces of wood in my home designs; however, it has become increasingly difficult to get ahold of such fine wood because the expense has discouraged its use. Nevertheless, I decided to use these beautiful large sections of wood in my design.

The 1st floor is a gallery and salon making use of the natural scenery of the surrounding area, and the 2nd floor space expresses the dynamism produced by the detail of solid wood and strong atmosphere created by handwork.

The front door is made of a Zelkova cut in 1951, soon after the end of the War. Acer pictum boards with beautiful grain are used for the paper sliding doors, and hard, red coated pearwood is used for the doorframes and banisters. Cedar boards from before the war that have figured grain from the sawblade were cut into approximately 7 mm thick and 450 mm wide pieces. Even when we stack 20 of these, they match without misalignment. I am always amazed at the skill that could cut these boards so precisely. They used approximately 200 boards for the walls and ceilings. Carpenters finished each of them at the site and coated them to protect them from hand and fingerprints. The Zelkova featuring a circular figure used for the decorative headboard in the guest room had been cured and kept in a dark storehouse for more than 50 years. You probably won't be able to find any more like this. I also applied the same wood to a side board on the upper part of a flower vase stand on the 4th floor of the *Ginza Kyubey Main Restaurant*, which we can see; but I don't have any more of it.

The exterior concrete block wall on the 1st floor is finished with black plaster; and the wooden exterior wall on the 2nd floor is finished with straight-grained cedar shingle roofing (24 cm long, 4.5 cm thick, and 9 cm wide). Although not used for about 50 years, I wanted to incorporate it into my design.

外観正面。Façade.

P.030 アプローチより玄関を見る。欅の90mm厚の無垢の大扉。1階外壁は黒壁硅石入左官仕上、下部腰部は豆砂利洗出。2階部分は杉の木羽板葺き。
View of the entrance. The door is made of the zelkova of thickness 90mm. The exterior wall of the first floor is black earth wall. Second floor is cedar wood single.
P.031 玄関欅一枚板の大扉ディテール。1951年に伐採された欅材。彫り込みは三重格子のデザイン。引手は鍛造で蜜蝋仕上。
Detail of door. The zelkova being used has been harvested in 1951. Door handle is iron forging.

Takao Habuka 031

吹抜けサロン見上げ。壁の黒い部分は榛名の黒土壁。天井は煤竹直径70㎝。View of the salon. The black part of the wall is a black soil wall. Ceiling is smoked bamboo.

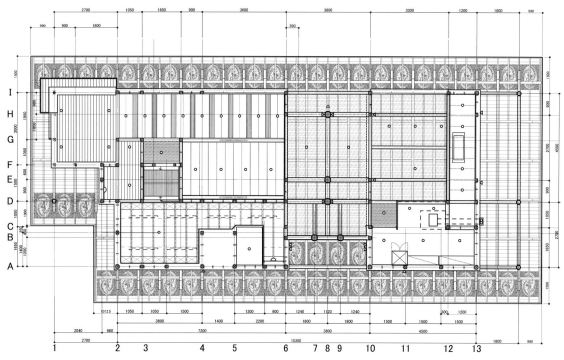

SECOND FLOOR CEILING PLAN 1:150

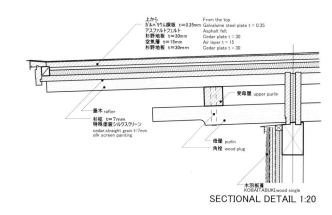

SECTIONAL DETAIL 1:20

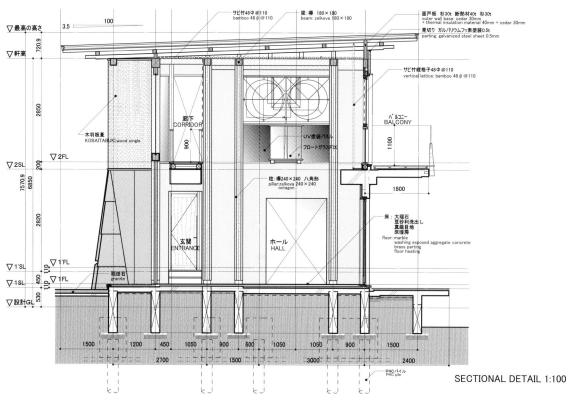

SECTIONAL DETAIL 1:100

2階渡り廊下より1階サロン見下ろす。Downward view of 1st floor, seen from the corridor on 2nd floor.

2階渡り廊下。吹抜け越しに和室を見る。View toward the Japanese-style room, seen from the corridor.

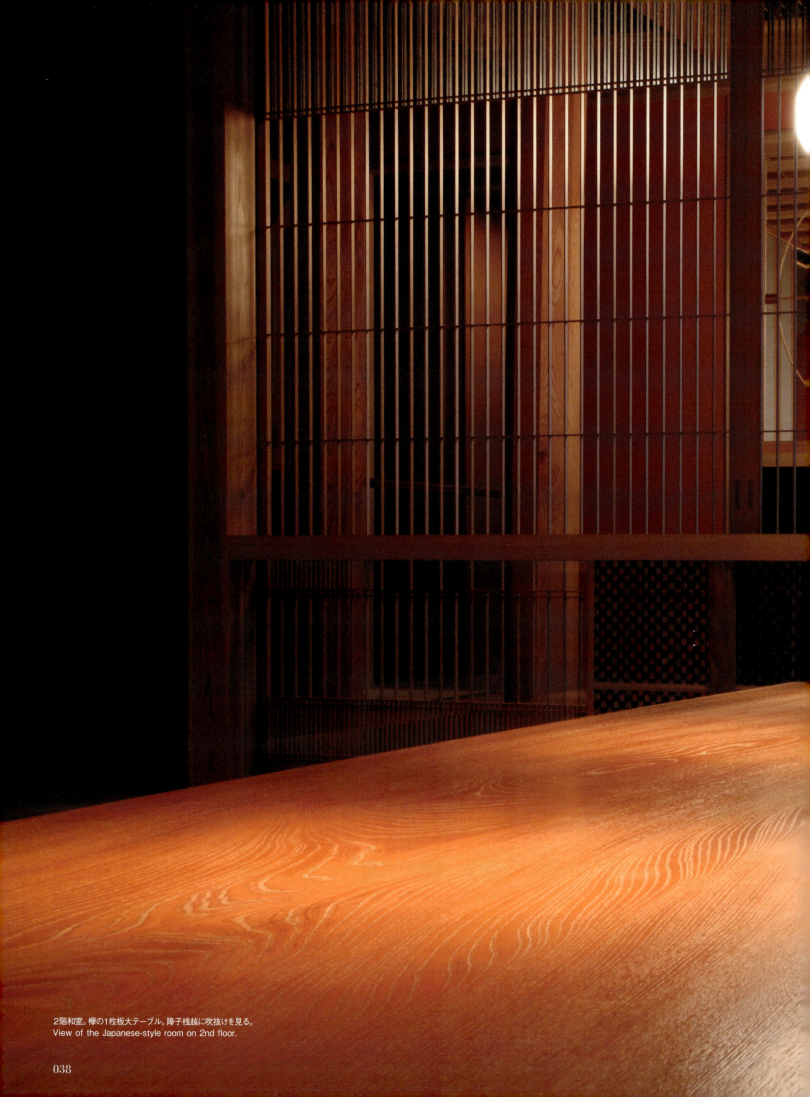

2階和室。欅の1枚板大テーブル。障子桟越に吹抜けを見る。
View of the Japanese-style room on 2nd floor.

P.040上 (up) 2階和室。View of the Japanese-style room on 2nd floor.　P.041上 (up) 2階ゲストルーム。View of the guest room on 2nd floor.

P.040-041 2階和室より吹抜け、ゲストルームを見る。ゲストルーム障子は円三角四角の完全無欠のデザイン。
View toward the guest room, seen from the Japanese-style room on 2nd floor.

2階ゲストルームより吹抜けを見る。Look toward the void, seen from the guest room on 2nd floor.

上 (up) 2階浴室夕景。幾重にも連なる山々を眺める。Evening of the bathroom on 2nd floor.
下 (down) 2階ゲストルーム飾り床。The alcove of the guest room on 2nd floor.

左（left）　ゲストルーム飾り床ディテール。化粧受け柱は梨材。
The alcove of the guest room on 2nd floor. The small pillar is made of the pear.
右上（right up）　ゲストルーム。欅の玉杢板と表装裂地のデザイン。
The headboard of the guest room. Zelkova and *Kireji* are used.
右中（right middle）　廻縁ディテール。斜め茶色の材は梨材の車知栓。細かな部分にも大工の技が光る。
Detail of the crown molding. Small brown wood is made of the pear, and is a connecting material of wood called "*Shachisen*." Craftsmanship technique appears in detail.
右下（right down）　渡り廊下手摺ディテール。材料は硬く滑らかで塗装の乗りの良い梨材。
Detail of the corridor handrail. Material is hard and smooth pear.

Episode

木製建具製作者・渡辺文彦の仕事

2003年に「第37回全国建具展示会」へ「組子・屏風」を出品し、内閣総理大臣賞を受賞。2007年には弱冠32歳、最年少で「現代の名工」に選ばれる。

その技は機械を遥か超えた次元である。真似はできない。彼の言葉に「機械は人の手を真似たもので、手を超えることはできない……」とある。

今回、渡辺氏には様々な建具を作っていただいた。欅の無垢の大扉の彫刻や、桟の太さ2mmから3mmの障子の桟の軽やかさ、円形の幾何学模様の桟の障子。どれも目を見張る精度を持っている。それを支えるのは彼の神業ともいえる手の感覚と、建具に込めた執念であろう。

寸分違わぬ精度で障子を組み、さらにその上から鉋を掛けるという、通常やらないことをやる。そんなことをすれば、木がさくれてしまったり、格子が崩れてしまったりしてもおかしくはない。そんなことが行えるのは、研ぎの技術が抜群に良いからである。鉋を持てば3〜4μm単位で木を削る。切れる刃物は彼の技術を極限まで高め、隙のない砥ぎ澄まされた手業が残る。

渡辺建具店　新潟県加茂市下条甲478-1

Work by Fumihiko Watanabe, a wooden fixture artist

Fumihiko Watanabe received the Prime Minister's Award for his "Folding screen made of muntin" at the 37th National Exhibition for Fittings in 2003. He was chosen as a modern artisan when he was only 32 years old, the youngest in the history of the award.

His techniques go well beyond what machines are capable of. Not one machine can do what he does. He says, "Machines are made to be similar to human hands, but they cannot surpass human dexterity."

I asked Mr. Watanabe to make a number of fittings for homes that I designed. These include a sculpture on a large Zelkova door, light paper sliding door frames 2 to 3 mm thick, and paper sliding doors with circular geometrical patterns. The detail of his work catches everyone's eye. I believe that his incomparable skill and enthusiasm in creating fittings make it possible to produce such excellent work.

He assembles paper sliding doors perfectly, and then planes them, which is unusual. If we try this, the wood may split or the lattice may deform. Mr. Watanabe's techniques for adjusting material with a plane are outstanding, and this allows him to work his magic without causing the least amount of damage. He planes in 3 to 4 μm increments. With a sharp tool, he exerts his skill to the maximum, and produces sophisticated, really perfect work.

Watanabe Fittings: 478-1 Shimojo-Ko, Kamo City, Niigata Prefecture

新潟県加茂市の渡辺文彦の工房にて欅の大扉の仕上りを確認する羽深。
Habuka and Watanabe Fumihiko confirm the finish of the door.

渡辺文彦。玄関大扉の三重格子の彫刻を彫る　使用している鑿はこの仕事のために作成。
Mr. Fumihiko Watanabe is carving a sculpture of triple lattice on the entrance door.

P.046-047 障子ディテール。通常は桧の桟を使うところを、扱いにくいが品があり美しい杉の桟を見付け3mmで使用してる。濃い色の桟は神代朴の木。
Detail of the *Shoji*. In general, the Shoji is made of cypress, but this shoji is made of cedar which is hard to handle but beautiful.
P.046下 (down) 障子と天井の煤竹。白い線は木綿のロープを隠し留めている。*Shoji* and the ceiling of smoked bamboo. White lines are cotton rope.

P.047下（down）吹抜け柱梁ディテール。欅の八寸角八角形の柱と欅の梁が設計者自身が開発した仕口追締め金物によりクサビを打込むことで締め付けられ隙間無くスッキリと納まる。
Detail of the columns and beams. Octagonal columns and beams are made of the zelkova.

台付欅の家
House of Zelkova

| 羽深隆雄 | 住宅 | 1994年竣工 |

リビング吹抜見上げ。トップライトの光と和紙。柱、梁は欅材。Looking up at top light over living room.

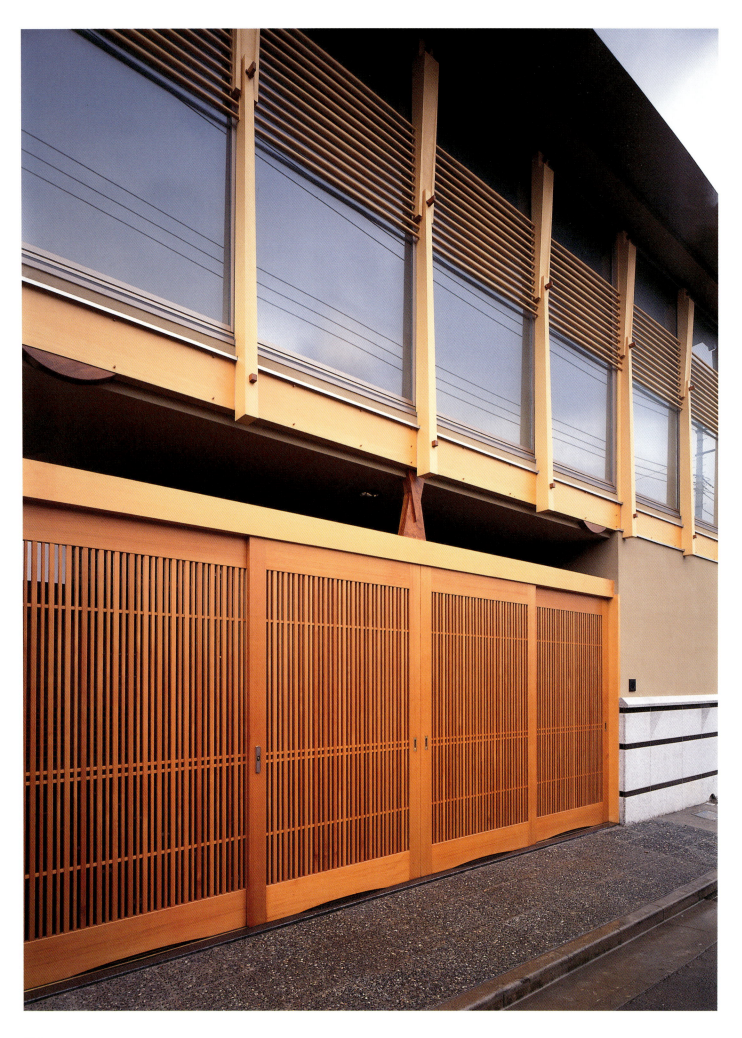

核となる中庭の欅

　この住宅は埼玉県川越市の北西に位置し、周辺地域はゆったりとした区画に整備されて、よい住環境を有している。ここに住宅を設計することは、北側道路という敷地の条件のなかで、現にある住環境をいかにして視覚から切り離し、独自の豊かな住環境をつくり得るかにかかっていた。

　小江戸川越としてのイメージがあるにしても、地縁的背景のない没個性町名で、そこにはその地域と何の関連性もなく住宅が建てられている。この新しい住居群の中で、単体としてでもその関連性を求め蘇らせることに意義があると考えた。それは民家や商家、蔵のもつイメージをそのまま継承するのではなく、現代のプログラムにそれを落とし込み、感性のフィルターを幾重にも重ね濾過することで唯一、可能になるのだ。

　プランはコの字型の平面が中庭を囲い、その中庭に面して高さ4.8mの木製建具（1〜2階まで通しの3枚引込み戸で上部梁に吊り込まれている）がある。この大きな戸が「内」と「外」を惑わせ、そして動きを誘発する。中庭と駐車場との界域では、木製格子戸により「内」へと誘い込まれる。光と風と雨を伴って「内」に入ると、台付欅の大木が空間に溶け込み、「外」と一体となる。

　住宅の計画は、いつも融通性がなければならない。そのひとつの手法として、家族がともに空気を察知しながら、互いの領域を守ることが必要である。また、さまざまな変化に対応するため、壁による仕切りは最小限に抑え、すべて工場製作の家具で仕切った。そこには細かな住居としての装置が組み込まれており、和室の押入れまでも家具によりデザインされている。

　この住宅で使用している仕上材は、一部特殊な木材を用いているほかは、土系のやわらかくやさしい材料で統一され、天井・壁は自然なテクスチュアとなり、木に馴染んでいる。建物を象徴する空間である居間の欅柱は、八・五寸角で底面より3.6mのところから上下に向かい正八寸角に絞り込み、同系色で濃淡3色に塗り分けられている。これにより、欅の強すぎる質感を和らげ、家具と同化させることで周囲との調和を図った。ほかには化粧ブレース材、および和室の敷居に梨材を用いている。梨は強く、堅く、一度納まると狂いがなく、使い減りからくる〝ささくれ〟もないため珍重され、私もよく好んで使う木材である。

　ほかにも貴重な木材を使っているが、限りある量を有効に使い材の良さを引き出せば、一般的な範囲でも使えなくはないだろう。それには材木屋や製材所にまめに足を運び、探すことから始めなければならない。そして木材についての深い知識が少しでもあれば、探し出すことは可能なはずだ。

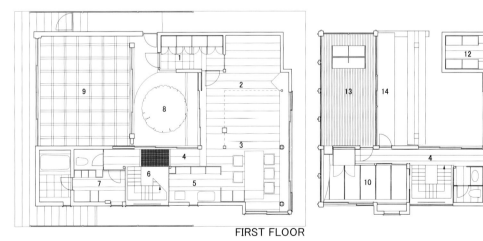

FIRST FLOOR　SECOND FLOOR　PLAN 1:200

1 玄関 Entrance
2 居間 Living room
3 食堂 Dining room
4 廊下 Corridor
5 台所 Kitchen
6 池 Pond
7 洗面所 Washroom
8 中庭 Courtyard
9 駐車場 Garage
10 和室 Japanese style room
11 子供室1 Children's room1
12 ウォークインクローゼット Walk in closet
13 子供室2 Children's room2
14 バルコニー Balcony
15 主寝室 Bed room
16 吹抜 Void

P.050 外観。1階木格子引戸の奥は駐車場。
Facade.

台付欅のある中庭よりリビングを見る。正面引込戸は高さ4.8m。
View toward the living room, seen from the center court. Sliding door is 4.8 meter high.

2階和室。右手透かし彫りは押入れの扉。View of the Japanese style room on the 2nd floor.

A Zelkova tree is the centerpiece of the inner court

Located in the northwest part of Kawagoe City, Saitama Prefecture, the individual lots are rather large, giving a feeling of space. Because the lot faces north, which affects the view, it was important to design the home in a way that created a conceptual separation from the surrounding houses.

Although the name, Oedo Kawagoe, may evoke images of the past, the residential area has no conceptual relationship to the history of Kawagoe City, and the designs of the homes do not incorporate a feel of the past. I thought it would be nice to reestablish a relationship with the history and character of the city in this new residential area. That does not mean I wanted to simply mimic the traditional styles, but to blend them into ideas filtered through modern sensitivity. This process alone makes it possible to reestablish a relationship between the new and the old.

I designed this house in a U-shape surrounding an inner garden. Three 4.8-meter high wooden doors hanging on the upper beams cover the 1st and 2nd floor corridors facing the inner garden. These large doors produce different atmospheres created by inner and outer scenes, and produce interesting movement in the scenery. Around the inner garden and parking area, wooden lattice doors invite us to venture inside. Walking inside with the sunlight, wind, or rain, we see a large Zelkova blending into the space and unifying the inside and outside scene.

I believe that house designs always need to have some flexibility. One of the ways to maintain flexibility is to design the home in a way that allows each family member to feel the presence of others while protecting individual space. In addition, in this house plan, I minimized the use of walls as partitions by using order-made wardrobes to enable adjustments to various changes in the family. I included several such features. Even the closet in the Japanese-style room is designed with built-in wardrobe and chest-of-drawers.

With the exception of some special woods, I chose soft and gentle soil-type materials for the finish. The ceiling and walls have a natural texture that blends with the tree. The Zelkova pillars in the living room measure about 26 cm^3 and serve to symbolize the house. The pillars narrow to about 24 cm^3 3.6m from the base, and are colored in three different shades. This softens the strong Zelkova texture and unifies the pillars with the furniture to harmonize the surroundings. In addition to this, I used decorative brace material liberally, and pearwood for the sills in the Japanese-style room. Pear is strong and hard, and does not change after being fit into a space. It also does not split with use, which people, including me, value.

I also used other rare wood. I believe it is important for us to optimize the effect of hard-to-get material. The search for such material starts early with frequent visits to suppliers, and it requires knowledge and experience to get what we are looking for.

上 (up) リビング壁詳細。腰壁は欅、巾木は板屋楓の銘杢。Detail of living room wall.
下 (down) リビング。Living room.

リビングより中庭越に駐車場を見る。View toward the parking, seen from the living room.

手業の装飾——
羽深隆雄の意匠

文=細野 透

　和風建築の名手、羽深隆雄は「手業の装飾」を持ち味としてきた。そして現在、60代になって取り組み始めた先進医療建築「会津中央病院　EAST CENTER（第2期棟）」において、「手業の装飾」の新たな可能性を模索している。

「仙寿庵」の装飾

　羽深隆雄の作風は「豊饒な和風建築」あるいは「現代の桃山」。彼を支えてきたのは「手業の装飾」、すなわち花鳥風月を基調とした「琳派的な造形」、およびコンピュータ・グラフィックス（CG）に支えられて登場した「フラクタルの造形」である。

　琳派は桃山時代に誕生。大和絵の伝統を踏まえつつ、豊饒な装飾性を特徴とし、絵画を中心に書や諸工芸をも包括してきた。本阿弥光悦と俵屋宗達が創始し、尾形光琳・乾山兄弟が発展させ、近代まで続いた造形芸術の流派である。

　一方、フラクタルとは「自己相似図形」、すなわちどんなに小さな部分をとっても、その部分が全体と似ているような図形をいう。

　たとえば、桜の大樹の姿を頭に思い浮かべてほしい。大地に太い幹がすっくと立って、途中から大きな枝が分かれ、次に中くらいの枝が分かれ、さらに小枝が分かれている。大きな枝を眺めると、一本の樹の形をしているし、中枝も小枝もまた1本の樹の形をしている。このように、部分（枝）が全体（大樹）に似た自己相似図形になっている。

　同じことが、雲の形でもいえる。空全体をおおっている雲は、何個かの大きなブロックから構成されていて、各ブロックも段々に小さなブロックに分かれている。じっと眺めると、やはりまた部分（ブロック）が全体に似た形をしていることが分かってくる。

　海岸線、川の枝分かれ、山の形などでも同じことがいえて、これを、「自然界はフラクタル造形に満ちている」と表現する。

手業に潜むフラクタル性

　フラクタルに関する理論は、ベノア・マンデルブローによって、1975年に発表された。マンデルブローは1924年ポーランド生まれのフランス人数学者で、米国エール大学教授だった。

　自己相似性を数学的に表現すると「ある数式を何回も繰り返して計算しなさい」というロジックになる。これを人間が手で計算するとなると、膨大な手間暇がかかってとても大変だ。しかし、コンピュータを使って計算し、CGの技術でビジュアルに示せば、その結果を割と簡単に知ることができる。

　CG分野には、自然の風景を描いたり、樹を描いたりするソフトがあるが、これはフラクタル理論にもとづいて作られている。このように、フラクタル理論の有効性はコンピュータ時代の訪れによって、はじめて明らかになった。

　フラクタルは自己相似性なのだが、これを少し広く解釈して「同じことの繰り返し」ととらえると、画家、工芸家、職人の手の動き、すなわち手業にもフラクタル性が潜んでいることが分かる。

　天才画家ファン・ゴッホが描いた《糸杉と星の見える道》（1890年）という有名な作品がある。その絵の中の題材は、糸杉も、空も、大地も、すべてが風に揺れて動いているかのように、うねうねとしている。これは、素早い絵筆のタッチで、同じ動作を何度も繰り返しながら描いた作品だといわれている。

　大工の棟梁が木に鉋をかけるときも、独特のリズムで鉋をシュッシュッと引いている。名人が仕上げた木は、表面は滑らかなのだが、よくよく見ると大工の手の痕跡が残っていて、ほれぼれしてしまう。

　左官、鍛冶、銅板職人などにも、みな独特のリズムがある。画家、工芸家、職人の手業。それは、自然界から伝わるリズム、ゆらぎ、人間の呼吸、物づくりに携わる者としての魂などを、作品に転写していくプロセスなのだろう。名人、達人の手業の痕跡はいつも美しい。

フラクタル造形を取り入れる5つの方法

　羽深隆雄は和風建築の頂点となった高級旅館「仙寿庵」において、琳派の流れを汲む「職人の手業」と、フラクタル造形を生み出した「CGの手業」を融合させるという大業に挑戦して、見事な花を咲かせることに成功した。

　そこでは5つの方法でフラクタル造形を取り入れた。第1に、デザインにフラクタルの自己相似性を取り入れて、空間の構造性を獲得したこと。

　「仙寿庵」の発注者は、18室ある客室のすべてに露天風呂をつけてほしいと希望した。敷地の東側には谷川が流れ、さらに向こう岸（東側）は高い崖になり、木が茂っているので、人目を気にする必要がない（fig. 1）。

　したがって、全客室に露天風呂をつけるためには、谷川に沿って客室を雁行して斜めに配置すればいい理屈になる。雁

fig.1 「仙寿庵」俯瞰。雁が編隊を組んだような棟。
Overlooking *Senjuan Hotel*, buildings in formation like flying geese.

fig.2 「仙寿庵」花鳥風月の回廊。ケーブルの影が土壁に浮かぶ。
Hallway of natural beauty at *Senjuan Hotel*. Cable shadows float above mud-plaster wall.

fig.3 「仙寿庵」花鳥風月の回廊の壁面。漆喰に土壁塗。
Walls along hallway of natural beauty at *Senjuan Hotel*. Mud-plaster coating on mortar.

行とは、雁の群れが斜めになって飛行することから生まれた言葉だ。そもそも、この土地の上空を春と秋の2回、雁が渡っていく。それゆえに、ここでは自ずと「雁の姿」がキーワードになった。

羽深隆雄は3つのコード（体系）を使って雁の姿を潜ませた。まずは遠景のレベル。少し離れた高い場所から建物を眺めると、6、7羽の雁が斜めに飛んでいるような姿をとらえられる。ただし、眺める角度によって、雁に見えたり見えなかったりするので、潜んでいると表現した方がいいのかもしれない。

次に、建物の平面図のレベル。平面図を子細に眺めると、6、7羽だと思っていた雁の1羽1羽が、実は数羽ずつの編隊であることが分かってくる。遠景では一羽の雁の姿をしているのだが、その1羽の中に前室、次の間、本間などの形で数羽の雁が潜んでいる。雁は意外な大群だったのだ。

そして、「花鳥風月の回廊」（figs. 2&3）。回廊のガラスは、ガラスに取りつけられた金物と、スチールパイプの柱に取りつけられた金物との間に、ケーブルを張って支えているのだが、このケーブルと金具のディテール（細部）が、雁が飛ぶ姿を思わせる形をしている。

雁の姿がはっきりと目に焼き付くのは、空が晴れて回廊に日光が射し込んでいる瞬間だ。ケーブルと金具のディテールの影が、東側の土壁の上に写って、空を飛ぶ雁の編隊が見て取れる。いずれにしても、ケーブルと金具のディテールを雁ととらえることは、3つのコード（体系）を理解してはじめて可能になる。雁はコードの中に潜んでいるのだ。

「仙寿庵」では、遠景のレベル、平面図のレベル、回廊のケーブルと金具のディテール、という3つのコード（体系）で雁の姿が潜んでいたのだが、これはまさに全体と部分の相似というフラクタルそのものである。

数学の最新理論の成果が、こんなさりげない形で導入されているのを知ることは、創る者にとっても鑑賞するものにとっても等しく喜びであり、空間に対する人間の理解を深くすることに役立つ。豊饒な建築は語られることを待っている。語られるための手がかりが、ここ「仙寿庵」には豊富にある。

マンデルブロー集合の「炎」

フラクタル造形を取り入れる第2の方法は、CGで描いたフラクタル図形を、そのまま和の素材に写し取ること。花鳥風月の引用に加えて、新たにフラクタル図形を引用することで、デザインソースは一段と広がることになる。幸いにも、花鳥風月とフラクタル図形とは親和性がある。平たくいえば、相性がいい。

回廊の白い漆喰壁に茶色の土壁で描いた炎のイメージは、マンデルブローがコンピュータで描き、人類が最初に目にしたフラクタル図形となった「マンデルブロー集合」を引用したものだ。

CGのソフトを操作すると誰でも経験できるが、マンデルブロー集合は不可思議な形をしている。はじめに見えるのは、ちょうど瓢箪のような形をし、周辺に海岸線のような凹凸がつい

Takao Habuka 059

た湖に似た姿だ。この湖の地図の縮尺が、1万分の1だったとする。

コンピュータという舟に乗って、瓢箪の頂部にある窪みを目指してこぎ出してみよう。マウスというオールをゆるゆると漕いで、頂部の窪みに近づいて、よくよく見ると、そこにあるのは瓢箪の形に似た小さな湖だ。視界を広げるために、地図の縮尺1000分の1に切り替えて、全体を広く見渡すと、驚くことに出発点とほとんど同一の風景が広がっている。

さらに先へ進んで、縮尺を100分の1、10分の1と拡大しても、後ろへ後退して、縮尺を10万分の1、100万分の1と縮小しても、事情は変わらない。どこまで進んでも、どこまで後退しても、そこにあるのは部分が全体と相似した自己相似形の世界だ。マンデルブロー集合は果てしなく続く無限の世界である。このために、フラクタル図形に神の真理、宇宙の構造が潜むと考える人もいるほどだ。

回廊の高い位置に彫り込んだ、風と葛藤する雁の姿を象徴したカルマン渦も、やはりまた一種のフラクタル図形である。シベリアの大地から、ここ谷川岳の上空に至るまで、雁は数十万回、数百万回も羽ばたく必要があったことだろう。その繰り返しを象徴するために、カルマン渦が選択されたのだ。

ここで、強調しておきたいことがある。フラクタル図形の引用とはいっても、たとえば、コンピュータの計算結果をカラープリンターで紙に出力して、それを直接、壁に貼り込んだのでは薄っぺらなものにしかならない。フラクタル図形を、職人の手業で柔らかく転写するからこそ、親和性が得られて、味わいがより深くなるのだ。

墨流しというフラクタル

フラクタル造形を取り入れる第3の方法は、自然界に潜むフラクタル図形を、和の素材に写し取ること。羽深隆雄が好んで使う手法に江戸墨流し染めがある。これは、墨や顔料を水面にたらして波紋状の模様を作り、それを紙や布に写しとる染め方だ。単に墨流しともいう。

墨流しのパターンはどれもよく似ているが、どれひとつ同じものはない。墨流しでできる模様は典型的なフラクタル図形だ。人間が古くから使っていた手法なのだが、それがフラクタルだったと分かると、話は急に新鮮さを帯びてくる。なにか、活力が吹き込まれるのだ。

羽深隆雄は江戸・唐半の4代目、渡辺彰と協同で墨流しの手法に取り組み、和紙だけではなく、木の壁、土の壁にも墨流しのパターンを転写する技法を開発。さらには、雲母の墨流しの技法も復活させた。雲母とは、貝殻をすりつぶした顔料のこと。銀粉のようにきらきらと光る雲母を、水面に流して漉きとるのだが、粋な味わいがある。

墨流しは「仙寿庵」のいろいろな場所で見られる（fig. 4）。なかでも、料理茶屋の小溜まり（小ホール）の天井を飾る、楕円形の組み込み照明を飾る墨流し（fig. 5）は、日本でもトップクラスの出来映えだ。通草の葉が、月の光に透けて見える様子をモチーフにした、幻想的な作品だ。

「幾何学」＋「虹のフラクタル」

フラクタル造形を取り入れる第4の方法は、幾何学的な図形を、自然界に潜むフラクタル的な造形で包み込むこと。たとえば虹。虹のフラクタル的なリズムは、ふわっと柔らかい半円形を数回繰り返して描くことで表現できる。虹の役割は、幾何学図形を自然界のリズムで包み込み、親和性のある造形に転じさせてしまうことにある。

羽深隆雄が得意とする工芸のひとつに、組子建具がある。組子とは、細かく切った木を組み合わせて、いろいろな模様を描いたものだ。和風空間にある普通の障子には、細い木

fig.4 「仙寿庵」玄関。土壁に江戸墨流し。
Entrance to *Senjuan Hotel*. Ink flow patterns (*edo suminagashi*) on mud plaster.

fig.5 「仙寿庵」照明の陣笠部分は江戸墨流し。
Cap shade "Jingasa" portion of lighting is *edo suminagashi* at Senjuan Hotel.

fig.6 「仙寿庵」式台の組子障子。
Shoji doors with wood-strip fittings at stepped entrance in *Senjuan Hotel*.

fig.7 アルミスパンドレルの凹部に土壁を塗りこんだ壁面。
Wall face with mud plaster filled into concavities of aluminum spandrels.

fig.8 江戸墨流しを見るマンデルブローと羽深隆雄。
Mandelbrot and Habuka look at *edo suminagashi* together.

で作った縦の桟と横の桟が走っている。これが組子障子になると、桟が縦、横、斜めに自由に走り、菱、花、松葉などのパターンとなって表れる。組子は伝統的な工芸のひとつなのだが、ある悩みを抱えている。デザインソースが固定化して、古くさくなって、飽きられてしまう恐れがあることだ。

羽深隆雄は伝統的な組子のパターンを一新し、新しいパターンを創作しようと決意。そのとき用いたのが、縦、横、斜めという直線をベースにした幾何学図形に、虹、風、雨、月のまわりに見える光の輪などの自然現象からフラクタル的なリズムを抽出して、オーバーラップさせる手法だった。

これにより、今までになかったダイナミックな表情の組子障子が誕生し、モダン和風の空間との親和性が高くなった。この組子障子は「仙寿庵」のいろいろな場所で見られる（fig. 6）。羽深隆雄は、空間に連続性をもたせて柔らかく仕切るときの一種の切り札として、組子障子を使うからだ。

工業製品の表面を職人の手業で覆う

フラクタル造形を取り入れる第5の方法は、工業製品の表面を、職人の手業に潜むフラクタル的な感覚で覆ってしまうこと。

和風建築は基本的には木、土、紙などの自然素材で作られるのだが、21世紀を迎えた現在では、ステンレス、アルミ、ガラス、プラスチックなどの工業化製品と無縁ということはあり得ない。工業化製品をいかに柔らかく取り込むか。それがモダン和風の重要な課題になっている（fig. 7）。

「仙寿庵」では、工費と工期を節約する目的で、壁の下地にリブ付きのアルミ材を使い、その凹部の上に土壁を塗って、職人の手業でモダン和風と親和性のある空間に仕上げた場所もある。野球にたとえると、ピンチヒッターとしてフラクタル造形を登場させたことになる。

羽深隆雄が誇りにしているエピソードがある。ベノア・マンデルブローは、フラクタルに関する研究が評価されて日本国際賞を受賞し、記念講演のために2003年4月に来日した。その際に「仙寿庵」を訪ねて墨流し作品を見たいと希望したが、日程の調整がつかずに現地見学を断念。代わりに、羽深隆雄が和紙と絹布に写しとった墨流しの作品を持参したところ、マンデルブローは「これはまさしくフラクタルですね」と話し、実にうれしそうな顔で見入っていたそうだ（fig. 8）。

「会津中央病院」の装飾

大規模な現代建築では原則として、柱・梁・壁などの構造体をそのまま見せる。それに加えて、太陽光や熱をコントロールするための「エネルギーパネル」、画像を見せる「情報パネル」、緑を育てる「緑化パネル」などの機能的なパネルを取り付けるケースも少なくない。

外壁を「装飾パネル」で覆う

これに対して、羽深隆雄は「会津中央病院 EAST CENTER（第2期棟）」において、外壁を「装飾パネル」で覆うという、かなり珍しい手法を採用した。この装飾パネルは、コンクリートパネルの中に、円形または四角形の陶板タイルを割り付けて造る。聞くと、この陶板タイルは、会津で流紋焼きタイルの窯元を営む弓田修司の作品。発注者から「地場産業を支援するため、流紋焼きタイルを使用してほしい」と要望されたという。

装飾パネルの中で特に目立つのは、柱と梁の交点に位置する、「大きな四角形に四つの円を置いたパターン」である。これはPC梁とPCa柱の接合部納まりの凹部を隠す役割を持つ。次に目立つのは、PCパネルの四隅に位置する「中ぐらいの円形に四つの円を置いたパターン」である。

さて、この「四角に四つ円」あるいは「円に四つ円」は何をモチーフにしているのか。一見すると、フランスの建築家ジャン・ヌーヴェルが設計した、パリに立つ「アラブ世界研究所」のガラス窓の装飾に使用したアラベスク紋様を連想させる。しかし、羽深隆雄には、文字・蔓草・幾何学図形を基調とするイスラム美術のアラベスクを、採用しようとする背景が見当たらない。

羽深隆雄に聞くと、限られた中での表現として、円、四角、三角はデザインの基本形で「密教の曼荼羅に例えられたこと

Takao Habuka 061

がある」と答えたが、私は曼荼羅とは思わない。曼荼羅とはそもそも、仏教の世界観を表すために、仏や菩薩などを体系的に配列して図示したもの。けれども、この「四角に四つ円」や「円に四つ円」は、世界像とか宇宙観を示すような構造性を持っている訳ではない。換言すると、曼荼羅というよりは、むしろ「麻の葉、鹿の子、市松、亀甲」などの図案を単純に繰り返していく、日本の伝統的な紋様を連想する。

意匠パネルに「宇宙と銀河・生命と遺伝子・太陽」を表現

「会津中央病院 EAST CENTER」の1階ホールには、人間の細胞に始まって銀河系に至る全宇宙を表現した、高さ1.65m、幅5mの大きな意匠パネルが3枚設置されている（fig. 9）。パネルはそれぞれ「宇宙と銀河」、中央が「生命と遺伝子」、右が「太陽」が表現されている。

「生命と遺伝子をデザインしたパネル」は大きく6の要素から構成される。上部中央には大理石モザイクによって「iPS細胞の断面図」が描かれ、その左右両脇パネルはUV塗装によって江戸の粋の色として日本独特の色調の銀鼠色のシルバー塗装で仕上げられている。iPS細胞とは、京都大学の山中

fig.9 「会津中央病院 EAST CENTER」意匠パネル。左から「宇宙と銀河」「生命と遺伝子」「太陽」を表している。
Design panels of *Aidu Chuo Hospital East Center*. From the left, portraying "The Universe and Galaxy," "Life and DNA," and "The Sun."

fig.10 「会津中央病院 EAST CENTER」意匠パネル「遺伝子の塔」の正面。上部中央は喜井豊治によるiPS細胞をモチーフとした大理石モザイク。
Front of design panel "Tower of DNA" at *Aidu Chuo Hospital East Center*. The upper middle section is marble mosaic by Toyoharu Kii, under the motif of the iPS cell.

伸弥教授らが作成した人工多能性幹細胞で、その偉大な業績により、2012年のノーベル生理学・医学賞を受賞した。

また下部中央パネルの中央部にはミラーガラスエッチングによって「遺伝子の二重螺旋」が描かれ、その左右両脇にはステンレスエッチングによって「遺伝子の配列記号」が描かれる。

次に「宇宙と銀河を表すパネル」の上部中央パネルには、ミラーガラスエッチングによって「地球の表面を流れる層積雲のクラウドストリート＝水の循環」が描かれている。また下部中央パネルの中央部にはミラーガラスエッチングによって「銀河系」が描かれ、その左右両脇にはステンレスエッチングによって「遺伝子の配列記号」が描かれる。

さらに「太陽を表すパネル」の上部中央パネルには、ミラーガラスエッチングによって、同じく「地球の表面を流れる層積雲」が描かれている。また下部中央パネルの中央部にはミラーガラスエッチングによって「太陽風」が描かれ、その左右両脇にはステンレスエッチングによって「遺伝子の配列記号」が描かれている。

3枚のパネルを眺めると相似性の中で微妙に変化していることがわかる。更に、それぞれの示すものを改めて読み解くと、「銀河・宇宙」莫大で広大な宇宙の一部が銀河系であり、その銀河の形成するうちのたったひとつが地球であり、そこには生命の源である水が存在する。

「太陽」銀河系を形成する一部の太陽系、その太陽の影響を受け、脈動し水が循環する地球。「生命・遺伝子」その循環する水から生命は生まれ、その人体を構成する細胞の数は60兆にも及ぶと言われている。全てがある種の相似性と関連性を持って流れるフラクタルの意匠だと理解できる。そして、未来に向けて無限の可能性を秘めたiPS細胞。患者と医療スタッフに勇気と希望を与える目的で設置されたという。

大理石モザイクという手業

縦82.5cm、横165cmもの「iPS細胞の断面図」を、大理石モザイクによって描いていく手業はすさまじい。制作したのはモザイク作家の喜井豊治氏である（fig.10）。これを縦横4mmのモザイクタイルに分割するとして、簡単な計算をしてみよう。

82.5cm÷5mm≒165個
165cm÷5mm≒330個
165個×330個≒5万5000個

必要なモザイルタイルの個数は約5万5000個になる。しかし、1枚の大理石を5万5000個に割ったとしても、大理石には黒色に近いもの、灰色に近いもの、白色に近いものなど様々な部分がある。すなわち、求める色のモザイクタイルを確保するためには、5万5000個の数倍ものタイルを用意した後に、色彩的に合格点が付けられるものだけをピンセットで拾い出して、割った角度を微妙に調整しながら取り付けていくという、根気のいる作業が待ち受けている。仮にひとりで作業したとすると、最低でも4から5ヵ月程度はかかるガチガチの手業になるという。

エレベーター扉に「医療スタッフのシルエット」

エレベーターの扉は左と右に開くため、1台当たり扉が2枚、2台だと計4枚になる。その扉にはステンレスのエッチングによって、情報回路を示す縦・横・斜めの直線が描かれ、その背景には錯視の効果をねらったオプティカルデザインの図形が配置されている（fig.11）。

情報回路のうち、情報量が集中する部分は黒く塗りつぶされているため、結果として医療スタッフのシルエットに似た形が浮かび上がってくる。それをじっと眺めていると、左から順にスタッフが「集中・混迷・模索・打開」している姿のようにも見える。

「会津中央病院 EAST CENTER」は、最新機能に裏付けされた先進医療建築ではあるのだが、羽深隆雄が施した手業の装飾により、外観は「生命樹（外壁パネル）」、内観は「銀河・遺伝子・太陽（意匠パネル）」、「医療スタッフのシルエット（エレベーターの扉）」などの物語性をまとって、我々を迎え入れてくれるのである。

fig.11 「会津中央病院 EAST CENTER」EV扉エッチング。
Etchings on elevator doors at *Aidu Chuo Hospital East Center*.

Handcrafted Ornamentation: Designwork of Takao Habuka

Toru Hosono

Master of Japanese-style architecture, Takao Habuka has maintained handcrafted ornamentation as his special trait. Today in his 60's, Habuka engages in an architectural endeavor for advanced healthcare. *Aidu Chuo Hospital East Center (Phase II)* explores fresh possibilities in handcrafted ornamentation.

Ornamentation of *Senjuan Hotel*

The style of Takao Habuka can be described as enriched Japanese-style architecture, or contemporary Momoyama. Handcrafted ornamentation, such as artform of the Rinpa School steeped in themes of traditional natural beauty, and fractal artform rendered with the aid of computer graphics, has undergirded his output.

The Rinpa School arose during the Momoyama Period, featuring rich adornment and following the tradition of *yamato-e* painting. Founded by Hon'ami Koetsu and Tawaraya Sotatsu, the school encompassed painting as well as literature and various crafts. The Ogata brothers Korin and Kenzan developed it further, and the school survived to modern times as fine art.

Fractals are self-similar graphics, where no matter how small a portion you examine, the entire graphic is similar to that portion. Imagine the form of a large cherry tree in your mind. A fat trunk rises straight up from the ground, large branches spread out, from which medium-sized branches spread out, from which small branches spread out. The large branches also appear to look like individual trees, but then the medium-sized and small branches also begin to look like trees. This example describes how a portion (branch) is similar to the entire picture (large tree) in a self-similar graphic.

The same phenomenon is found in clouds. The clouds covering the sky are arranged from several enormous blocks, each of which is subdivided again into blocks, and then into groupings at smaller and smaller levels. A patient observation reveals that a portion (block) is similar to the whole.

Coastlines, the branching of rivers, and mountain formations can present the same arrangement. In short, nature is filled with fractal formations.

Fractal Character Hidden in Handcraft

Benoir Mandelbrot was a French mathematician born in Poland in 1924, and later became a professor at Yale University. He published his theory on fractals in 1975.

The mathematical expression of self-similarity turns into logic dictating iterative computing of a certain equation. Human calculations by hand would be onerous, taking a huge amount of time and effort. Calculations by computer and visualization by computer graphics, however, enable the results to be learned relatively easily.

Software is available in the computer graphics domain for drawing natural scenery and trees, for example, and is based on fractal theory. The validity of fractal theory, in fact, became evident for the first time with the arrival of the era of computing.

Fractals have self-similarity. If a broad definition were "repeating the same thing," then the movements made by painters, craftsmen, and workmen, in other words handcraft, could potentially retain fractal characteristics.

Road with Cypress and Star (1890) is a famous piece by the painting genius van Gogh. The objects in the painting, such as the cypress trees, the sky, and the ground, all seem sinuous, as if they are swaying in the wind. The effect is said to result from painting the work with fast brush strokes that repeat the same movement over and over.

When a Japanese master carpenter applies a plane to wood, he draws the plane with a signature rhythm and sound. The master's finish is smooth on the surface; however, a close inspection will reveal vestiges of the handwork—remarkable and admirable.

Plasterers, blacksmiths and copperplate workers all have their signature rhythms, too.

The handcraft of painters, artisans, and workmen engage in a process of transferring into their work the rhythms and flux from nature, human breathing, and even their souls as individuals involved in creating. The traces left by handcraft of masters and experts are always beautiful.

Five Ways of Incorporating Fractal Artform

At the high-grade *Senjuan Hotel* that delivered the zenith of his Japanese-style architecture, Takao Habuka took on the enormous challenge of merging the handcraft of workmen in the tradition of the Rinpa School and the handcraft of computer graphics rendering fractal artform. A spectacular success resulted.

Fractal artform was incorporated in five ways. First, self-similarity of fractals was adopted in the design to acquire structuring of space.

The client of *Senjuan Hotel* desired an outdoor bath for all 18 guestrooms. The Tanigawa River flowed to the east of the lot, and the bank on the other side (east) was a high cliff with trees. There would be no need to worry about lurking eyes in accommodating this request (Fig. 1, P.058).

To build outdoor baths for all of the guestrooms, logic would suggest a diagonal arrangement of the guestrooms along the river in a flying-geese pattern, a description that emerged from the diagonal flight formation of geese. Interestingly, geese cross the skies of this area twice a year in spring and autumn. "Form of a goose" naturally became a keyword here.

Takao Habuka stashed geese patterns into three codified systems here. The first was the distant view. Gazing at the building from a height slightly away, the form appears to be six or seven geese in the diagonal flight formation. Depending on the angle, however, these geese appear and disappear. A better description would be to say that the flying geese stay concealed.

The next codified system is in the building's horizontal projection. A detailed examination of the plans reveals that each of the alleged six or seven geese actually constitute a flock of several geese in formation. The distant view may show one goose, but inside that goose resides an anteroom, drawing room, main room, and so forth as several geese. The geese are actually a huge flock.

The third system is found along the "Hallway of Natural Beauty." The enclosing glass for the hall is supported with cables stretched between brackets mounted to the glass and brackets mounted to the steel-pipe beams. The details of the brackets and these cables evoke the form of flying geese.

The pattern of geese clearly registers during the moments when sunlight streams into the hall on sunny days. The shadows of the cables and bracket details appear on the mud-plastered wall to the east, like a formation of flying geese. The cables and bracket details only look like geese after the three codified systems are understood, however. The geese are concealed within.

At the *Senjuan Hotel*, geese were hidden within three codified systems: the distant view, the horizontal projection, and the cables and bracket details of the hallway (Figs. 2&3, P.059). This arrangement actually relates to fractals, in which the whole and part are similar.

Knowing that the fruit of a recent theory in mathematics has attained such a subtle introduction is a delight equally shared by the creative side and the appreciative side, and also aids in deepening people's understanding about space. Enriched architecture awaits this conversation. *Senjuan Hotel* has plenty of lead-ins to be topics of such a conversation.

Mandelbrot Set: Flames

The second way of incorporating fractal artform consisted of transferring fractal images drawn by computer graphics directly onto Japanese base materials. The reference of fractal images in addition to references of traditional natural beauty expanded the sources of design by another rung. Fortuitously, traditional natural beauty and fractal images have affinity. They are quite simply, compatible.

The illustration work of flames drawn by brown mud-plaster on the mortared white walls of the hallway employed the Mandelbrot set as a reference. Using a computer, Mandelbrot drew the set, which rendered the first visualized fractal image for humans to see.

Anybody who manipulates computer graphics software can experience the peculiar shape of the Mandelbrot set. The first visual looks like a gourd, or a lake with rough edges around it like a coastline. Let us assume the scale of the lake's map is 1/10,000.

Next, the computer takes us on a ride, like a boat. Let us row toward the indentation at the top of the gourd. We lightly row the oars, called the mouse, approach the indentation at the top, and look quite carefully to see a small lake similar to the shape of a gourd. We alter the map's scale to 1/1,000 and enlarge the view to look entirely across. Surprisingly, the same vista as our original starting point stretches out.

Moving ahead to expand the scale to 1/100 or 1/10, or moving backward to reduce the scale to 1/100,000 or 1/1,000,000 changes nothing. Regardless of moving forward or backward, the world is self-similar where the portion is similar to the whole. The Mandelbrot set continues infinitely in its world. That is why some people believe that God's true reason, or structure of the universe is hidden in fractal forms.

As another class of fractal image, Karman vortices symbolizing the conflict between geese and winds are carved along the higher reaches of the hallway. The geese must have flapped their wings tens and hundreds of thousands of times from Siberia to reach the skies here above Mt. Tanigawa. The Karman vortex was selected to symbolize that repetitive motion.

With reference of fractal images, it should be emphasized that paper output of computed results on a color printer would appear exceeding flat if mounted directly on a wall. The workman's handcraft provides the gentle transfer of the fractal images that yields an affinity, a deeper meaning.

Fractals in Ink Flow Patterns

The third way to incorporate fractal images transferred fractal images hidden in nature to Japanese base materials. A technique that Takao Habuka likes to employ is dyeing with ink flow patterns (*edo suminagashi zome*). India ink or pigments are dropped on the surface of water to create ripple patterns, which are transferred to paper or fabric. This dyeing technique is also simply called *suminagashi* in Japanese.

These ink flow patterns all look similar, yet each is unique. The patterns that *suminagashi* render are typical fractal images. People have employed the technique for a long time, but the story has suddenly become refreshed in learning that it forms fractals. Life force seems to be infused with the technique.

Takao Habuka worked on *suminagashi* methods jointly with Akira Watanabe, fourth-generation master of Edo Karahan. They developed techniques to transfer ink flow patterns to not only *washi* (traditional Japanese paper), but also to wooden and mud-plaster walls, and also revived the technique of *suminagashi* with powdered shell pigment. Called *ummo* in Japanese, the shiny shell powder like silver powder is flowed on the surface of water and then skimmed off for an elegant result.

Suminagashi is found in various places at *Senjuan Hotel* (Fig. 4, P.060). The work that adorns the embedded oval lighting in the ceiling of the small hall of the restaurant house (Fig. 5, P.060) is splendid, among the top class in Japan. The motif of the dreamy work presents an *akebi* leaf, translucent in moonlight.

Geometry + Rainbow Fractal

The fourth way of incorporating fractal artform consisted of enveloping geometric shapes with fractal artform hidden in nature. The fractal rhythm of a rainbow, for example, can be expressed by a few repetitive illustrations of floaty, gentle semicircles. The rainbow serves to envelope geometric shapes with nature's rhythm and to convert them into compatible artform.

Takao Habuka is skillful in the craftwork of fitted wood strips *Kumiko Tategu*. Wood-strip fittings are combinations of finely sliced wood that can portray various patterns. Ordinary *shoji* doors in Japanese-style space have vertical and horizontal crosspieces made of wooden strips. With crafted fittings, however, the crosspieces run freely in vertical, horizontal, and diagonal directions and portray rhomboidal, floral, and pine-needle leaf patterns. The craft is traditional, but faces a problem. The sources for designs are fixed; the worry is obsolescence and relevance.

Takao Habuka resolved to create new patterns by renovating the traditional wood-strip patterns. The technique employed was to overlap extracted fractal-like rhythms from natural phenomena like rainbows, the wind, the rain, and rings of light around the moon over geometric shapes based on straight lines running vertically, horizontally, and diagonally. The result led to *shoji* doors with wood-strip fittings of unprecedented dynamic expression, and greater compatibility with modern Japanese-style space. These are found in a variety of places at *Senjuan Hotel* (Fig. 6, P.060), primarily because Takao Habuka employs fitted *shoji* doors as a special class of technique to gently partition spatial continuity.

Handcrafted Coverage of Industrial Product Surfaces

The fifth way of incorporating fractal artform consisted of covering the surfaces of industrial products with fractal-like sensations lying within handcraft.

Japanese-style architecture is fundamentally built from natural base materials like wood, earth, and paper, but cannot be created in the 21st century without relating to industrial products like stainless steel, aluminum, glass, and plastic today. An important challenge for modern Japanese style concerns how to gently incorporate these industrial products (Fig. 7, P.061).

To save on time and cost of construction, *Senjuan Hotel* employed ribbed aluminum members as backing for walls. In some places, mud plaster was applied to their concave parts to finish space with compatibility and modern Japanese style by handcraft of workmen. In this case, fractal artform was trotted out like a pinch-hitter in baseball.

Here is an episode that Takao Habuka is proud of. Earning acclaim from his fractal research, Benoir Mandelbrot was awarded the Japan Prize. In April 2003, he came to Japan for a commemorative lecture. He requested a visit to *Senjuan Hotel* to view the *suminagashi* work, but the itinerary could not be coordinated. Although Mandelbrot gave up on that visit, Takao Habuka brought *suminagashi* pieces transferred to *washi* and silk cloth. Mandelbrot remarked, "This is truly fractal," and Habuka looked on with sincere pleasure (Fig. 8, P.061).

Ornamentation of *Aidu Chuo Hospital*

As a general rule for large-scale modern architecture, structural members like pillars, beams, and walls are presented as constructed. Moreover, the buildings frequently have functional panels, like "energy panels" to control sunlight and heat, "data panels" that display pictures, and "green panels" to grow green plants.

Covering Exterior Walls with Ornamental Panels

For *Aidu Chuo Hospital East Center (Phase II)*, Takao Habuka instead adopted a rare method of covering exterior walls with ornamental panels, which were made by arranging circular or square ceramic tiles within concrete panels. The ceramic tiles were the work of Shuji Yumita who operates a *Ryumon-yaki* tile foundry. The client requested, "*Ryumon-yaki* tiles should be used in support of local industry."

The especially prominent ornamental panels are at the intersections of pillars and beams with a pattern of four circles placed on a large square. The panels serve to conceal the concave joints of the PC beams and PCa pillars. The second-most conspicuous pattern is four circles placed on a mid-sized circle, and located at the four corners of the PC panel.

What was the motif for "four circles on a square" and "four circles on a circle"? A cursory examination reminds one of the Arabesque patterns used in the glass window ornamentation for the Institut du Monde Arabe in Paris, designed by French architect Jean Nouvel. Takao Habuka, however, had no background that would lean toward selection of Arabesque, Islamic art with themes incorporating text, vines, and geometric shapes.

When asked, Takao Habuka replied that circles, squares, and triangles were fundamental shapes of design among the limited possible expressions, which were also compared to mandalas of esoteric Buddhism. I don't consider these mandalas, which systematically arranged and illustrated Buddhas and Bodhisattvas to express the world of Buddhism. But the "four circles on a square" and "four circles on a circle" do not possess structure to present a worldly image or perspective of the universe. Instead, the patterns evoke traditional Japanese patterns that continuously repeat illustrated designs of entwined hexagons, dappled white spots, checks, honeycombs, etc.

Design Panel Expressions of The Universe and Galaxy; Life and DNA; The Sun

Three large design panels, each two meters high and five meters wide, are installed along the ground floor hallway at *Aidu Chuo Hospital East Center*. The panels express the entire universe, beginning with the human cell and expanding to our galaxy (Fig. 9, P.062), and depict "The Universe and Galaxy" to the left, "Life and DNA" in the center, and "The Sun" to the right.

The panel designed with "Life and DNA" is composed of six large elements. "Cross-section of iPS Cell" is created with marble mosaic in the upper middle section. The upper sections to the left and right are finished with a silver-grey coating by UV paint that is a distinctive Japanese tone, a fashionable color of Edo. Prof. Nobuya Yamanaka et al. of Kyoto University, recipient of the 2012 Nobel Prize for Physiology or Medicine for their enormous success, created the iPS cell (induced pluripotent stem cell).

Mirror-glass etching has rendered the "Double Helix of DNA" at the lower middle section of the central panel. "Genetic Code" made by stainless steel etching is depicted to the left and right.

In addition, the upper middle section of "The Sun" also depicts "Cumulous Clouds Flowing Over the Earth" made by mirror-glass etching. The lower middle section, though also mirror-glass etching, depicts "Solar Wind," and is flanked by "Genetic Code," made by stainless-steel etching.

Next, the upper and lower middle sections of "The Universe and Galaxy" are, respectively, "Cloud Street of Cumulous Clouds Flowing Over the Earth = Circulation of Water" and "The Galaxy," both made by mirror-glass etching. The latter is flanked by "Genetic Code," made by stainless-steel etching.

The viewer can appreciate the three large panels as they vary subtly amidst their similarity. I offer a further reading of "The Universe and Galaxy": our galaxy is part of a vast and expansive universe, Earth is merely one celestial body that makes up the galaxy, and water—the font of life—exists on Earth.

"The Sun" relates to the Solar System, which forms part of the Milky Way Galaxy. Earth receives the sun's influence, cycling its water and teeming with life. "Life and DNA"

reminds us that life was born from cycling of water. The number of cells in the human body is 60 trillion. The iPS cell harbors unlimited potential for the future—an installation intended to instill courage and hope in the patients and healthcare staff.

Marble Mosaic by Handcraft

"Cross-section of iPS Cell" is 82.5 centimeters high and 165 centimeters wide. The marble mosaic is mind-boggling, the creation of mosaic artist Toyoharu Kii (Fig. 10, P.062). The following simple calculation divides the dimensions by 4-millimeter square mosaic tiles.

$$82.5 \text{ cm} \div 5 \text{ mm} = \text{approx. } 165$$
$$165 \text{ cm} \div 5 \text{ mm} = \text{approx. } 330$$
$$165 \times 330 = \text{approx. } 55,000$$

The required number of mosaic tiles is about 55,000. But a single slab of marble divided into 55,000 pieces would not provide for the various portions that might be close to black, grey, or white in color. In other words, the necessary quantity of mosaic tiles for the desired color assortment would be a multiple of 55,000. Then, only those pieces graded with passing scores for their hues would be extracted by tweezers, and subtly adjusted in angle and size. The work is marked by perseverance that would apparently consume one artist with handcraft for at least four or five months.

Silhouettes of Healthcare Staff: Elevator Doors

The elevator doors open to the left and right, two doors per unit, four doors total. On these doors, stainless steel etching has produced straight lines running vertically, horizontally, and diagonally to depict data circuits. Optical design graphics are placed on their background for an effect of visual illusion (Fig. 11, P.063).

Among the data circuits, the parts where data is concentrated are rendered black. These black parts consequently merge into images similar to silhouettes of healthcare staff. By viewing these images for a while, the four "staff" seem to represent, in sequence from the left, focus, confusion, exploration, and breakthrough.

Although *Aidu Chuo Hospital East Center* is advanced healthcare architecture equipped with the latest facilities, we are greeted with stories through the handcraft ornamentation implemented by Takao Habuka. "Life Tree" (exterior wall panels) dresses the exterior. Design panels of "Galaxy, DNA, Sun" and elevator doors with "Silhouettes of Healthcare Staff" adorn the interior.

食事処天井見上げ。マーブル模様は江戸墨流しで漉かれた和紙。Ceiling of Chaya restaurant. Marble pattern is *Edo Suminagashi*.

私の桂離宮
─桂離宮の空間操作

　私は目的をもって初めてその敷地に立つと、全神経が張りつめ、鋭く、極度に緊張する。私の仕事は、この地を育んだ豊かな自然をいかに感じ取り、引き出すかにかかっているからだ。

　設計にあたってのクライアントからの要求は、全室から谷川岳が展望でき、全室露天風呂付きにしてほしいということのみであった。そして計画に入り、考えが煮詰まるたびに敷地を訪れ、確認した。ここを訪れる方々が、豊かな環境の中でゆったりと時空の流れに身をゆだね、わずかな時を谷川の大自然と共生することに意義があると考えたからである。

　いつからか定かではないが、私にはいつも桂離宮が無意識のうちに心のどこかに見え隠れしていたように思えてならない。「繊細、幾何学的、雁行、リズミカル、簡素、調和、モダン、光と影……」、桂離宮を表すキーワードは数多くある。それらを育む設計手法をたどってみると、実に緻密に「押さえて、振って、そして開いている」ことに気づかされる。それは程よいリズム感となって周りを包み込み、まるで小石を投げると池に広がる波紋のように広がり、静かに消えていき、そのイメージだけが鮮明に余韻となって残る。

　こうしたイメージは、自然の場の力を読みとることから始まり、飛び石を渡っていくかのように展開される。そして、場の力が足元から伝わり、自然を察知し、さらに目線の高さや方向が絡み合って、期待となり、創造となっていく。それはチラチラと見え隠れすることさえも、巧妙にデザインされたものであることが見てとれる。穂垣、笹垣、土塀は目線を切らないように、適度にアンジュレーションをつけて低く抑えることで、背景への期待と想像力をかきたてている。このランドスケープの妙が、桂離宮を訪れる人を内なる空間へと心地よく誘う。

　自然の形態や場面は異なっているが、谷川温泉の「仙寿庵」に、この一連の空間操作や手法を、新たな発想を織り込みながら巧妙に取り入れた。それは敷地に近づくにつれ、背丈よりも少し高いコンクリートの長い塀が、背後の建物をチラチラと垣間見せることから始まる。そして塀越しに見え隠れする建物に期待感を徐々に募らせながら、自然に低く抑えられた風除室へと誘い込まれる仕掛けとなっている。

　式台をしつらえた玄関は、全体を包み込むように大きな勾配天井の空間となっていて、見上げた目線を式台正面に戻すと、土壁に江戸墨流しを漉き込んだ、やや低めの壁面により仕切られている。目線を完全に遮らない微妙な高さは、ここでも桂離宮の手法を意識している。「押さえて、振って、開く」。ここではまだ、谷川の雄大な自然は見えない。

　玄関は、桂離宮のあられこぼしとまではいかないが、斜めに張った石の間に豆砂利を洗い出すという手の込んだ仕上げとしている。少し斜めに振った式台には、ステンレスの細い糸で織られた畳が7帖敷き込まれ、脇の障子から差し込む光をここで取り込み、畳が鈍く光る。ステンレスの畳は、絹糸を織り込んだようにスベスベとして温かく、その足元の感触を確かめながら、次なる場面を見ることに心はせかされる。そして曲線と直線が複雑に交差する、繊細な組子障子を開けると、そこは桂離宮の月見台のように大きく開け、高さ6m、長さ40mの曲面ガラスに映し込まれた谷川の大自然とようやく出会うことになる。

P.070　早朝の「仙寿庵」。
Exterior view at early morning.

Katsura Rikyu
– Spatial structure of Katsura Rikyu

When I stand at a site for the first time after I start a job, the nerves in my body tingle and I become extremely nervous because I know how important it is for my work that I sense the nature that has cultivated the charm of the location.

The client asked me to give all the guest rooms an open-air bath and a panoramic view of Mt. Tanigawa. During the planning, I visited the site repeatedly for inspiration. I did this because I feel it's important to share the feeling that people have when they visit a place. I realized the importance of letting myself be taken by the flow of the nature that surrounds me and becoming one with it, even if only for a short period of time.

Although I am not quite sure when it started, I cannot help thinking that Katsura Rikyu has always been a part of my unconscious mind. There are many words that express Katsura Rikyu, words such as sensitive, geometrical, flying geese pattern, rhythmical, simple, harmony, modern, light and shadow. Seeking a design concept that included all of these made me realize that the design of Katsura Rikyu was based on the *jo-ha-kyu* concept. This design concept generated a comfortable rhythm that wrapped itself around the surrounding environment, and then spread like a ripple in a pond before diminishing gradually, leaving only a clear image as an aftereffect.

Such an image is created through an understanding of the power nature at the location exerts; and this image expands quickly, like it's jumping from one stepping stone to another. The power of this image flows up from its origin and helps us to observe the nature that surrounds us, sparking our anticipation and imagination through an integration of the level and direction of our gaze. We get a glimpse of an ingeniously designed inner space. Keeping the height of the bamboo trunk fences (*hogaki*), bamboo leave fences (*sasagaki*), and mud walls low by applying just the right amount of undulation to prevent them from interfering with the guest's eyesight increases the anticipation and directs the imagination toward the background. These remarkable characteristics of the landscape give visitors the comfort to proceed further and further into the inner space at Katsura Rikyu.

Although the form and location differ, I applied the same spatial techniques and methods to the natural surroundings of Senjuan Hotel at Tanigawa Hot Spring while incorporating new ideas. As visitors approach the location, the long concrete fence standing slightly higher than the average person produces a glimpse of the building. This gradually increases the visitor's excitement about seeing the entire building, and brings them to a windbreak room whose ceiling is naturally low.

The entrance features a step up and a ceiling with a steep inclination that appears to wrap the entire space. If you return your gaze from the ceiling to the entranceway, you see a rather low soil wall partition that incorporates an Edo marbling print pattern. The well-balanced height of the wall, which does not completely block the visitor's eyesight, applies the same concept used at Katsura Rikyu. From here, we cannot yet see the magnificent nature of Tanigawa.

Although not as elaborate as the scattered hailstone pavement (*arare-koboshi*) at Katsura Rikyu, the entrance featuring pea gravel between diagonally placed paving stones is quite impressive. Tatami mats made of thin stainless steel threads are installed on the slightly diagonal step at the entrance, and the sunlight coming through the sash on the side illuminates them to produce a smooth, warm radiance as if they were made of silk. Visitors feel the texture of the mats, which entices their desire to see the next room. Opening the sensitive sashes that have a complicated muntin structure of curved and direct lines, you'll see the magnificent nature of Tanigawa reflecting on a high, wide curved glass window through a large opening like the Tsukimidai at Katsura Rikyu.

大浴場。Main bathing hall.

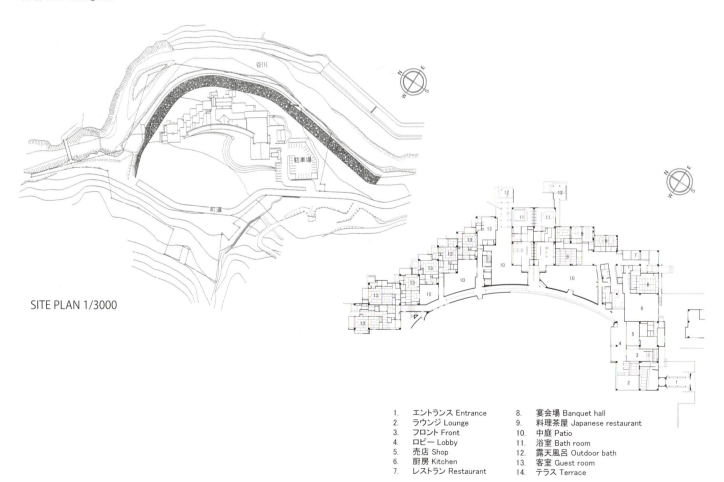

SITE PLAN 1/3000

1. エントランス Entrance
2. ラウンジ Lounge
3. フロント Front
4. ロビー Lobby
5. 売店 Shop
6. 厨房 Kitchen
7. レストラン Restaurant
8. 宴会場 Banquet hall
9. 料理茶屋 Japanese restaurant
10. 中庭 Patio
11. 浴室 Bath room
12. 露天風呂 Outdoor bath
13. 客室 Guest room
14. テラス Terrace

FIRST FLOOR PLAN 1/1200

P.074 DPGガラスの曲面廊下。漆喰と土壁仕上。上部にカルマン渦の彫込意匠が見える。
Curved corridor at dusk. Wall decorated with mortar and mud. Carmen motif grooves are curved into the ribs.
P.075 夕景の「仙寿庵」。漆喰と土壁。Exterior view at night.

Takao Habuka 075

P.076 玄関式台を見る。ステンレスの畳が左手の障子の光を呼び込み鈍く光っている。View of the entrance. Stainless steel threaded tatami mats shimmer.
P.077 式台からフロントへのアプローチ。床は畳敷き。View toward the approach, seen from the reception. Floor is tatami mat.

Takao Habuka 079

庭を取り入れ
独自の環境を確保

　1918年（大正7年）開業と古く、皇室や国賓をはじめ国内外よりの要人の宿泊も多く、土地の老舗旅館としての知名度も高い。環境は磐越西線の磐梯熱海駅から徒歩5分と近いにもかかわらず、周囲は高い樹木に囲まれた独自の恵まれた環境を有していて、名園「水月園」には猪苗代湖よりの豊かな川の流れがえんえんとそそぎ、庭中央の大きな池を回遊して緩やかに流れている。

　エントランスアプローチは、M型の空間で列柱が配され、天井には伝統的手法で製作された江戸墨流し和紙が貼られていて、その先の透明ガラス越しの風除室は「シムス」の堀木エリ子氏による特殊和紙が微妙に透け、空間に深みと色彩を落している。目線を下げ正面に移すと、コンクリート造形の漆喰の壁をくりぬいた円の中から川が流れ、庭の奥深さを感じさせる。訪れる人はこのイメージをもって内部へと引き込まれていく。

　「空間の構成は場景による」。

　ロビーでは、一尺角のケヤキ柱9本が水中より浮かび天井高く立ち上がり、ロビーと2階料亭の空間を一体化している。柱頭では楓（かえで）の木に和紙を貼ってつくられた直径約3〜4mの花弁が、トップライトの光により時空を透かし込む。

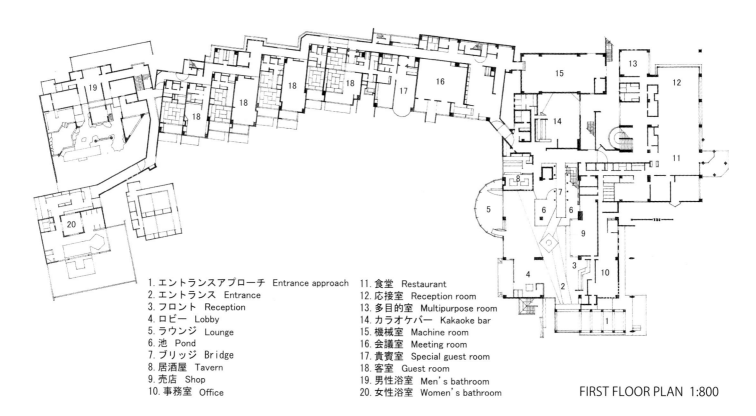

1. エントランスアプローチ　Entrance approach
2. エントランス　Entrance
3. フロント　Reception
4. ロビー　Lobby
5. ラウンジ　Lounge
6. 池　Pond
7. ブリッジ　Bridge
8. 居酒屋　Tavern
9. 売店　Shop
10. 事務室　Office
11. 食堂　Restaurant
12. 応接室　Reception room
13. 多目的室　Multipurpose room
14. カラオケバー　Kakaoke bar
15. 機械室　Machine room
16. 会議室　Meeting room
17. 貴賓室　Special guest room
18. 客室　Guest room
19. 男性浴室　Men's bathroom
20. 女性浴室　Women's bathroom

FIRST FLOOR PLAN 1:800

P.079　エントランスホールより庭からの流れを望む。
View toward the flow from the garden, seen from the entrance hall.
P.081　エントランスアプローチ。天井は江戸墨流し仕上。
View of the entrance. Ceiling is *Edo Suminagashi Washi* paper.

Takao Habuka 081

Incorporating a garden to produce a unique environment

Opened in 1918, the *Shikisai Ichiriki Hotel* is known as the hotel-of-choice for royalty, state guests, and other VIPs from Japan and around the world. Although it is only a five-minute walk from Bandai Atami Station, it is surrounded by lush tall trees. The famous park, Suigetsuen, is blessed with an abundance of water from Lake Inawashiro slowly flowing into the large pond located in the middle of the garden.

Pillars lined the M-shaped space at the entrance approach, and traditional Japanese paper with Edo marbling pattern is applied to the ceiling. Specially-made Japanese paper by Eriko Horiki from SHIMUS creates exquisite transparency in the windbreak room, and the clear glass partition produces depth and color in the space. Looking downward, a flowing stream can be seen through a circular opening in the plaster-coated wall on the concrete structure, which emphasizes the depth of the garden. Guests are attracted by the atmosphere and drawn to the inside.

"The scenery that surrounds a structure completes it." Nine square 30cm³ Zelkova pillars reach from the water toward the ceiling to unify the space occupied by the lobby and the restaurant on the 2nd floor. At the top of each pillar, petals made with Japanese paper applied to maple wood form a flower measuring approximately 3 to 4 m in diameter that is lighted from the top.

When creating the design for the restaurant, I decided to include the garden to ensure a unique atmosphere. Planning a loose U-shape building, I positioned the guest rooms facing the garden on the deep west side of the site to provide a quiet and comfortable atmosphere. Using the building to block the stone pit on the hill behind, I laid out each exterior wall in a flying geese pattern to produce the deep shade of the traditional Japanese style. Looking to add elegance and softness, I added a loose camber on the formal roof tiles.

P.082 正面外観ディテール。白い漆喰と本瓦の屋根。
Detail of the Exterior wall.
P.083 顔料と雲母による絵の描かれた漆喰。
White mortar painted with pigment and seashell powder.

ロビー吹抜け部見上げ。300×300角の欅柱と直径4000mmの楓材による骨組みの和紙組の花弁。
Looking up at the giant petals from 2nd floor hallway.

銀座久兵衛
Ginza Kyubey

| 羽深隆雄 | 商業施設 | 2006年竣工 |

別館
Annex
京王プラザホテル店
Keio Plaza Hotel Tokyo
本店(改装)
Main Restaurant (remodeling)

欅の如鱗杢に施された截金。
The *Kirigane* drawn on the zelkova. *Kirigane*: The use of finely cut gold leaf as a decorative technique for Buddhist icons.

エントランス。Main entrance.

逆説の美学による空間構成

「銀座久兵衛 別館」は、東京銀座、金春通りの「久兵衛本店」の斜め向かいに計画された。地下1階、地上5階建ての既存コンクリートの躯体を残し、地下1階、地上1階、2階と、三層がそれぞれ趣の異なった鮨店となっている。

地下1階はイス式、1階はお座敷カウンターの掘りごたつ式となっていて、久兵衛独特の鮨ネタのガラスケースはなく、付け台は1枚の無垢の檜の良材で削り出した。2階は雰囲気の異なるお座敷テーブル席で、床板を外すとテーブルを前に板前さんが鮨を握れる仕掛けになっている。この大テーブルは、江戸の粋な色のひとつである、銀鼠のUV塗装で仕上げた。

この設計では、伝統を理解した上での私なりの和風モダンが求められた。その方法論とは、日本にある逆説の美学である。花は散り美しく枯れることにより永遠となり、秘すれば花という、能の極意からなっていて、「押さえて、振って、開く」世阿弥の『風姿花伝（花伝書）』による。能の空間構成は「序破急」で説明することができるが、ここでは、まず入口からちらちらと奥が窺えることで想像力を煽る、繊細な組子障子までが「序」、狭いエレベーターホールの格子引戸までが「破」。そして一挙に視界が開ける、客席の「急」で完結するのだ。

銀座久兵衛
別館

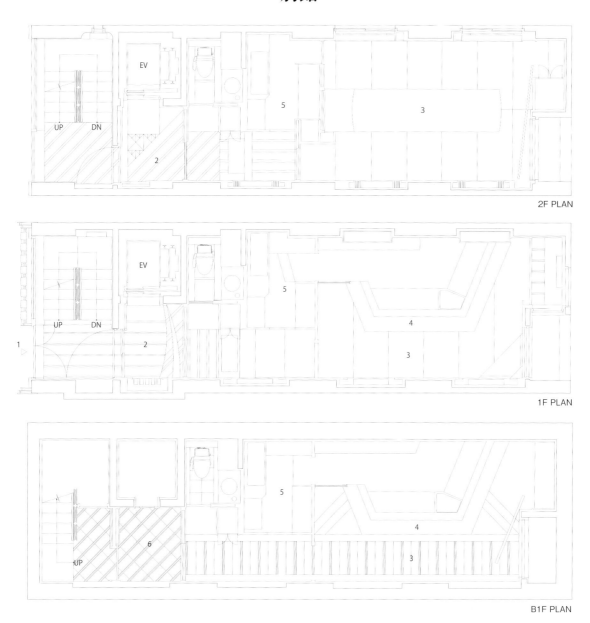

1 Entrance 2 EV hall 3 Dining 4 Counter 5 Pantry 6 Anteroom

1階客席。右手に截金が見える。
Overall view of 1st floor. *Kirigane* on the right wall.

Space configuration with the aesthetics of paradox

The plans for Ginza Kyubey Annex sushi restaurant called for the building across the street from *Kyubey Main Restaurant* on Komparu Street in Ginza, Tokyo to be refurbished. Retaining the existing concrete structure with one underground and five aboveground floors, the underground, 1st and 2nd floor spaces feature different Kyubey styles.

The underground space has western-style tables and chairs while the 1st floor features *horigotatsu*-style counter seating without the traditional display case for the fish. The counter is beautiful solid cypress. The 2nd floor space has Japanese-style low table seating that accommodates families and groups. The room is designed with a recessed space that allows the chef to make and serve sushi at the table. The large table has a UV coating in ash grey, a unique Edo-style color.

I had to understand the tradition to achieve a Japanese-modern architectural design. The methodology is rooted in traditional Japanese paradoxical aesthetic. A flower becomes eternal after it has blossomed and withered, an aspect of Noh drama expressed by the notion that "a hidden secret produces a dramatic surprise." This concept is described by Japanese aesthetician, actor, and playwright, Zeami Motokiyo (1363-1443) in his book, "*Fushi Kaden (Kaden-sho)*." The spatial structure of Noh can be explained by *Jo-ha-kyu*, the concept of modulation and movement applied in a wide variety of traditional Japanese arts. It consists of an "introduction (*jo*)," "break (*ha*)," and "approach (*kyu*)." I applied the Jo-ha-kyu concept to the design of this building. The introduction (*jo*) is from the entrance, which allows the guest to catch a glimpse of the inner space and imagine what is to come, to the muntin and sash, followed by the break (*ha*) toward the lattice door at the narrow elevator hall, and ends with the approach (*kyu*) to the guest seats.

Ginza Kyubey
Annex

P.092 地階客席。Overall view of underground level.
P.093 地階壁面詳細。Detail of the wall.

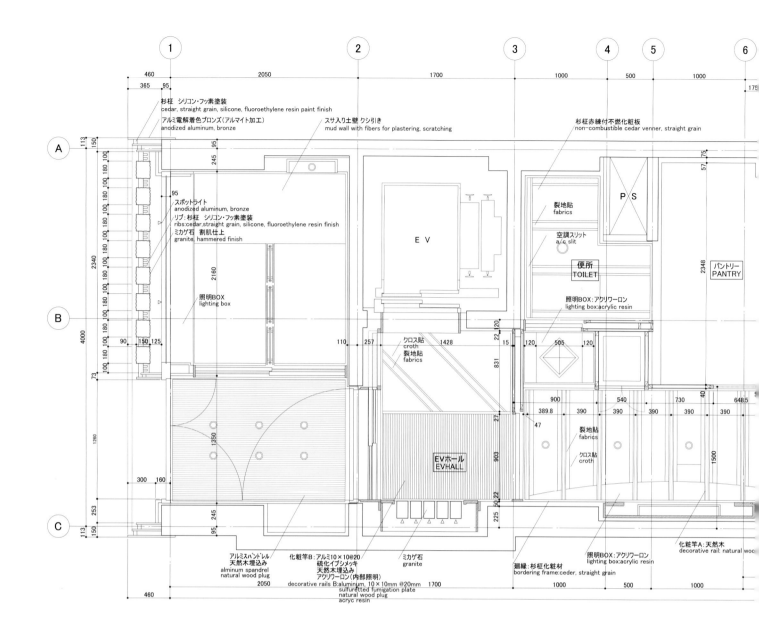
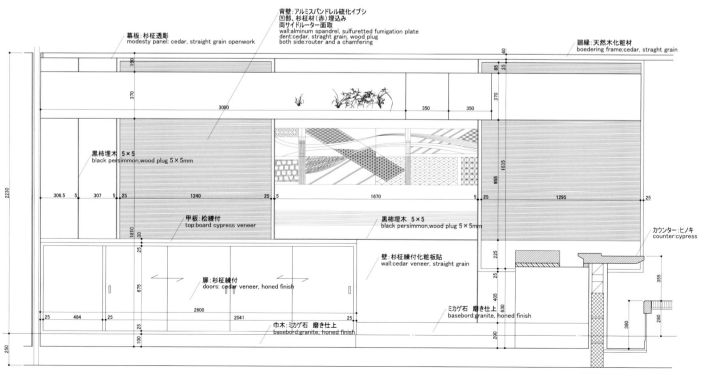

INTERIOR ELEVATION 1:30

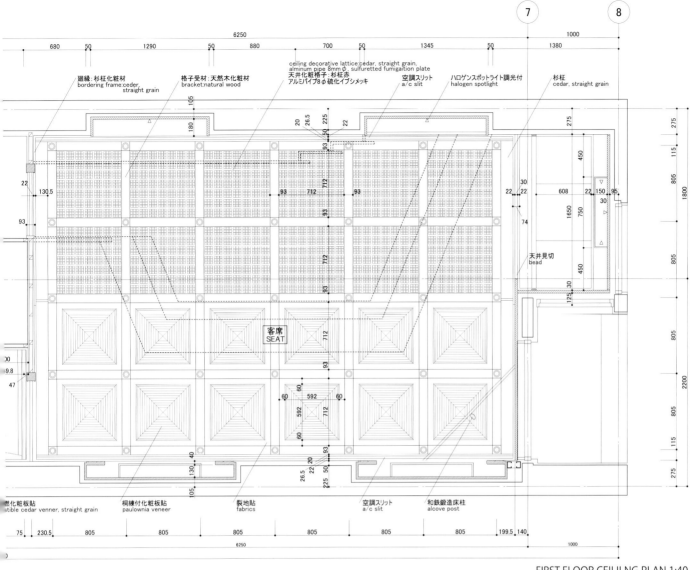

FIRST FLOOR CEILING PLAN 1:40

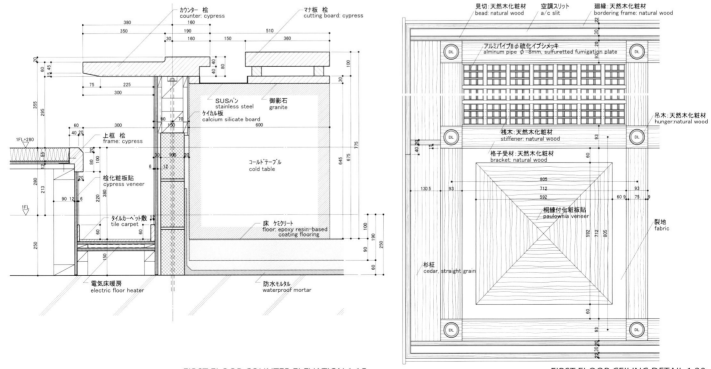

FIRST FLOOR COUNTER ELEVATION 1:15

FIRST FLOOR CEILING DETAIL 1:20

Takao Habuka   095

京王プラザホテル店。客席。Overall view of the chair counter.

左右で異なる趣のある空間

2006年4月「銀座久兵衛 別館」の全館リニューアルが竣工し、その後、「銀座久兵衛 本店」の全階部分改修が、週末や連休中の施工というタイトなスケジュールで完了した。「京王プラザホテル店」の計画は、そのあとの2008年2月にスタートしている。

38年近く経った京王プラザホテルの創業時からの店舗は古く、改修を機に倍の広さとなった。店舗としては厳しい7階に位置し、庭園を右手に長い廊下に面し、間口22.8m、奥行き4.3mと細長く、さらに中央に耐力壁があるため、変形プランとなった。本設計ではこれを逆手に取って、それぞれ異なる趣のある空間を求めることにした。

向かって右手側の内装は檜柾で統一し、畳敷きの久兵衛スタイルのお座敷カウンターとなっていて、付け台は黒の漆で仕上げ、緩やかな角度が付けられている。ここでも鮨ネタは見えないが、焼方の動きが見える、鮨屋としては珍しい演出となっている。

一方、左側の内装は杉柾を使用し、カウンターの形はもう一方と同じ鶴翼といわれる、板前とお客さんがコミュニケーションを取りやすい久兵衛独特の八の字型。このために用意された檜の良材を20mm削り出し、付け台一体のカウンターとなっている。

厨房の動線は狭いがバックで繋がっており、宴会場への対応も可能。ふたつの個室は可動間仕切りで仕切られるほか、ホテルでは不可欠となるテーブル席も用意されている。

ここで最もこだわったのはエントランスから入ってすぐの、緩く角度を振った意匠スクリーン。カウンターもこれに平行に振ることで、狭いバックの動線も確保される。今回のデザインはここに集約されているといっていい。檜の横桟格子の中に組子が仕込まれ、両側を色が濃く艶のある梨材で軽やかに締めて横桟をつかむスクリーンは、繊細で緊張感のあるディテールを生み出している。高い技術に裏打ちされたデザインは、ここを訪れた人の心を捉え、心豊かな記憶として刻み込まれることだろう。

銀座久兵衛
京王プラザホテル店

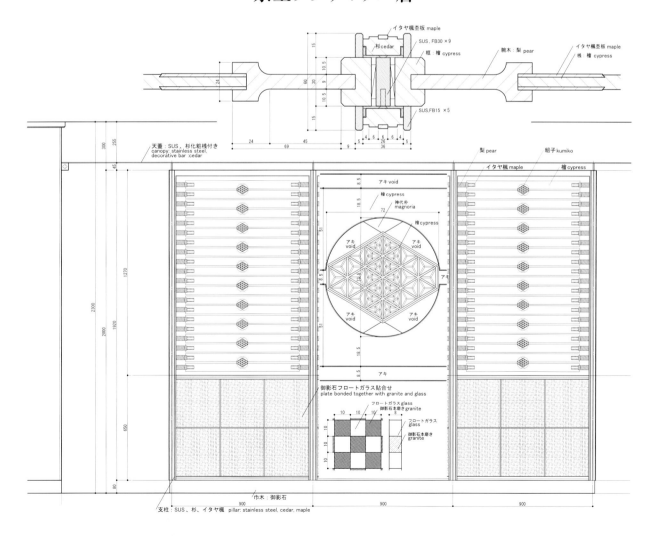

Ginza Kyubey
Keio Plaza Hotel Tokyo

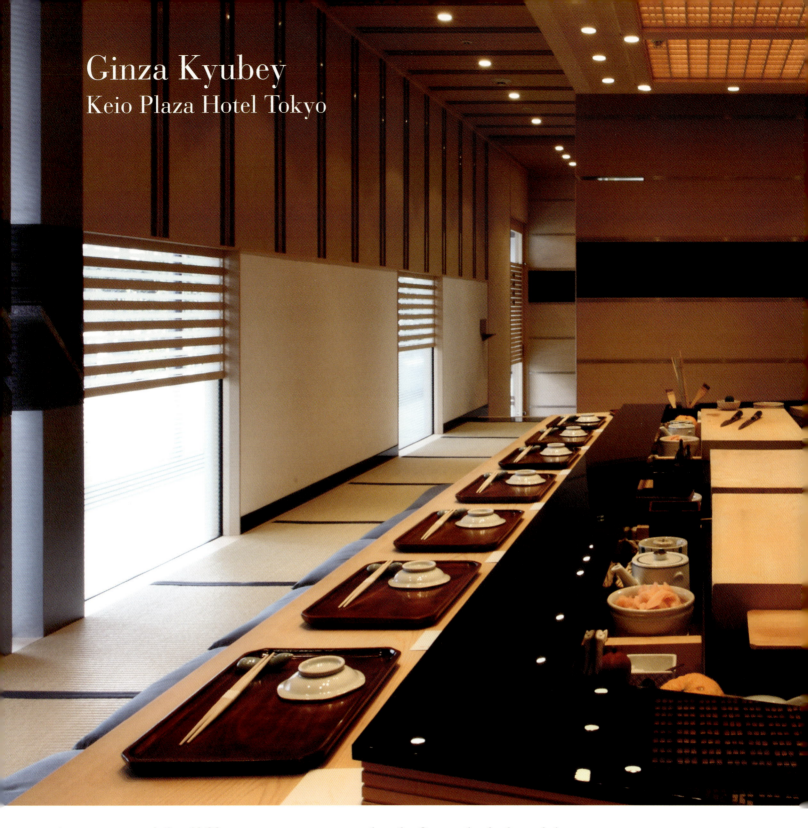

A space with different tastes on the left and right sides

The entire *Ginza Kyubey Annex* building was completely remodeled in April of 2006. Following this, partial remodeling on all the *Ginza Kyubey Main Restaurant* floors was completed on a tight schedule of weekends and holidays. We started on the *Keio Plaza Hotel Tokyo* location in February of 2008.

Since the *Kyubey Keio Plaza Hotel Tokyo* location had opened with the hotel 38 years ago, it was a little long in the tooth. After this remodeling, the restaurant was also expanded to double its previous size. It is located on the 7th floor, which is not really a favorable location for a restaurant because of its narrow frontage (22.8 m) and depth (4.3 m). Adding to this was the vertical slab in the middle of the building, which presented a design challenge. Using this to my advantage, however, I decided to plan each floor as a unique space.

The right side of the interior from the front is cypress, and the low counter table is in front of the tatami-mat seating, which is a design unique to Kyubey. I gave the counter table a gentle slope and a black lacquerware finish. Removing the display case traditionally included to allow guests to see the fish they are ordering provided a more dynamic view of the activity behind the counter. This lends a

uniquely interesting quality to the dining experience.

The left side of the interior from the front is cedar. The counter describes the shape of the Japanese character, "eight" (also known as *kaku-yoku*, the shape of a crane wing), which provides an ideal spatial relationship for comfortable conversation between the sushi chef and guests. A twenty-millimeter thick slab of high-quality cypress is curved to form an elegant counter.

Despite the narrow space, the line of flow in the kitchen is conveniently connected in the back to allow the chefs to service a large-party. The space can be separated into two rooms by a movable partition, and western-style table seating can also be arranged.

I placed a priority on the gently inclined screen nearest the entrance. Placing the counter parallel to this screen ensured a smooth visual flow in the narrow back space. My total effort in designing the restaurant focused on this. The horizontal cypress sash is framed with dark, glossy pearwood. This screen expresses sensitive detail. The design is supported by highly-advanced techniques to provide guests with an unforgettable experience.

座敷カウンター客席。右手ガラスが焼方。奥が厨房。カウンターは桧無垢材、黒い付台は漆塗り仕上。
Tatami mat counter. The counter is made of the cypress. The black part of the counter is lacquered Tsukedai.

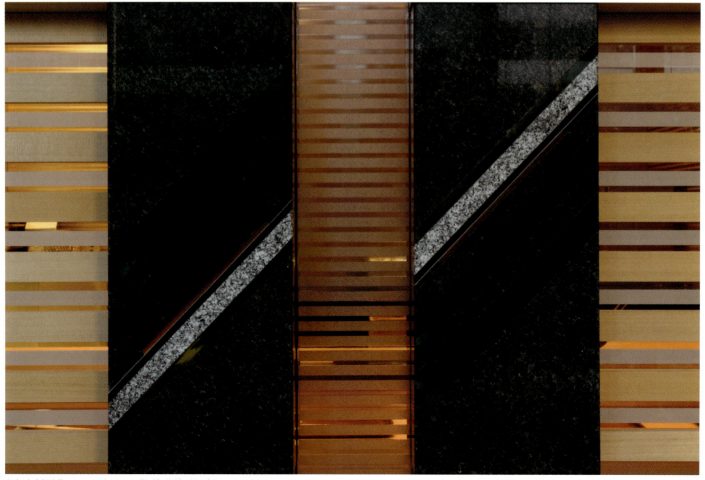

上（up）木製建具スクリーンディテール。梨、桧、楓材の組み合わせ。Detail of the wooden screen. Pear and cypress, maple wood are used.
下（down）200×200角の御影石と透明ガラスの斜め切意匠。Details of pillars using stone and glass.

上 (up) 木製建具スクリーン。組子ディテール原寸。Wooden screen. Detail of the kumiko actual size.
下 (down) 玄関木製建具ディテール。Detail of the entrance door.

本店4階客席。Overall view of 4th floor.

銀座久兵衛
Ginza Kyubey

本店(改装)
Main Restaurant "remodeling"

上 (up) 組子障子ディテール。数種の銘杢を使った組子障子。右手は御影石とガラスの市松模様の特殊なパネル。
Detail of the Kumiko-Shoji. Various wood is used for Kumiko-Shoji. On the right there is the a special panel of checkered patterns made of granite and glass.
下 (down) 本店1階客席天井。客席部の天井は1階から5階まで改装している。
Detail of the ceiling. The ceiling from the first floor to the fifth floor was refurbished.

Takao Habuka 103

会津中央病院
Aidu Chuo Hospital

| 羽深隆雄 | 病院 | 2009年〜 |

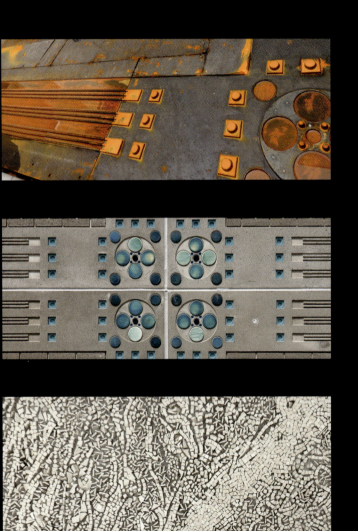

中庭よりPCaパネル意匠を見る。左手は既存棟よりの渡り廊下、右手にステンレスバフ仕上げの意匠パネルが見える。
View toward the facade, seen from the courtyard. There is a corridor on the left. On the right there is a pond and monument of stainless steel.

EAST CENTER 第2期
East Center (Phase II)

WEST2 第1期
West2 (Phase I)

中庭よりの外観見上げ。撮影＝小林浩志　View toward the facade, seen from the courtyard. Photo by Hiroshi Kobayashi

メディカルサイエンスと
建築アートの融合

　2009年5月第1期工事が完了し、約5～6ヶ月後、第2期工事の計画がスタートした。併わせて第1期完了とともに、既存建物の中で主力で規模も大きい、入院患者の最も多い、地下1階地上8階建てで延床面積約9000㎡の免震レトロフィット工事がスタート。2010年1月末にレトロフィットが完了し、その1年と40日後、2011年3月11日、東日本大震災が起こる。まさに免震構造の安全性を実証するかのようで、その偉力を見せられた思いであった。

　第2期工事となるEAST CENTERは、病院機能の根幹を有し、各階ごとにその機能が複雑多岐にわたっている。1階は外来、2階は手術室、3階は救命救急、4階はICU・HCU、5階内視鏡、6階脳卒中病床、7階は脳外科外来とNCUとなっていて、1～3階はスロープで高さを調整して既存施設と繋がっている。

　構造は、第1期と同じ、耐力壁がなく将来にわたり多様なプランの変更に対応可能なPC・PCa構造を主体構造としていて、基本スパンを15×7m、12×7mとしている。だが、敷地傾斜によ

会津中央病院
EAST CENTER

り1〜3階に段差が生じるために、あまり例のない1階レベルと3階レベルで、マットスラブを段違いとした免震構造を取り入れざるを得なかった。

「病院施設には、患者一人ひとりがそれぞれ、様々で複雑な問題を抱えて来院される」。

ここでもまた、今までの病院建築とは異なる場面が設定されている。それは既存の天井の高い渡り廊下に始まり、中庭のモニュメントとホールに集約されていて、そこは静かに、そして、穏やかに心が浄化され内部に惹き込まれる仕掛けとなっている。そこでは、「宇宙」「地球」「生命」をテーマとした3枚組の意匠パネルが目に飛び込む。その大きく象徴的で印象的なパネルのイメージをもって、ごく自然に、自由に誘い込まれるように、各フロアへと導かれていく。それは、本来病院建築として最も必要とされるメディカルサイエンスと建築アートの融合の場を創造している。

病院建築を設計するにあたり最も重要なことは、患者一人ひとりが自由を取り戻すため治療を受ける心、そして再び生きる力と勇気を、建築空間を通して甦らせ、患者自ら心の中で仕上げていくプロセスの手助けとしての場を創ることにある。

Takao Habuka　109

Aidu Chuo Hospital
East Center (Phase II) Construction

Integration of the Medical Sciences and the Art of Construction

In May 2009, Phase I construction was completed. About 5 to 6 months later, Phase II construction started. Immediately after the completion of Phase I, seismic isolation retrofit started for the total area of approximately 9,000 ㎥. The building has one floor under and eight floors above ground. This is a relatively large building and has the largest number of patients among the existing buildings. After the seismic isolation retrofit was completed at the end of January 2010, the Great East Japan Earthquake struck just about two months later, on March 11, 2011. While we cannot forget the terrible loss of life and irreparable damage this earthquake caused, we were relieved that the isolation structure we applied prevented damage to this building.

Constructed during Phase II, the EAST CENTER has the standard hospital functions, and each floor is equipped with a broad range of specialized functions. The 1st floor has an outpatient clinic, the 2nd floor has operation rooms, the 3rd floor has an emergency room, the 4th floor has an ICU and HCU, the 5th floor has endoscopy rooms, the 6th for has beds for stroke patients, and the 7th floor has a neurosurgery outpatient clinic and an NCU. The 1st to 3rd floors are connected to the existing buildings by slopes and height adjustments.

As with the structure of the buildings constructed in Phase I, the basic structure is PC/PCa, a structure that does not have weight-bearing walls, which allows for a wide range of changes in the future. The basic span is 15x7 m and 12x7 m. However, because the 1st to 3rd floors would have gaps due to the inclination of the land, I applied an isolation structure by installing a mat slab at different levels between the 1st and 3rd floors, something that is rarely seen.

Providing gentle care for people in need

The design of this hospital structure is different from existing hospital buildings. Passing through the existing corridor with its high ceiling, you see a monument in an inner garden before reaching a hall. It provides an atmosphere that calms you and encourages you to go further. You see three picture panels expressing the theme of "space," "earth," and "life." The significantly symbolic impression of the pictures invites you to each floor. These details function to create a space that integrates medical science, the most important aspect of a hospital, with architectural art.

The most important aspect of hospital design is to create a space that supports and lifts the spirits of individual patients undergoing treatment.

P.108-109　3階。救命救急・夜間診察アプローチを池越しに見る。　撮影=小林浩志　View of the ambulance approach on the 3rd floor. Photo by Hiroshi Kobayashi
P.110　枝垂桜越しに外壁を見上げる。Looking up at façade through cherry blossoms.
P.111　中庭池モニュメント。透明ガラスエッチングとステンレスバフ仕上げの意匠パネル。Pond and monument in the courtyard. Transparent glass etching and specular stainless steel panel.

既存との渡り廊下。正面に意匠パネルが見える。
View of the Corridor.

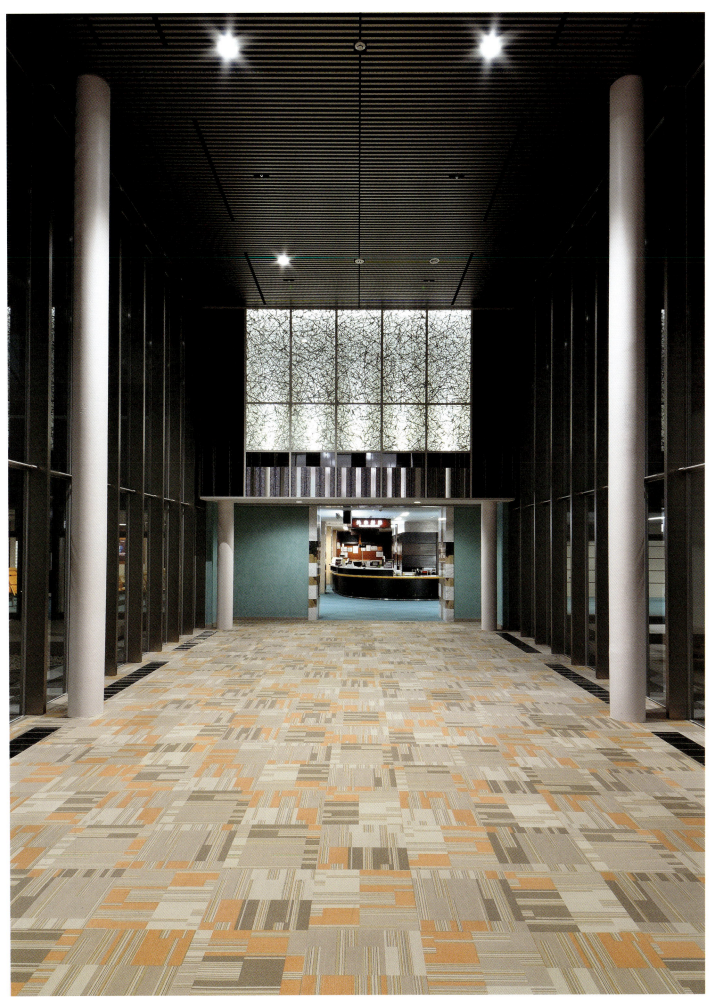

P.114 渡り廊下よりホールに向かう。上部曇りガラスはスリット付きのプロフィリットガラス。
View of the Corridor. At the top there is a window made of profilit-glass.
P.115 連絡通路より既存棟との接続口を見る。View of the existing side of the corridor.

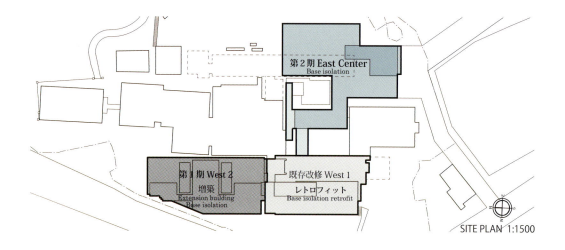

SITE PLAN 1:1500

FIRST FLOOR PLAN 1:900

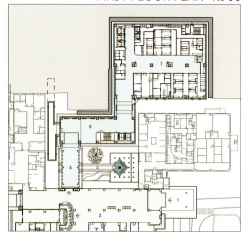

1. エントランス entrance
2. ホール hall
3. 総合受付 reception
4. 渡り廊下 corridor
5. 中庭 courtyard
6. ホール hall
7. 待合ホール hall

THIRD FLOOR PLAN 1:900

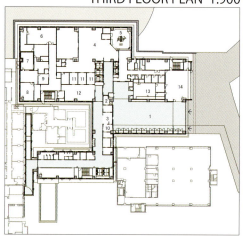

1. 車寄せ carriage porch
2. 洗浄室 the wash chamber
3. 受付 reception
4. 初療室 emergency room
5. 手術室 operating room
6. DSA 検査室 DSA room
7. MRI 検査室 MRI room
8. CT 検査室 CT room
9. 一般撮影室 X-ray room
10. 夜間外来風除室 windbreak room
11. 夜間外来診察室 consultation room
12. 夜間外来待合 hall
13. 救急ワークステーション office
14. 救命救急車庫 ambulance garage

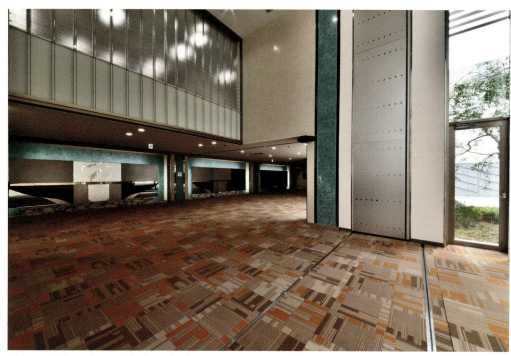

1階ホールから外来のアプローチ。左手下方には3枚の意匠パネルが見える。
Approach from the first floor to the outpatient hall. Visible three design panel on the left lower.

1階。外来フロア、エレベータホール。1st floor. Elevator hall.

1階。外来診察待合ホール。Outpatient waiting hall on the 1st floor.

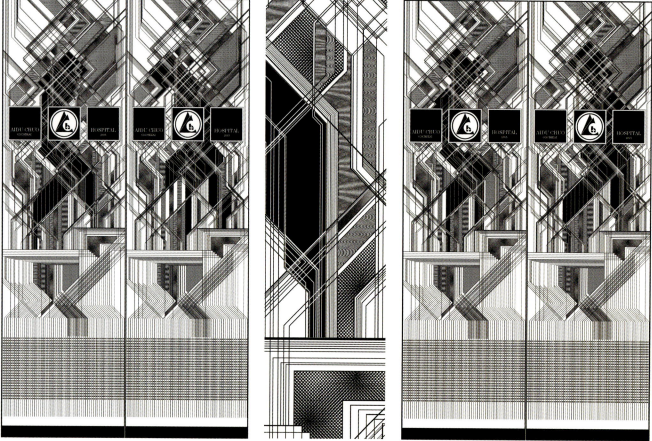

上（up）1階エレベータホール。エレベーター扉はステンレスエッチング。Elevator hall on 1st floor. The elevator door is etched stainless steel.
下（down）ステンレスエッチング原画。Original picture of the etching.

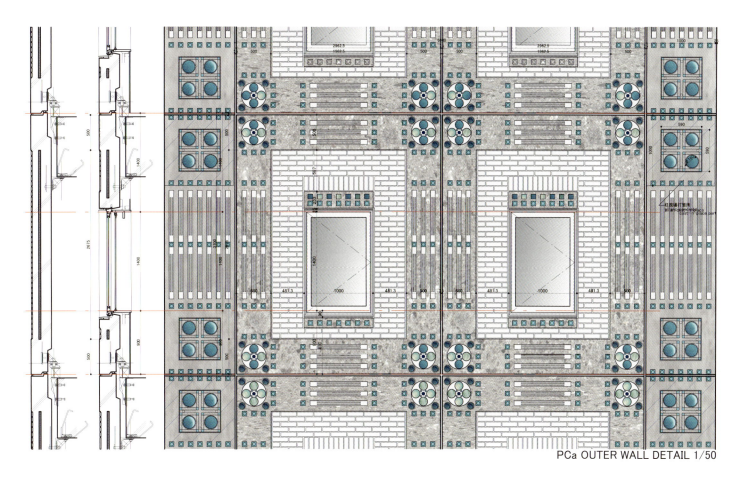

PCa OUTER WALL DETAIL 1/50

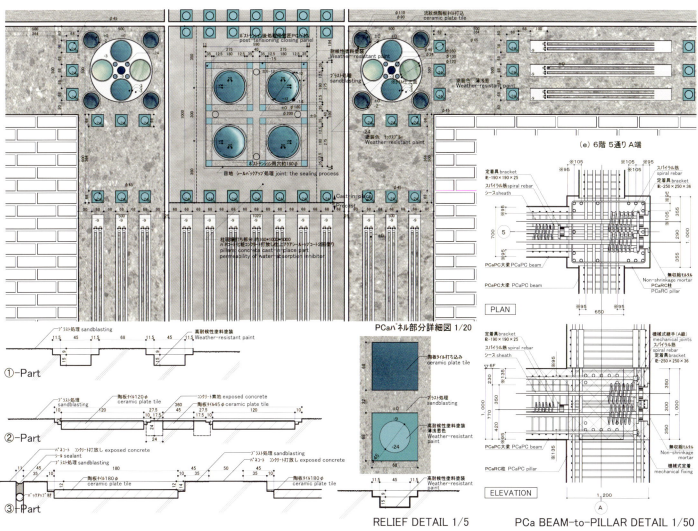

RELIEF DETAIL 1/5   PCa BEAM-to-PILLAR DETAIL 1/50

Takao Habuka 119

中央部意匠パネル。上部は喜井豊治氏によるiPS細胞(人工多能性細胞)を表現した大理石モザイク。下部はミラーガラスエッチングは遺伝子の2重螺旋を表している。その左右はDNAをデザインしたステンレスエッチング。
The center part of the triple design panel. At the top there is a marble mosaic that expresses IPS cells by Mr. Toyoharu Kii. At the bottom there are stainless steel plates and the mirror which etched the pattern designed DNA.

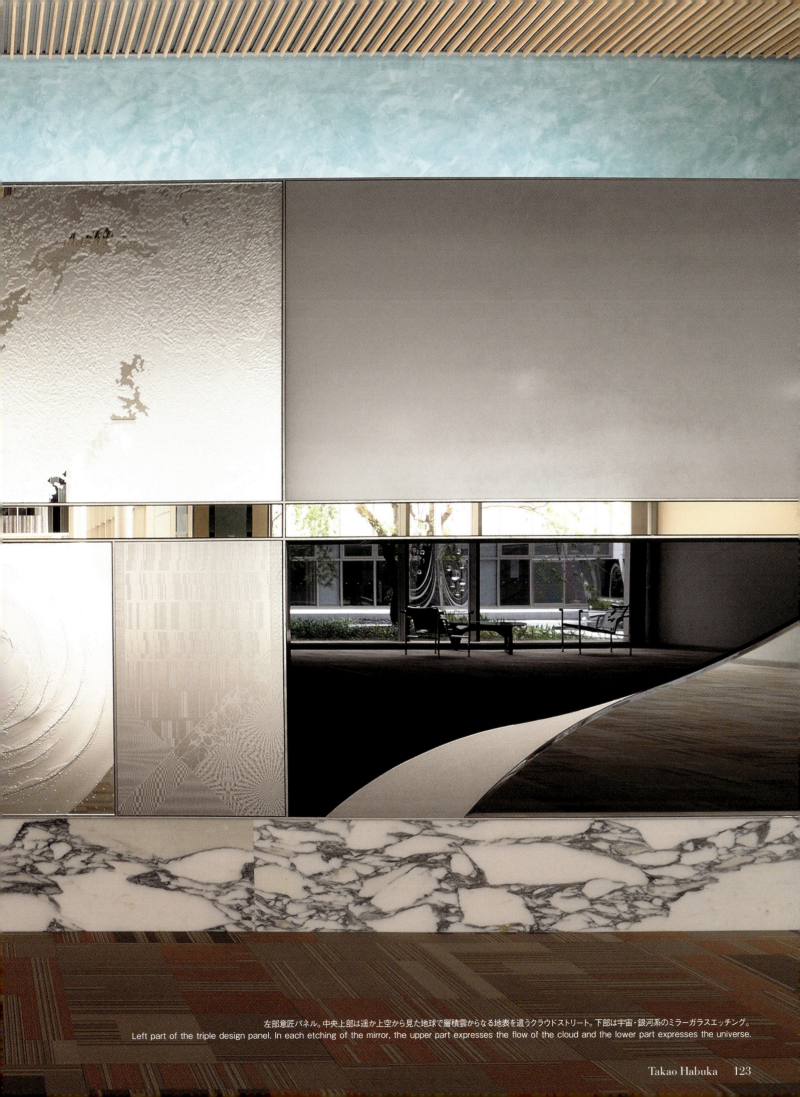

左部意匠パネル。中央上部は遥か上空から見た地球で層積雲からなる地表を這うクラウドストリート。下部は宇宙・銀河系のミラーガラスエッチング。
Left part of the triple design panel. In each etching of the mirror, the upper part expresses the flow of the cloud and the lower part expresses the universe.

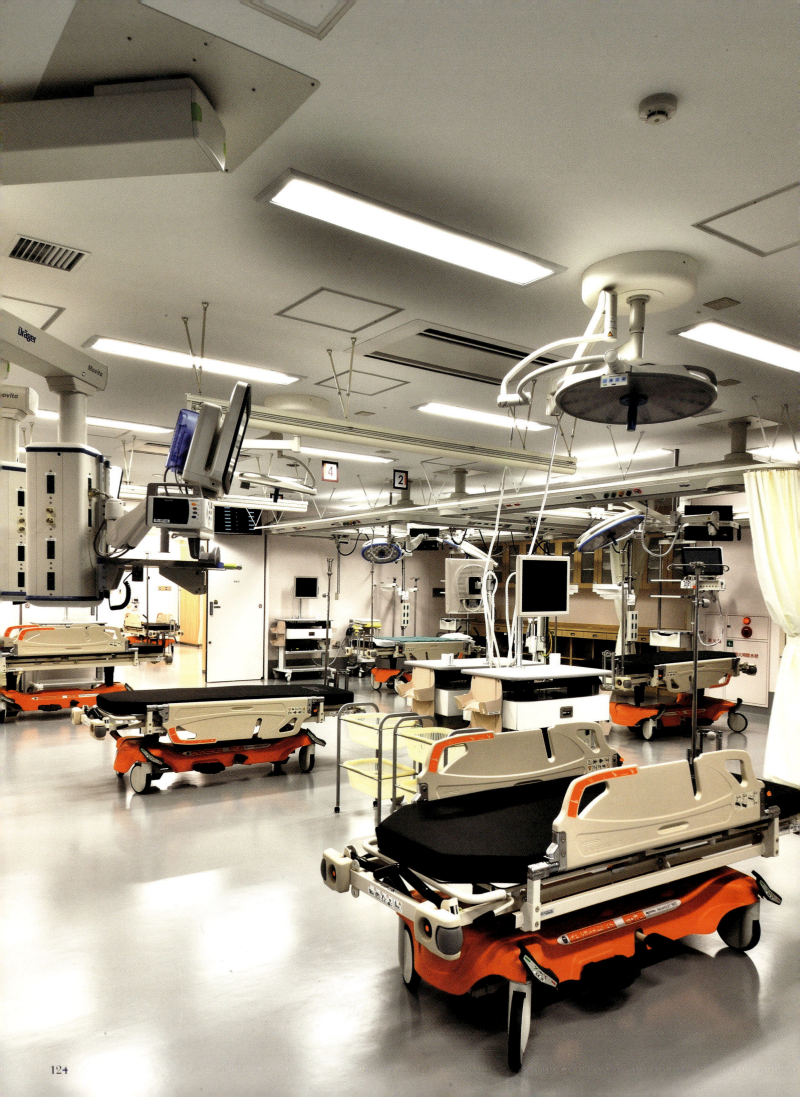

P.124 3階。救命救急初療室。Emergency rooms on the 3rd floor.
P.125上 (up) 7階。特別外来診察室。Special outpatient clinic on the 7th floor.
P.125下 (down) 1階。外来フロアへのアプローチ。Corridor to the outpatient hall on the 1st floor.

会津中央病院
WEST2 第1期

地下1階。多目的パブリックフロア。池に浮かぶ階段を見る。手前は池に掛かる御影石の橋。
Multi-purpose public floor on the Basement floor. View of the stairs floating on the pond.

明るく広がりのある「おもてなし」の空間

　大きな病院の増改築である。一般的に新築を除き病院建築は過去に増改築を数回繰り返し、その結果、迷路のような状態になりやすい。

　今回の計画では、まず既存施設を丹念に調査し、それを基に将来の増改築の方向性を見定め、ハードを決定し、医療を「おもてなし」と捉えた。さらに精神的に癒されるホスピタリティーを基本とし、従来の病院のイメージからの脱却を図り、建築空間により生きる力と勇気を呼び起こし、心豊かにする静かな動的空間を求めた。

　それはW2棟1階にある。ここを核として待合、診察、検査へと自分の位置がわかり、向かうべき方向が視認できる。明るく広いホールはトップライトの光が差し込み、光と影が静かな時を知らせる。その壁面には幅7.5mの熱帯魚の水槽が設けられ、吹き抜けを介して水の階段が交差し、ここから静かな動的空間が始まる。そこは1日の流れを感じとれる健康的で明るく広がりのある空間となっている。

　さらに、本来病院建築で考えなければならないメディカルサイエンスと建築アートのコラボレーションによる、新たな病院建築を目指した。

　今回の増築は柱、梁、外壁を工場製作のPC、PCa構造とすることで、7ヶ月の工期の短縮を実現させた。増築部は基礎免震とし、既存棟は地階柱の中間免震レトロフィット工法とし、三次元可動のエキスパンションジョイントで連結させている。

1階より吹抜けを見る。地下1階は多目的パブリックフロア。左手に7.5mの水槽が見える
View toward the void, seen from the 1st floor. There is the aquarium on the left.

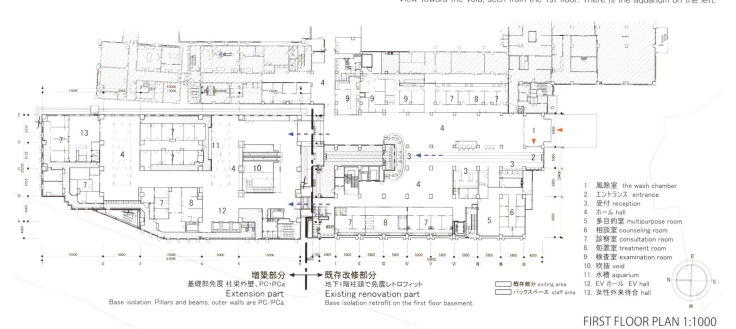

1. 風除室 the wash chamber
2. エントランス entrance
3. 受付 reception
4. ホール hall
5. 多目的室 multipurpose room
6. 相談室 counseling room
7. 診察室 consultation room
8. 処置室 treatment room
9. 検査室 examination room
10. 吹抜 void
11. 水槽 aquarium
12. EVホール EV hall
13. 女性外来待合 hall

FIRST FLOOR PLAN 1:1000

Aidu Chuo Hospital
West2 (Phase I)

Bright and expansive hospitality

Hospitals tend to become mazelike after repeated refurbishments and extensions, and I wanted to avoid this in my design.

In this plan, I examined the existing building in detail to determine the possibilities for future extension and reconstruction, and decided to focus on "hospitality" in the design. Breaking away from the existing image of hospitals, I sought a calm but dynamic space that creates a feeling of comfort as it lifts spirits.

A calm but dynamic space is located on the 1st floor of the W2 building. Standing in this space, you can see the waiting room, consultation and examination rooms, allowing you to recognize your location and where to go next. The bright and expansive hall receives sunlight from the sunroof. The light and shadow in the hall quietly tell you the time. A tropical fish tank measuring 7.5 m wide is installed in the wall, and water-colored stairs are positioned in the middle of the stairwell, from which a calmly dynamic space begins. This is a healthy, bright and expansive space where people can feel the flow of the day.

Using these detailed elements, I aimed to establish a new hospital style through a collaboration of medical science and architectural arts.

1階ホール。トップライトより優しく光が差し込む。御影石削岩石に7.5mの熱帯魚の水槽。
View of the hall on the 1st floor. Granite cutting rock and the tropical fish aquarium width 7.5m.

7階サロンよりレストラン入口を見る。View of the restaurant entrance, seen from the salon on the 7th floor.

上（up）7階レストラン。Restaurant on the 7th floor.
下（down）特別病室。応接スペースや執務デスクが設えてある。カーテンは電動式。
Special hospital room. There are sitting area and an work desk. Curtain is motorized.

Takao Habuka 133

論考1

素材・手仕事・装飾——梵 寿綱と仲間たち
鈴木博之

建築の本質は「空間」として完結した単位が基本として存在するのか、それとも「場所」的に広がってゆくものなのか。これは我々が建築に対して抱く大きな問題である。この問題は、建築の本質は世界の文化圏を超えて普遍的に同一なのか、それとも文化圏ごとに異なる性格をもつものなのかという疑問につながるし、建築の本質は時代を超えて変らないものなのかという疑問にもつながってゆく。

梵寿綱という建築家と、その仲間というべき作家たちの建築を考えるとき、建築の普遍性と特殊性という二つの側面は、極めて重要な問題となる。ここで梵寿綱について、彼自らが述べる所を最初に引用しておこう。

「梵寿綱と仲間たち」は英語でVon Jour Caux and his Troupeとなります。「Troupe」とは「しがない旅役者」のことで一夜の観客の雰囲気で即席に脚本の筋書きや演出の調子を変えて舞台を設え共感した観客からの「おひねり（ご祝儀）」で生計果てしない旅を続けます。

のっけから晦渋で韜晦した説明であるが、梵寿綱について考えようとすると、こうした精神を理解しなければならない。

空間か場所か

イタリアの哲学者ウンベルト・エーコは、建築の始まりを「洞窟」と「階段」という要素から説明している。「洞窟」とはひとを包み込み、保護するシェルターとしての建築の要素であり、「階段」とはひとに行動を促す存在としての建築のありかたを示す要素である、と。

エーコによるこの説明は大変興味深く、建築の本質を鋭く解き明かしてくれているように思われた。建築は人間にとっての安らぎの場としてのシェルターである。と同時に建築は、じっとして動かない存在であるにもかかわらず、人々に動きを与え、大げさにいうなら社会の活動をもたらす存在である。それを「階段」という要素に代表させるところがしゃれていると思った。彼の説明によれば、ひとは階段を前にしたときにおのずから昇るか下るかの行動に迫られる、というのである。

しかしながらこの説明を反芻するうちに、一つのことに気づいた。日本には「洞窟」住居はほとんど存在しなかったという事実と、日本の建築にはほとんど「階段」も備えられていなかったという事実である。日本の原始住居は竪穴式住居に代表されるように平地住居が圧倒的であった。穴居住宅はほとんど存在していない。そして日本の建築は平屋ばかりであったから、内部に階段をもつこともなかった。

日本には平屋しかないというと、そんなことはない、原始時代はいざ知らず、歴史時代になってからは五重塔もあれば天守閣もあるではないかと反論されるかもしれない。しかし五重塔の内部を見てみれば解ることだが、塔の内部には床もなく天井もない。つまり五重塔の内部にはひとが上る上階など存在しないのだ。第一、ふつうのひとで五重塔に登ったことのあるひとなど、まずいないだろう。五重塔はひとが上るようには造られていないのだ。五重塔は五階の塔ではなく、あくまでも屋根だけが五層に重ねられた、外部から眺められる存在なのだ。

同じように天守閣も日常的にひとがいる場ではなかった。確かに天守閣の内部には急なはしご段のような階段があるし、上階にも床が張ってある。けれどもそこに日常的にひとが上ることはなかった。天守閣に籠るとすれば、それは城を枕に討ち死にする覚悟を決めたときだけだろう。天守閣もまた、城下かから遥かに眺められる象徴的存在だったのである。城主は天守閣の下に造営された広大な平屋の御殿に暮らしていた。

同じように二階をもつ都城や寺院の楼門なども、上階は一種の異界と思われていた。羅生門の伝説、南禅寺の山門から絶景かなとよばわったという石川五右衛門の伝説を思い起こせばよいであろう。

実際に人々が上ることのあった金閣や銀閣といった楼閣建築の場合は、そこに上ることがそれだけで非日常的イベントであったからこそ珍重されたのである。遊廓の二階座敷なども同じことだ。つまり、伝統的な日本の建築において、二階にひとが暮らすという習慣は存在しなかったのである。つまり日本の伝統は木造平屋の建築によって築かれてきたのである。

それでは木造平屋の建築は、西欧の建築的伝統とは異なる世界を形成したのだろうか。

木造平屋の建築が発展的に展開する場合には、広い領域に建物が点在する形式をとるか、建物がつぎつぎに横に

（水平方向に）拡がってゆくか、この二つが考えられる。前者は寺院の伽藍などをイメージすればよいであろうし、後者は二条城二の丸御殿や桂離宮のような建物を想像すればよい。後者は建物が雁行といわれる一種のジグザグ型の水平展開をしている。これは平屋の建物をそのまま巨大にしてしまうと、建物内部は暗くなってしまって使い物にならないからだ。建物を水平方向に展開する場合には光や風が取り入れられるように、建物を雁行させるのがもっとも効果的なのである。

　ここで一つの問題が起きる。平屋の建物が広い領域に点在してしまったり、水平方向に拡がってしまうと、重要な部分となるはずの奥の方は、外部からは窺い知れなくなってしまう。「いとも畏き辺り」などといって、大切なものは目に見えるところからは隠されるとする日本的な意識は、こうした建築形式の伝統と無関係ではない。

　平屋の建築が水平に展開する建築は、同時に部屋々々がそれぞれ外部と直接的に接する。したがって少なくとも主要な部屋はそれに面する外部、すなわち庭をもっていた。雁行する桂離宮のような建物の広がりは、外部と建物をもっともうまく接触させる手法を示したものである。しかしながらこうした内部と外部の接触という性格は、古代の寝殿造りの邸宅から中世・近世の書院造の座敷、寺院の方丈といわれる居住部分、そして町家の座敷にいたるまでに共通する。主要な部屋は庭をもつ、これが水平展開する平屋の建築のもう一つの特徴となる。

　日本建築の魅力として、屋根と並んで庭園の美しさがたたえられることが多いのも、水平展開する平屋の建築的伝統に由来していると考えられる。水平展開する建築にとって、庭園は建築と同等の重みをもつ存在だからである。無論西欧にも庭園の美しさでしられる建築は数多い。しかしながらそうした庭園の多くは、建築が内包する部屋とは別個の存在感を自立的に主張している。建築と密接に結びついた中庭の場合でも、それは一つの立方体的な空間として構想されていると感じる。平屋の建築にとっての庭、とりわけ日本建築における庭は部屋と相互に依存しあい、相互に貫入し合うようなあり方を示している。日本建築の部屋部屋は庭に向かって開かれ、庭は部屋に対してその顔を向けるのである。

　それではこうした建築のあり方を何と呼べばよいであろうか。西欧の建築が空間的であるのに対して、これは水平に拡がる場所的な建築と呼ぶべきであろう。もともと我が国の建築における座敷などの主要な部屋は、空間として完結した存在ではなく、庭園に向かって開かれた存在、あえていうなら空間ではなく舞台のようなものなのである。日本建築の

部屋は空間を形成するものではなく、場所を生成するものなのである。そうした部屋がつらなってゆく建築は、敷地全体をどのように構成していくかを問題としてきた。日本の都市もまた、建築と庭をモザイク状にちりばめて水平に連なる、場所的な都市ということになるであろう。

　「場所」は、即物的に敷地とか現場と考えられるけれども、そこにはそれぞれ個性があるという考えもまた、歴史的にかなり古くから存在していた。西欧には古代から「ゲニウス・ロキ」という概念があり、私はそれを「地霊」と訳しているのだが、これは中国における「人傑地霊」という言葉を踏まえたものである。両者はともに、場所がもっている潜在的なちからを言い表わしたことばなのである。場所には場所のちからがあり、可能性が秘められているという考えである。古びた迷信くさい概念だといわれるかもしれないが、こうした言葉は逆に我々が現代都市のなかで失ったものを教えてくれる。新しいビルが建ち並ぶオフィス街は、いまや世界共通だ。東京の大手町は、シカゴやニューヨークの一部と見えなくもない。じっさいこうした世界共通の都市風景は方々にあって、ニューヨークのマンハッタンを舞台にした映画やテレビドラマを作るときには、しばしばカナダのトロントでロケをするのだと聞いたことがある。ちょっと画面を見ただけでは区別がつかないくらい、高層ビルの林立する風景が似ているからだ。

　世界の都市景観の共通性といえば肯定的に響くが、それは現代都市における「場所性の喪失」にほかならない。我々は、いまや場所を失って生活しているのではないのだろうか。普遍的という名のもとに、建築は場所性を失い、我々を抽象的な空間のなかに捉え込んでしまった。しかしながら建築は人間をその内部に含み込む構造体である。たしかに時代の精神は後戻りできない。時代が目指す方向はインターナショナルであり、世界の共通性であるかもしれないが、そこでの生活には場所の感覚が必要ではなかろうか。現代の建築は、抽象的な空間と時間の産物を目指すのではなく、そのなかに含み込まれる人間の意識に立った、場所性と時代性とを獲得してゆくべきであろう。

情報化時代の場所

　情報化によって、我々は場所をとらずに膨大なデータが処理でき、引き出せ、活用できることになった。現代の我々が扱う情報量はほんの十数年前に比べてどれほど大きいものか、比較するのが難しいほどである。しかも情報はパソコンやインターネットのなかに置いたままにしておいて、必要に応じて取り出せばよい。しかもそうした情報をどこからでも

引き出せる時代が訪れている。情報は場所をとらないだけでなく、場所を選ばなくもなりつつあるのである。その意味では、蔵書やメモを増やす努力、そして情報を求めて方々へ足を運ぶ努力が圧倒的に軽減されたといってよいだろう。もっとも、私は勤勉ではないし、物忘れもひどいから、情報を取り出し忘れる、情報のありかを忘れる、情報を尋ねる時間がない、といったことはしょっちゅうである。そこで「何が情報化なのだ、よくわからない」という冒頭の愚痴になる。

情報が氾濫しているというけれど、それだけでは何の意味ももたない。情報とは公表されたり、印刷されたり、ダウンロードされたりして、はじめてそのすがたを現すものだからだ。目に見えるかたちになるまでは、情報は宙をさ迷っているように思われる。それを捕まえてはじめて情報は使えるようになる。情報にどこからでもアクセスできるといっても、それがどこにあるかを知らなければならない。

そうした情報のあり方を示すものとして「サイト」という言葉がある。ウェブサイト、ネットサイトなどだ。これは私の専門領域である建築の歴史の世界では、現場ということになる。工事現場である。発掘現場もサイトである。つまりは場所ということだ。考えてみると、情報に関わる言葉には建築のアナロジーではないかと思われる例が多い。コンピュータ・アーキテクチュアという言葉をよく聞くし、情報漏洩や情報への不正アクセス防止のための手だてをファイアー・ウォールといったりする。防火壁である。どうも情報技術は建築や場所の類推によって理解を得ているらしい。

情報は「場所」を必要としていると感じたとき、情報の本質を感じたように思った。場所のもつ意味もまた、そのときに見えてきたように思われた。情報を取り出すサイトは、現在ウェブ上のサイトであると同時に、現実の場所に遍在しはじめている。あらゆる場所であらゆる情報に接近できる状況が現れつつある。それが情報化時代のあたらしい局面なのであろうか。しかしながら、それほどの変化がそこにはあるのか。

かつてヴィクトル・ユーゴーは「これが、あれを滅ぼす」というフレーズによって、ゴシックの聖堂に彫刻のかたちで掘り込まれた可視的な聖書の世界が、新しく生まれてきた書籍というかたちの印刷物によって滅ぼされてゆく事態を言い表したが、今、情報化の時代がこれまでの印刷物の世界を滅ぼすのであろうか。しかし、現在の状況はこれがあれを滅ぼすという択一的なものではなく、共存的なものであろう。

一つの類推として、考古学あるいは発掘においてしばしば使われる「in situ」という言葉が思い浮かぶ。「in situ」とは文字通りには「その場所において」という意味である。ある史料が伝来したものではなく、その現場において発掘さ

れたものであれば、信頼度はもっとも高いので、そうした史料は「in situ」において発見された史料として尊重されるのである。このことは情報の信頼性においても当て嵌まるであろう。情報にとって「場所」のもつ意味は、変わらず大きく、意味のあるものであり、情報をとり出す場所はウェブ上に存在するとともに、現実の世界においても存在するのであるから。

情報と同様に建築もまた切実に「場所」を必要としている。建築は一つの「場所」には一つしか建たない。それぞれの建築はかならず世界で一つしかない場所を占めて建っているのである。その事実をもう一度考え直してみることが、将来の建築のあり方を教えてくれるのではないだろうか。ここで私が「風土」といわずに「場所」というのには、意味がある。

建築の固有性などというと、すぐさま風土性、地域性、伝統性などという方向に話がどんどん向かいがちである。しかしながらそうした方向には、前向きの姿勢が感じられない。一つの地域なり伝統なりに閉じこもっていってしまいそうな危険性がある。また、建築の個性を国民的伝統という方向で解釈してしまうと、ただちに偏狭なナショナリズムの建築が生まれてきそうである。じつを言えば、社会主義諸国で作られつづけた権威主義的な建築（モスクワ大学などを想像していただきたい）は、こうした「伝統主義」にきわめて近いものだったように思うのだ。文化的意味をもった記号をちりばめることによって建築の個性を回復しようとしたのがポストモダニズムだった。けれどもそれがただちに陳腐化してしまったという教訓を踏まえるならば、風土性、地域性、伝統性などという方向での建築の個性化に含まれる危険性も予測できよう。だからこそ「風土」ではなく、「場所」ということばに注目したいのである。「場所」には必要以上の伝統・風土・地域などの背景がまとわりついていない。

我々が情報に接することができるのはサイトという名の「場所」を通じてであり、そこから我々は別の場所に向かって飛び出してゆけるらしい。それはサイトとしての場所の意味であると同時に、場所本来のちからでもあるらしい。ときどき刑事物のドラマなどで「現場百回」といったせりふが出てくるけれど、現場すなわち場所にはやはり何かのちからがある。足を運ぶことで見えてくるものがあるのは事実であろう。それは情報化時代になっても同じなのではなかろうか。

サイトのおもしろさは、何が現れるか解らないところにある。発掘現場としてのサイトはその最たるものだし、工事現場も何が起きるか解らない。そして町なかのあらゆる場所もまた、何が潜んでいて、何が現れるところか解らない。むしろ、何を見つけるかがサイトでの勝負だ。町を歩き回ることは場所に蓄積された情報を探しに行くことだ。場所とは歴史

や情報が蓄積する形式のことではなかろうか。ウェブ上をうろうろすることも同じだ。影もかたちも無いように思われる情報も、サイトという名の場所を通して降りてくるのだ。我々は場所に網を張って情報を待ち受ける。

梵 寿綱と仲間たち

そうした時期、我々に忘れられかねない建築のあり方を示すのが、梵寿綱である。空間と場所、機能と装飾、そして近代建築が目指した普遍性と、日本建築がもつ個性的な場所性の展開、こうした問題は梵寿綱の建築を見ると、激しく揺すぶられる。近代建築が解決してきたと思われる多くの命題が、梵寿綱の作品を前にすると、改めて問い直されているように感じられる。空間とは何か、場所とは何か、情報化時代におけるサイト（site、場所）とは何か、我々はもう一度考え直してみる必要性を感じる。

私が彼の建築にであったのは、すでに半世紀近い昔、1969年のことであった。ある建築雑誌に紹介されたその建物は、「ある美瑠〔塚田ビル〕」[*1]という名前であった。6階建位の、それ程大きくない普通の町中の建物であったが、それは細かい部分に異常なまでに注意の込められた建物であった。ステンレス製のドアの把手に浮き彫りされた梅鉢のような模様、また、床のパターン、ガラスブロック、そうした全てに円と正方形を基調としたパターンが配され、緊密な紋章の世界が構築されていた。パターンは静謐でありながら緻密な体系を形作っており、建物は凝縮した細部が綿密に張り巡らされていた。いわゆる町中の事務所建築に、これ程までの不思議な細部のつらなりを込めることが現代において可能であろうとは思われない程であった。そしてこの時、その設計者として、梵という名の設計事務所の存在を知ったのである。

梵寿綱は本名を田中俊郎といい、そのキャリアの出発点にアメリカでの建築体験をもつ建築家である。1962年にアメリカに発った彼は、「ハウス・アンド・ガーデン」誌に勤め、後にシカゴのアート・インスティテュートに学んだ。この留

fig.1 「阿維智」玄関ホールタイル 原画。
Entrance hall tiles, original art of *Gladiator's Nest*.

学中に彼は東京の三宅坂に計画された国立劇場の設計競技に応募して、佳作入選を果たしている。この案を見ると、極めて緻密なデザインであり、近代建築の合理的細部設計の精神に貫かれた、ひと言でいえば近代建築の典型的手法による作品である。この後も、彼はシカゴでの美術展に応募して複数回入賞している。このような、いわば目覚ましい成果を上げて、アメリカとメキシコの周遊を経て帰国した。

このような経歴を見るならば、梵寿綱は近代建築の主流を歩む建築家となるべき存在であったと感じられる。そうした彼が、梵寿綱という名を選び取り、細部装飾に満ちた建築をつくり出す道を歩み出したのはなぜか。まず、梵寿綱の成立について考えてゆこう。

梵寿綱は自分の創造のマニュフェストともいうべき文章を1969年末に雑誌「建築」に発表している。「三祈指帰」と題されたその文章は、空海の「三教指帰」を意識したもので、一人の優婆塞がニーチェと思われる意志の人と、道元と思われる無常の人とを遍歴し、空海と思われる大師に巡り合うという哲学的な内容を持っている。しかしながらそうした文章に予想される過去への回帰の志向は、そこには見出されない。「三祈指帰」はつぎのように書き出されている。

私のもっている世紀の交換の意識のなかで最も不幸な事は、それが過ぎ去った時代の上に漸進的に築かれるといった単純な引継ぎの上に成る変化ではなくて、完全に事態を根底から変えてしまう性質のものだということであった。

fig.2 「無量寿舞」外観。
Exterior of *Eternal Home*.

じつはこの文章を、私は1977年に書いた梵寿綱論の記事*2で引用しているのだが、こうした点については、何も付け加える必要はない。ここで考えてゆきたいのは、梵寿綱はどのように現在を迎えているのかということである。

帰国して大学で講師を勤めはじめた田中俊郎は、建築計画やシステム・デザインを教えたという。ミース・ファン・デル・ローエやバックミンスター・フラー流の合理主義建築の最先端を持ち込む彼の姿がそこに見られる。この講義を受け、そこに引き込まれていった若い学生の一人が、ここでのもう一人の主人公、羽深隆雄であった。彼は田中（梵）の建築の捉え方、建築に対する考え方に惹かれ、彼の設計事務所に出入りするようになる。

やがて両者はそれぞれ別々に仕事しつつも、観念的には同一のものをもちつづけ、施工に携わる職人を共有したり、融通無碍というべき連合を形成するようになるらしい。梵寿綱にいわせると、こうである。

生命の伝承が実父母由来の家族の血統によるものではなくて、「縁」あって巡り合った人間同士の生命の饗応と記憶によるものだとの、経験的な認識を育ててきた私・田中俊郎は、養父が亡くなったときを機縁に、設計事務所名として掲げていた「梵」と、養父の戒名の「寿綱」をつなげた「梵　寿綱」の雅号を名乗ることになりました。

そして、社会的な姓名を捨てることで、各個人の寿命を超えて永続する人工的存在物である建物に、生きた時代の束の間の生命の輝きの響きや、綾なす生命を伝える語り部を天職として、建築家の作務を果たす決意をしたのです。

その翌年の1974年に、「心の内奥への巡礼・彼岸への誘い」を空間構成の主題とした「阿維智」（fig.1）を、『新建築誌』に発表しました。「阿維智」はクライアントの会社名「アイチ」に由来しますが、密教根本経典・大日経の「阿字観（瞑想法）」の「阿（根本となる真言）」と「智（人間の智慧）」を「維（綾織成す）」との言霊を主題として、空間構成を試みました。

表音文字のアナグラム（言葉の単語を入れ替えて新しい意味を生みだす言葉遊び）は、綴りが異なる単独の意味を持つ新しい文字を生み出します、が、象形文字である漢字のアナグラムは、一語一語の形象が意味を持っていて、組合せや配置で複合された新しい意味を暗示します。

そこで建物の社会的な名称をアナグラムすることで、「阿維智」以降の作務を、「秘羅樒」、「斐醴祈」、「和世陀」、「無量寿舞」、「精霊の館」、「和泉の扉」、「きらめく器」、「性源寺」、「舞都和亜」などと、編み出した主題となる「言霊」の暗喩を手掛りにした建物を、竣工時に一般公開する「アート・コンプレックス」運動を始めました。

そして、羽深隆雄については、つぎのように述べる。

建築はその時代に生きた人々の生命の息吹を語り伝えますがその時代の建築が残らなければその時代そのものが消えてしまいます。技術や表現様式や思想以外に伝承や後継すべきものは何か？　—

fig.3 「和世陀」外壁ディテール。
Exterior wall detail of *Waseda el Dorado*.

言で言えば「時代的生命への共感」なのではないかと思います。その意味で羽深隆雄は僕の後継者なのです。

　このように梵寿綱の言葉を引用しても、実のところ私には彼の言わんとするところが理解できない。漢字の組み合わせによる建物名称の性格づけもよく解らないし、そこから生じるという「アート・コンプレックス」運動も、何を目指すものか、はっきりしない。唯一感じられるのは、彼の手がけた建物の存在感が多くの人々に強烈な印象を与え、そこから一種の芸術家集団、職人集団、クライアント集団のごときものが生まれていたという事実のリアリティである。羽深隆雄もそうしたもっとも梵寿綱に近い位置にいる一員であるということだ。したがって、彼らの建築を分析する作業は、彼らの建築そのものに基づく分析に終始することになろう。

空間から場所へ

　梵寿綱の建築作品は普遍的空間を目指すのではなく、固有性を備えた唯一無二の場所をつくり出そうとする。向台老人ホーム「無量寿舞」（fig. 2）は、高齢者が人生の最後を迎えるための場所である。公共的性格から、こうした施設に宗教色を持ち込むことは禁止されているのであるが、ここにあるのは社会福祉施設という無色透明な施設建築ではない。この建物の中心を成しているのは、霊安室なのである。それを知ったときには、思わずぎょっとするが、この施設の究極の目標が、安らかな死を迎えることであるとするならば、そのための部屋である霊安室こそ、この老人ホームのクライ

マックスなのだと理解される。ここには「大いなる手」をかたどった彫刻があり、人を迎え入れる。

　施設全体にわたって鏝仕上げの多彩さを見せる壁面装飾、木彫、ステンドグラスなど、多様な職人仕事による仕事がみられる。これらはこの施設をかけがえのない唯一無二の場所にすることに役立っている。この老人ホームに入る人々は、ここを施設としてではなく、人生の最後の場所として味わう。梵寿綱はさまざまな職種の職人やアーティストたちをこの現場に呼び入れ、腕を振るわせることによって、ここを機能的な空間から、機能を超えた全体性を備えた場所に変貌させていく。こうした仕事の方向性は、彼がオーガナイズする建築のすべてに見られるものであり、その結果、彼の建築はすべて普遍性よりは固有の場所性を備えた「一回限りのできごと」というべき性格を帯びる。

　写真家の篠山紀信が、この建物にモデルや人形を配して、彼の幻想的な世界を写真のなかにつくり出している。彼はこの建物がもっている個性、独創性、超越性といった性格を感じ取ったからこそ、この建物を主題として写真による世界をつくり出そうとしたのであろう。梵寿綱の建築は、ジャンルを超えて他のアーティストに響きあうのである。それはモダニズムとは対極の質を秘めた性格である。

　近代建築の特徴であり、その長所でもあると言われてきたものは、建築が機能的であり方法的であり、普遍性をもつという点であった。普遍的方法に根ざすからこそ、近代建築は世界のあらゆる場所において成立することができたのであ

った。梵寿綱の手法は、近代建築のもつ普遍性を意図的に逆転させ、建築を一回限りのパフォーマンスの結果として生み出すものである。

早稲田に彼が作り上げたマンション「和世陀」(fig. 3) も、都内各所に見られる彼の作品と同様、個別性が際立つ装飾が建物を覆い、かけがえのない都市のオアシスとなっている。場所をつくり上げること、そのために多くの職人やアーティストたちの技倆が傾注されること、それが彼の建築づくりである。

梵寿綱の後継者ともいわれる羽深隆雄の建築のつくり方も、場所を形成してゆくという手法において、まったく同一だといってよい。羽深が自らのために建てた埼玉県の都幾川近くの別荘を見るならば、固有性を目指す建築のすがたが、ここにも共通して存在していることに気付くであろう。

都幾川の別荘「湧雲の望楼」(fig. 4) は、100年もつ建物をつくり上げるという目標でつくられたという。羽深の実家は新潟県の高田市（現在は上越市）の材木商であった。彼はこの材木商の二代目の長男に生まれる。実家は電柱の腕木に用いる欅材を扱うことが多く、その材をストックし、卸していたという。おそらく建築に用いる木材は産地と分ちがたく結びついたものなのであろう。高田に生まれ育った彼は、木材を通じて材料と場所の関係を身をもって知ったに違いない。やがて彼は川越に自邸の台付欅の家を建て移り住むことになるのだが、この新しい場所に彼は自分のアイデンティティを見出していたのであろう。川越から遠くないこの都幾川のほとりが別荘の場所として選ばれ、さらにこの場所をかけがえのないものにするための工夫が重ねられる。

この建物は近代建築が目指してきたものの対極に位置する。つまり、空間構成としての建築ではなく、場所を体感するための建築である。入り口から建築内部に入ると同時に、人は斜面に向かって開ける場所のアウラを全身で感じることになる。この建物に用いられている材料も、その仕上げも、すべてがここを特別な場所にするために用いられているのである。別荘のなかで寛ぎながら、我々はこの建物をつくり上げている素材の意味とちからを、改めて考えさせられる。そして、ここではすべての努力が場所の意味とちからを感じさせるために用いられていることに気付くのである。

都幾川の別荘は、都心からそれほど遠い距離にあるわけではないが、ここを訪れた人は、明らかに都心とはことなる別の場所を体験したことを感じるであろう。場所の意味とちからを顕現させるものこそ、建築なのだ。その点において、梵寿綱の建築と羽深隆雄の建築は太いつながりをもつ。

羽深隆雄の作品のなかで、ある意味では最も有名なもの

fig.4 「湧雲の望楼」にて、羽深隆雄（右）と筆者。襖に使用された岩野平三郎が漉いた雲肌麻紙を見る。撮影=小林浩志
Author and Takao Habuka (right) at *Wakigumo no Boroh*, viewing the kumohada mashi (traditional Japanese paper) made by Heizaburo Iwano and used on a traditional sliding door. Photo by Hiroshi Kobayashi

が、東京銀座の寿司屋「銀座久兵衛 別館」(fig. 5) であろうが、ここもまた新しい和風建築をつくり出すというだけでなく、ここにしかない場所を生み出すことに、あらゆる努力が傾注されているように思われる。つまり現代の食文化の空間を一般論として成立させようとするのではなく、特殊解であっても構わないから、これが久兵衛という店にしかない仕上げであり、これが久兵衛という場所なのだと示したい、そしてさらにいうならば、これが銀座という場所なのだという表現を考えているのではないかと思われる。それこそが、普遍性よりも特殊性に賭ける創造であり、空間よりも場所を目指す態度だと思われるのである。

材料から素材へ

建築の場所性を顕現させることにおいて、梵寿綱の建築と羽深隆雄の建築は共通性をもつが、建築にそのような性格を与えるために素材のちからを用いるという点においても、

この両者は共通性をもっている。建築をつくり上げる材料、つまり建築の基本的構造材と仕上げ材の両面で、彼らは建築が素材によって何を語りかけるかを、我々に考えさせる。

梵寿綱が、自分の処女作であった小さな住宅の改造工事について語った文章がある。彼はその家を建てた棟梁と語りあうなかで、建築を構成する材料をいかに個性に満ちた素材に還元するかを考えてゆく。

軸組みは、筋違いや釘や構造金物等を一切使わず、柱に通し梁と通し貫、楔締めや大栓入れを原則とし、腰羽目や化粧格子も、建前の時に組木細工のように組み込んで固めました。限られた予算内での道楽仕事ですから、古い瓦を再利用したり、栗石を玄関土間に敷きつめたり、松の足代板で腰羽目を加工したり、杉の大貫から焼板天井を作ったり、手間を惜しまず工夫を重ねてゆきました。

廊下の天井板は、銘木屋の店先の溝板をもらってきて曳き割り、「うづくり」で磨きあげた、径五寸余りの生き節乱杢板ですし、外部の駒返しは捩れて使えなくなった栗の土台を、チョウナでなぐり仕上げとし、芯を通して貫き収めて込栓で締めたものです。

棟梁が伝えたかったのは、素材を生かした建物を造る技術ではなくて、素材の心によって生かされてくる建物を、仕上げて行く心遣いであったのだと思います。

すでに三十年の月日が経過していましたが、取材に訪れた日の夕刻、棟梁手作りの彫刻腕木の照明器具の風化したガラス絵は、私が持参した手作りのステンドグラスに取り換えられました。長い闇の時を経て新しい伝承の小さなあかりが灯されたのでした。*3

彼は一般的な建築材料に手を加え、仕上げ直すことによって、ものとしての原点にまで材料を還元してゆくのである。そこに現われるのは工業製品、規格材といった商品化された建築材料ではなく、物質的な存在感を漂わせる素材そのものである。彼の建築は素材を身にまとうことによって、本質的な存在になる。

早稲田に建てられたマンションでは、壁面にはモザイクタイルが貼られ、床には石張りのモザイク仕上げが施され、手すりや扉には金属細工が用いられ、さらにはステンドグラス、壁画も用いられて、建物全体が目くるめくほど多彩な素材の集合体となる。こうした仕事は、梵寿綱の作品に共鳴する多くの芸術家や職人たちによるものである。梵寿綱は彼らの手腕を自由に振るわせ、彼らを互いに、騒々しいまでに競わせる。

近代建築が捨て去った、あるいは否定した多くの要素、

fig.5 「銀座久兵衛 別館」1階。
First floor of *Ginza Kyubey Annex*.

fig.6 母屋の継手の仕口。この複雑な仕事が強い継手を生む。
Angled splice for a purlin. Intricate work creates a strong joint.

fig.7 尻挟み継ぎに、さらに一仕事加え欅材の丸栓を追加した母屋の継ぎ。
Purlin joint to which zelkova round peg is added, an extra step to the tail-wedged joint with cotter.

装飾性、個別性、一回性などがここにはある。方法論として、これは普遍性に欠けるもののように思われるのだが、彼のこの姿勢は多くの協働者を呼び起こすし、クライアントやテナントの共感も呼び覚ます。無論こうした方法が、現代における建築の創作法として主流を占めるようになるとは思えないが、彼自身、自らが主流となろうと考えたりはしていない。自分の存在を認めさせ、その仕事が共感を得られればよいのである。それが「梵寿綱と仲間たち（Von Jour Caux and his Troupe)」なのであり、「Troupe」が「しがない旅役者」のことであるように、彼らは一夜の観客の雰囲気で即席に脚本の筋書きや演出の調子を変えて舞台を設え、共感した観客からの「おひねり（ご祝儀）」で生計し、果てしない旅を続ける、ということになるのである。

梵寿綱に学んだ初期の一人である羽深隆雄もまた、素材に関して極めて深いこだわりをもっている。とりわけ羽深の場合、実家の家業であった木材を巡る経験が深い。先にも述べたように、電信柱の腕木に用いられる欅を基に数多くの良材を多くストックするようにもなった。木材の場合、第二次世界大戦後、製材の方法が大きく変わったことが印象的であったという。

機械化が進むまで、製材は木挽きと呼ばれる職人が大鋸を用いて手で挽いた。彼らは材木を前にして、2、3日は何もしないで見ているという。その後、やわと鋸の目立てを始め、道具を整えてから、ようやく材木を挽きはじめるのだという。そのようにして製材された板には、鋸の目が残り、板の息づかいのようなものが籠るという。これは木材という建築用工業製品ではなく、素材としての存在感を宿した板そのものである。昭和30年代からチェーンソーが一般化し、木材の伐採に用いられるようになるし、製材も帯鋸となり機械化されてゆく。それでも木材に素材としての存在感を見出しつづけ

るのが、羽深の流儀である。

そのひとつとして羽深隆雄は、木はすべて無垢の自然乾燥材とし、立木を想像して木性を読んで適切に使う。10.2mもある母屋材の継ぎ手にもこだわり、従来柱の根本の継ぎ工法に用いられる金輪継ぎの変形で、さらに強化される中央に栓を打つ尻挟み継ぎを用いている（figs. 6 & 7）。

木材だけでなく、金属細工、和紙、指物などの職人を通じて、羽深は建築を構成する素材を根源にまでさかのぼらせる。素材の存在感は、彼の建築には饒舌なまでに現われる。欅の驚くほど幅広の一枚板、八角形につくり出された柱、杉や梨や煤竹といった素材、さらにはコンクリートにレンズ用ガラスまでも打込み、新たな発想を加えて使いこなす。

1976年から羽深は自らの設計事務所の中に「Look East」という集まりをつくる。この集まりは鍛造、鋳造、ガラス、大理石モザイク、和紙、木工、左官などのアーティストや職人たちから構成されていて、それぞれの技量を磨きながら、互いに刺激を与え合う場であった。ここでは多様な素材がそれぞれにふさわしい技術によって建築に組み込まれていった。

羽深はこうした素材を彼のコントロールのもと、緻密な全体像を生み出すように組み合わせる。こうした面では、芸術家や職人の腕を自由に振るわせる梵寿綱の手法とは、対照的である。彼らは作品の様式によって共通しているのではないし、製作法において共通しているというわけでもない。彼らを単純に新しい和風建築の表現を目指す建築家と整理することはできないであろう。梵寿綱は梵寿綱であり、羽深隆雄は羽深隆雄である。

生産から手仕事へ

木挽きが製材に変わっていったように、建築を巡る材料は工業化されてゆく。工業化の内実は素材であり、製造工程

である。建築材料は化学的素材からなるものになり、それらが機械化され工業化されたプロセスを経て生み出されてゆく。壁を構成する漆喰や土壁はセメント系の化学製品に置き換えられ、板材もムクの木材はほとんど無くなって、積層材や木質系の合板、突板あるいは金属パネルなどに置き換えられてゆく。

工業化された建築材料を用いる建築は、建設方式においても湿式から乾式に変り、部材のアッセンブルというかたちで組み上げられてゆくようになった。水で材料をこねたり、火を使って材料を煮たりする左官工事は嫌われ、完成された部材の組み合わせに置き換えられてゆく。そうした変化によって建築は工業化され、工程監理の容易な製造業に近づくことができるようになる。建築の施工は、建設作業であることから、部材の組み立て、さらに言うならば部材のアッセンブルになってゆく。施工の技術は、技能というよりも工程監理がその中心になってゆく。

このような変化が、建築を近代的な建設作業にしてゆくことを可能にしたが、そうすることで失うものもある。建築から固有性、個別性、一回性が失われ、建築もまた自動車や電気製品のような、カタログ商品に近づく。しかしながら建築は一つ一つ個別の場所に建てられるものであり、場所が異なる以上、厳密にいうならば同じ建築は二つとして存在しない。そしてまた、住宅であれオフィスであれ店舗であれ、建築を用いる人はそれぞれ別々であり、建築は人それぞれのかけがえのない生き方に結びついた、唯一無二の存在なのである。

梵寿綱とその仲間たちの建築は、建築のもつ一回性、個別性を重視したところに成立しており、カタログ商品としての建築の対極に位置する。したがってそれを作り上げてゆくプロセスも、素材に個別性をあたえる手仕事が多い。東京銀座の久兵衛別館に見られる職人たちの仕事は、截金や墨流しに典型的に現われるように、精緻でありながら不規則性と偶然性を秘めた効果をもっている。こうした技能の精密さは、機械的な正確さではなく、偶然の揺らぎを瞬間ごとにコントロールしてゆく息づかいの籠った緻密さなのである。おなじように、指物師の仕事も、ここではその厳密さにおいて極限まで細かい。しかしながらこうした細かい仕事の綿密さに圧倒されながら、こうした仕事は機械の如くに精緻であればあるほど、機械による生産ではなく、長年にわたる研鑽の賜物である職人の手仕事であることが感じられてきて、あらためてその精緻さに驚くのである（figs. 8 & 9）。

梵寿綱や羽深隆雄の用いるさまざまな技法や材料は、それらを使いこなしきることのできる人々の手の存在を前提にしているのである。彼らの建築には異なる金属を組み合わせたり、金属と木材を取り合わせたりする仕上げがしばしば見られるし、梵寿綱は異なる技術を持つ職人やアーティストたちを、平気で隣り合わせに仕事させたり、組み合わせたりする。職人やアーティストたちは互いを意識しながら調和を求

fig.8　渡辺文彦と湧雲の望楼の欅の大扉の仕上がりを確認する羽深。
Habuka, with Fumihiko Watanabe, looks at the finish of the large zelkova-wood door for *Wakigumo no Boroh*.

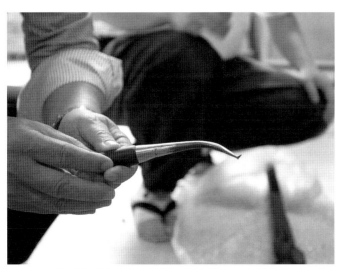

fig.9　fig.8の欅の大扉の彫刻のためにわざわざ造った特殊な鑿。これで小さな凹部をひとつひとつ仕上げていった。
Special chisel made just for sculpting the large zelkova-wood door in fig. 8. The chisel was used to individually finish the small recesses.

めたり、相手を凌駕しようとしたりする。

互いに異なる材料や技能のこうした取り合わせやせめぎあいは、そこに人間的な緊張感を生む。それは工業化され、標準化された近代産業としての建築には見られなくなってしまったものだ。彼らの建築に見られる精密さ、精緻さ、極限的な超絶技巧の数々は、メカニカルな緻密さではなく、熱の籠った手仕事が生み出す人間的なものなのである。

装飾のもつ意味

機械的ではなく手仕事的につくられる建築であり、多様な材料や技法を人間的な表情を込めて用いる建築は、梵寿綱とその仲間たちの建築を一種の近代建築批判の仕事としている。

機能一辺倒ではなく、個別性をもった一回限りの建築が、彼らの目指す建築なのである。したがって彼らの建築を「新しい和風」であるとか、「新・表現主義」などと、造形的・様式的なレッテルによって整理しようとすると、そこから漏れてしまうものが出てきてしまうであろう。

梵寿綱とその仲間たちの建築は、表現における共通性をもつのではなく、素材に対する態度、技術に対する態度、機能に対する態度などに共通性をもつのである。したがって彼らの建築を様式的スクールと分類するべきではない。

梵寿綱の建築には世紀末的あるいはロマン主義的な物語性をもった手仕事がちりばめられており、羽深隆雄の建築には抽象的でありながらほのかに和風のモチーフを感じさせる細部意匠が、職人的超絶技巧の粋を尽くしてちりばめられているのである。両者の造形モチーフや様式的傾向には、明らかに違いがある。だが、そうであるとしても、彼らの建築に共通して感じられる表現の質は、どう整理するのがよいのであろうか。

彼らの建築にとって重要な要素は、建築の表現を支えている独特の要素であり、それは一般の近代建築のように機能的な表現ではない。何度も繰り返してきたように、彼らの建築は機能によって普遍的な表現を求めようとするものではないからである。彼らの表現は、機能ではなく、一種の装飾（オーナメント）である。しかしここでも誤解を避けなければならないのは、彼らの用いる装飾というものは、一般的な飾り（デコレーション）ではなく、手業による意味の伝達を行なう要素をもった装飾だということである。

彼らの用いる装飾は、物語性を帯びた絵画的な装飾であったり、高度な技術に支えられた華麗なパターンであったりするが、それらは単なる飾りではなく、建築の一回性を表現する表現、例えるならば古代ギリシア悲劇に登場するコロス

（合唱）のような性格をもっている。

梵寿綱の建築に現れるコロスたちは、物語性をもったモチーフをつぎつぎに展開してゆく。その多くは具象的な女性像であったり、植物や動物のモチーフであったりする。梵寿綱はそれらのモチーフをつくり出すアーティストたちに、持ち場持ち場で自由に腕を振わせる。それはちょうど、コロスが指揮者の手をはなれて即興で合唱を繰り広げるようである。

それに対して羽深隆雄は職人たちの技術、手業に一糸乱れぬ技巧の合唱を求める。こうして、両極端と思われるやりかたで装飾的技巧を建築に持ち込んでおり、その装飾の性格も両者の建築では異なっているけれど、彼らの建築が共通して機能を超えた表現を身にまとっていることは事実である。

素材は違っても、装飾のジャンルは違っても、そして職人たちやアーティストたちの働き方も違っていても、彼らの建築は共通して建築の機能性を超越した表現を求めている。そこには個々の建築を越えて永遠の生命に連なるような超越的イメージが存在していた。それが彼らの建築に共通した装飾性を生み出している。

我々が彼らの建築に惹かれるのは、そこには日常の機能を超えた彼方を目指すまなざしがあるからである。それは世紀末的な表現を通じても、新しい和風を思わせる表現を通じても、可能なのである。

梵寿綱も羽深隆雄も、自分のやり方で建築をつくっている。当然、そこに持ち込まれる装飾の性格も、その創作の仕方も、それぞれ異なる。けれども両者は、筋道は違っても日常を超えた表現を求める点においては共通している。

かつて梵寿綱は、自らの理想とする建築家の系譜として、アントニ・ガウディ、フランク・ロイド・ライト、ジュリア・モーガン、グリーン＆グリーン、そして白井晟一、今井謙次、村野藤吾の名を挙げていた。*4

羽深隆雄はこの梵寿綱を通じて彼らを求め、そしてさらにはオットー・ワグナーを研究して、そこに自分の育った和の世界を重ねていった。二人がこうした理想を追いながら、超越性を求めたところに、彼らの関係がある。表現や技法やモチーフは異なっても、彼らは梵寿綱とその仲間たちと呼びうる共通の理想をもっているのだ。

（建築史家）

本稿は、鈴木博之が2013年12月23日に書き上げた。
鈴木は翌年2月3日に他界したため本稿が遺稿と思われる。

*1 本稿内において、建築名称は本書での掲載名とあわせたが、一部、旧名称を〔 〕内に残した。
*2 鈴木博之『建築』1977年。
*3 「寿舞について寿舞 梵寿綱の処女作」『住宅建築』1981年10月号。
*4 「深秘実践の生活者」『伊丹潤 JUN ITAMI 建築と都市』2008年、主婦の友社。

Essay 1
Material, Handwork, Ornamentation: Von Jour Caux and his Troupe
Dr. Hiroyuki Suzuki

Does the essence of architecture exist as a completed unit of "space," or expand as a "place"? This is a large question that we face in architecture, and relates to whether the essence of architecture is universally identical across cultural spheres around the world or possesses dissimilar characteristics in each cultural sphere, and to whether the essence of architecture remains unchanged across time periods.

Two facets in architecture, universality and peculiarity, are very important issues in discussing the architect Von Jour Caux and the architecture of his artists—his Troupe. The following citation quotes Von Jour Caux in this regard.

Von Jour Caux and his Troupe is the English rendering, where troupe refers to a humble band of traveling play actors. They improvise the story of a script or pace of a production to arrange the stage according to the audience's ambience of a single night, and continue their endless travels by living off of the tips from an empathetic audience.

The description sounds self-effacing and obscure from the onset, but this mindset needs to be understood in discussing Von Jour Caux.

Space or Place

Italian philosopher Umberto Eco explains the beginnings of architecture with elements of "cave" and "stairs." The cave is an element of architecture that encloses the human being as protective shelter. The stairs represent an element of implemented architecture as a presence to urge human behavior.

This description by Eco is quite intriguing, and seems to brilliantly reveal the essence of architecture. Architecture is shelter to provide a place of comfort for human beings. At the same time, although an immobile existence itself, architecture imparts motion to people, and in a broad sense enables activity in society. The representation with stairs as the element seems quite elegant. Eco explains that humans are compelled to either ascend or descend at their encounter with a flight of stairs.

I became aware of two facts while ruminating on this explanation. Most dwellings in Japan were never in the form of a cave, and traditional Japanese architecture was rarely constructed with stairs. Primitive Japanese dwellings, typified by the dugout or pit-house, were predominantly flatland dwellings, and cave dwellings were almost non-existent. In addition, since Japanese architecture was practically all single-story, no interior staircases were necessary.

Certainly, others can argue that Japan has built more than just single-story construction. Although we don't know about primitive times, Japan's historical periods saw the construction of five-storied pagodas and donjons (castle towers). But interestingly, an examination of the interior of a five-storied pagoda would not reveal any staircases, floors, or ceilings. There are no levels above ground inside a five-storied pagoda for a person to ascend to. Truly, nobody could have experienced going up inside a pagoda. The construction of a five-storied pagoda does not provide for any person to go "upstairs." It really doesn't have five stories, just a roof in five tiers, as a presence to be viewed from the outside.

In the same way, people did not ordinarily spend time in a donjon, although steep, ladder-like steps and upper floors did exist. Holing up in the donjon occurred only after a decision to seal one's fate in the castle. The donjon, therefore, was similarly a symbolic presence to be revered from below the castle walls. The lord of a castle actually lived in a large, single-story mansion built beneath the donjon.

In the same way, urban castles and tower gates of shrines had second levels that were believed to contain some sort of altered world. The legend of *Rashomon*, and the legend of Ishikawa Goemon who exclaimed about the vista from the gate of Nanzenji Temple support this explanation.

For truly multi-storied architecture like the Golden Pavilion and Silver Pavilion in which people could actually ascend, the ascendance itself was an extraordinary event and a prized occasion. Upstairs parlors in red-light districts were no different. In short, the practice of people living their everyday lives on the second floor did not exist in traditional Japanese architecture. The Japanese tradition was established with single-story wooden architecture.

Did single-story, wooden architecture create a different world from the Western architectural tradition?

The advancement of single-story wooden architecture has two conceivable directions: a format where multiple buildings dot a large area, or one building contiguously expands laterally (horizontally). A temple complex exemplifies the former, while Ninomaru Palace of Nijo-jo Castle or Katsura Imperial Villa illustrate the latter, which develop horizontally in a type of zigzag format called a flying-geese pattern. If a single-story building were simply enlarged to a huge size, the interior would become dark and useless. The zigzag pattern would be the most effective way to draw light and air inward in the lateral development of a building.

145

One problem did arise, however. Dotting a large area with single-story buildings or expanding horizontally caused the important reaches of the estate to become concealed. Described as "high places," important parts hidden from view became a Japanese mindset, which was not unrelated to the traditions of this architectural format.

Horizontal development of single-story architecture meant that the various rooms had direct, external contact. Thus, at least the main rooms had external parts that faced gardens. The expanse of Katsura Imperial Villa developed in a flying-geese pattern shows the best technique to enable external contact along such a building. Not a unique practice, this characteristic of contact between interior and exterior was common to estates of *shinden tsukuri* (ancient palatial architecture of Heian Period), drawing rooms of *shoin tsukuri* (traditional residential architecture in medieval and recent periods), *hojo* (living quarters) of temples, and parlors of merchant houses. Consequently, the other characteristic of laterally developed single-story architecture was that the principal rooms had gardens.

With respect to the attractiveness of Japanese architecture, the frequent praise of beautiful gardens and roofs is thought to originate from this architectural tradition of lateral development for single-story housing, because the gardens exist with equivalent weighting to the horizontally projecting architecture. Of course, garden beauty is also renowned in much Western architecture, but those gardens proclaim a self-standing existence separate from any rooms included in the building. Even for the case of a courtyard closely tied to the architecture, I sense such a space to be a discrete cube. The garden for single-story architecture, particularly in Japanese architecture, and the room mutually depend on each other and pervade each other. The rooms in Japanese architecture openly face the garden, and the gardens turn their "faces" toward the rooms.

What should this type of architectural format be called? If Western architecture is spatial, this format should be called horizontally expansive, placement architecture. In traditional Japanese architecture, the main rooms like the *zashiki* (general-purpose sitting room) did not exist as enclosed space, but were open-faced to the garden, more like a stage than a space. In this sense, a room in Japanese architecture creates a place instead of forming a space. Thus, the architecture of such rooms, successively connected, has pondered the problem of how to compose the entire property. Japanese cities are also seemingly placement-oriented, a mosaic of interspersed architecture and garden successively linked horizontally.

From a practical perspective, "place" may be considered the lot or the site, but historically, thinking since long ago has held that a place retained its own character. I have translated the ancient Western concept *genius loci* as "ground spirit," being mindful of the word *rén jié dì líng* used in China. Both words describe the potency belonging to a place. The concept suggests that each place has its own potency or hidden potential, and may sound like old superstition. Nonetheless, these words teach us what we have lost in our present-day cities. Office districts lined with new buildings are a universal phenomenon today. Otemachi in Tokyo could be part of Chicago or New York. This globally common, urban scene is ubiquitous. I heard, for instance, that movies and TV dramas set in Manhattan are staged in Toronto, Canada. A fleeting scene on the screen hardly divulges any difference, since the skyscrapers look similar.

Global commonness of urban vistas sounds positive, but refers to none other than a loss of siting characteristics. We seem to be living today without being in a place. Architecture has lost siting characteristics in the name of universality, and put us in abstract space. Nonetheless, architecture provides structural bodies that enclose people in their interiors. The spirit of this era cannot be turned back. The vector is international and possibly global commonness, but isn't there a necessity for a sense of place in living there? Architecture today should not strive for a product of abstract space and time, but acquire siting characteristics and time-period characteristics according to the awareness belonging to the people contained within.

The Place in Information Society

Digitalization of information has enabled the processing, access, and utilization of voluminous data without occupying a place. The amount of information we transact today is enormous compared to a decade ago; the comparison itself would be difficult. Moreover, information can be left in the personal computer or on the Internet and accessed on demand. The coming era will enable access to that information from anywhere. Information no longer occupies a place, and will no longer choose a place. In that context, efforts to augment private archives and papers, and to physically travel in order to gain information have been eased tremendously. Incidentally, I am not diligent and quite forgetful. Forgetting to access information, forgetting the location of information, and lacking time to query for information are regular occurrences, which lead to my grumbling about how meaningful digitalization— described above—really is.

Information may be flooding us, but this observation on its own is meaningless. Information reveals its form through public announcements, in print, or by downloading. Until produced in a visible format, information seems to be wandering around in space. Information is only useful after its acquisition. In addition, we must know of its location for ubiquitous access of information to function.

The word "site" describes how such information is situated, as in "website" or "Internet site." In the architectural history realm which is my professional discipline, the word refers to the physical site or construction site, as well as the excavation site, or in short, a place. Further contemplation finds many examples of words associated with information to be analogous with architecture. We hear the description "computer architecture" frequently, as well as "fire wall" to describe the means to prevent data leakage or illicit access to data. Information technology apparently gains comprehension through analogies to architecture and place.

So when I sensed that information needed a place, I also sensed the essence of information, and a starting point for the meaning held by "place." The sites for accessing information today are websites, but are also starting to pervade real places. Conditions are emerging where ubiquitous access enables the approach to all information from any place. Perhaps we are seeing a new development in the Information Age, even though this shift may not seem so monumental.

Victor Hugo's phrase "This will destroy that" described the eventual fall of the visual world of the Bible carved into the Gothic cathedrals as a consequence of physical printed matter in the form of the newly invented book off the press. Today, we wonder whether the Information Age will lead to the downfall of the world of printed matter. The conditions today, however, probably dictate coexistence and not destruction of one by another.

As one analogy, the word *in situ*, frequently used in archaeology and excavations, comes to mind. *In situ* literally means "in that place." An artifact excavated at a site has higher credibility than what historical records tell. Such historical material, therefore, is held in high regard as discovered *in situ*. The same applies to credibility of information. The meaning of "place" for information remains large and significant, since the places to access information are present on the Web as well as in the real world.

In a similar way to information, architecture earnestly requires a place. Architecture can physically be built in one place only. Each work of architecture is built and can only occupy a unique place in the world. Revisiting this fact may teach us how architecture should be positioned in the future. There is significance in saying "place" instead of "culture" here.

In discussing the characteristics of architecture, the conversation tends to head promptly toward local culture, regionality, and tradition. These directions don't feel positive, however, and bear the risk of becoming confined to one region or tradition. Moreover, interpreting individual characteristics of architecture in the context of a national tradition risks the emergence of architecture based on narrowly prejudiced nationalism. In my honest assessment, authoritarian architecture (for example, at Moscow State University) built for some time in socialist nations was quite close to this type of traditionalism. Post Modernism aimed to recover individual characteristics in architecture by interspersing symbols with cultural relevance. The rapid obsolescence of that attempt, however, tells us about the predictable risk contained in individual characteristics for architecture described along the lines of local culture, regionality, and tradition. Thus, the desire to focus on "place" rather than "local culture" is here. "Place" does not have tradition, local culture, or region clinging more than necessary to the background.

The "place" where we can get in touch with information is called a site, from where we can evidently fly off toward another place. That is the definition of a place as a site, and also the intrinsic potency of a place. In detective TV dramas we sometimes hear the line "[Check] the site 100 times," which suggests that the physical site or place does have some sort of potency. The facts become evident by physically going there. That seems no different in the Information Age.

Sites are interesting, because mystery remains over what might reveal itself. An excavation site is the best example, but a construction site may also present surprises. Likewise, nobody really knows what may be hidden at, or may emerge from any place in the city. The contest consists of what may be found at a site. Walking around the city means looking for information accumulated in places. A place might be described as a format that accumulates history and information. Wandering around the Web is the same. Shadowless and shapeless, information rains down from places called sites. We lie in wait for information by casting our nets at places.

Von Jour Caux and his Troupe

In this time period, Von Jour Caux posits what architecture should be, lest we possibly might forget. An examination of Von Jour Caux's architecture ferociously affects the mind that mulls questions over space and place, function and ornamentation, and universality envisioned by modern architecture versus development of unique siting characteristics held by Japanese architecture. The numerous challenges that modern architecture supposedly resolved seem to be reopened for debate in front of a Von Jour Caux building. I sense the need to reconsider: what is space, what is a place, and what is a site (place) in the Information Age?

My encounter with Von's architecture goes back nearly a half-century to 1969. An architectural journal had introduced the building called *Practice of Mandala* [*Tsukada Building*] . [*1] This ordinary urban building was not very large, about six stories high, but had received meticulous attention to details. Stainless-steel door handles with relief patterns like potted plum trees, and patterns based on circles and squares on everything from floors to glass blocks were arranged to structure a snug, emblematic world. Though tranquil, the patterns formed an elaborate system, and the building was thoroughly detailed in a concentrated fashion. This urban office building was so thoroughly filled with mysterious linking of details as to seem impossible at that time. I learned of the architect, and the existence of the architectural design office called Von.

Von Jour Caux's real name is Toshiro Tanaka, an architect whose career started with American architectural experience. He left for the United States in 1962, worked at *House and Garden*, and later studied at the School of the Art Institute of Chicago. During his studies abroad, he entered the design competition for the national theater planned at Miyakezaka in Tokyo and received an honorable mention. This proposal was an extremely elaborate design, a work steeped in the spirit of rational detailed planning of modern architecture. In sum, the work employed typical methodologies of modern architecture. He subsequently applied to enter art exhibits in Chicago, and netted prizes on multiple occasions. Gaining spectacular success, he returned to Japan after traveling around the United States and Mexico.

The personal history above would suggest that the architect Von Jour Caux was destined to walk the mainstream of modern architecture. Why then did he choose the name Von Jour Caux and begin walking the path of creating architecture filled with detailed ornamentation? We first study the founding of Von Jour Caux.

At the end of 1969, Von released a text that could be considered his own creative manifesto in *Kenchiku*. The title *Sanginshiki* for the text was a nod to *Sankyoshiki* by Kukai. The philosophical content relates the travels of a upasaka (devout follower of Buddhism) together with a willful person thought to be Niche and a transient person thought to be Dogen who happens to meet a master thought to be Kukai. The retrospective orientation anticipated for such a text, however, cannot be detected. The text of *Sanginshiki* starts in the following manner.

The unhappiest event in my mind about the turn of the century is not the changes that occur over a simple hand-off like gradually building over the past ages, but its nature to change matters fundamentally and completely.

I actually cited this in my article about Von Jour Caux in 1977, and have no need to comment further on this.*2 I do wish to discuss how Von Jour Caux is facing the present day.

Upon returning to Japan, Toshiro Tanaka began working as a

lecturer at the University and apparently taught architectural planning and system design. There we saw him bring into the classroom the cutting edge of rationalist architecture in the ways of Mies van der Rohe and Buckminster Fuller. The young student who attended the instruction and was drawn into this conversation was our other protagonist, Takao Habuka. He was keenly attracted to Tanaka's (Von's) assessment and approach with respect to architecture, and began frequenting his design office.

Over time, the two conducted their work separately, but continued to hold the same notions. They shared the craftsmen that worked on the construction, and formed flexible and versatile alliances. Von describes the arrangement as follows:

I, Toshiro Tanaka, had nurtured an empirical understanding about transference in life to be not along family bloodlines of your real parents, but to occur through the feasting and memories in life among human colleagues met through fate. Thus, at the fateful moment of the death of my foster father, I assumed the pseudonym Von Jour Caux as a combination of Von, which was the name of the design office, and Jour Caux, which was the posthumous Buddhist name of my foster father.

By dispensing with societal family and given names, I resolved to fulfill my architect's work as my life's work, by communicating as storyteller the brilliance and reverberation of life during such brief lifetimes, of richly varied life, to buildings that continue to stand as artificial existences in excess of individual human lifetimes.

The following year in 1974, the journal *Shinkenchikushi* presented *Gladiator's Nest* (Fig. 1, p.137) with the spatial composition theme of "Pilgrimage to the inner depths of heart, invitation to the other side."

The Japanese title *A-I-Chi* originates from the client's company name Aichi, but spelled with different kanji. Among the three selected kanji for the title, '*A* (fundamental truth)' and '*Chi* (human wisdom)' come from *Ajikan* (meditation method) of *Dainichi-kyo*, a fundamental sutra of Esoteric Buddhism. Together with '*I* (twill woven),' the spirits of the language of the three were melded into the theme for the spatial composition endeavor.

Anagrams of phonetic letters create new, alternatively spelled words that have their own meanings. Anagrams of pictographic characters like *Kanji* have meanings in each letter that imply new compound meanings according to combination or placement sequence.

Societal names in Japanese of the buildings were anagrammed with kanji and Roman characters for the projects subsequent to *Gladiator's Nest: Invitation far Beyond* 〔*A-I-Chi*〕, like *Hiraki: Woods of Guardian, Condo Hiraki: Wiseman's Stone, Waseda el Dorado: Rhythms of Vision, Eternal Home: Life-tide, Mundi Animus: Presence to be, Door to Fountain: Genius loci, Cradle Temple: From Beyond to Beyond* and *Trip to Carnival: Vibration of Human Soul*. The metaphors derived from these "language spirits" provided themes that supported the buildings, and we started the Art Complex Movement of public showings for the buildings upon completion.

He states the following about Takao Habuka:Architecture can recount

the life and breath of people who lived in a particular period, but the architecture of such a period has to survive, or else that time will be lost forever. What else should be passed on or carried forward other than technology, style of expression, and thinking? In brief, I believe that to be "empathy to life in a time period." Takao Habuka is my successor under that definition.

Despite the citation of Von's words above, I actually cannot understand what he is trying to say. The characterization of building names in combinations of kanji cannot be understood well either, and the Art Complex Movement that arises from there is unclear in its aim. My only feelings relate to the eminence of the buildings he worked on. They have made an intense impression on many people, and in fact, a kind of artists' group, craftsmen's group, and clients' group emerged in reality. Takao Habuka has been a group member as one of the closest to Von Jour Caux. The work involved to analyze their architecture, therefore, will start and end with analysis based solely on their architecture.

From Space to Place

The architectural work of Von Jour Coux aims not for universal space, but creation of a unique place featuring individual character. *Eternal Home* (Fig. 2, p.138) is a place for elderly people to welcome the end of their lives. The public nature of the institution prohibits the introduction of religious color, but the architecture is hardly a colorless and transparent welfare institution. The centerpiece of the building is the mortuary. Hearing this causes one to cringe reflexively. But if this institution's ultimate goal is to enable people to welcome a peaceful death, the mortuary, prepared for that purpose, can be appreciated as the climax of this elderly people's home. The sculpture of "Munificent Hands" welcomes people here.

Wall ornaments with artful variety and troweled finishing, wood carvings, stained class, etc., throughout the institution show the diversity of work completed by craftsmen, and aid in making the institution a precious and unique place. Those who relocate to this elderly people's home partake of their last place in their lives, not of an institution. Von Jour Caux invited a host of craftsmen and artists to this site and had them channel their talent. The functional space was transformed into a place furnished with totality beyond function. The direction taken has been observed in all of the architecture he has organized. Consequently, all of his buildings have been furnished with individual siting characteristics rather than universality, and don the character of a "one-time only event."

Photographer Kishin Shinoyama created his own fantasy world within photography by arranging models and dolls in this building. Undoubtedly, he sensed the individual character, unique creativity, and transcendence belonging to this building,

and fashioned a world through photographs with the building as its theme. The architecture of Von Jour Caux resonates with other artists across genres. This character, nevertheless, is at the opposite extreme in quality to Modernism.

Features of modern architecture that are also considered to be advantages include the functional, methodic, and universal aspects. Modern architecture succeeded in places all around the world, because it was rooted in universal methods. The methods of Von Jour Caux intentionally reverse the universality held by modern architecture, and render architecture as the result of a limited, one-time performance.

The residential complex *Waseda el Dorado: Rhythms of Vision* (Fig. 3, p.139) built in the Waseda neighborhood is similar to his buildings seen around Tokyo. Distinctively characteristic ornaments cover the building and create a precious urban oasis. His architectural process comprises the completion of a place, and the outpour of talent from numerous craftsmen and artists fulfills that completion.

The architectural process of Takao Habuka, described as the successor to Von Jour Caux, is identical with respect to the methods of forming a place. A look at the guesthouse that Habuka built for himself near the Tokigawa River in Saitama Prefecture shows the common presence of an architectural form striving for individual character.

Wakigumo no Boroh (Fig. 4, p.140) is the Tokigawa guesthouse built with the objective to construct a building to last 100 years. The household of Habuka's parents was originally near Takada, a city in Niigata Prefecture, and then a lumber trading business in Kawagoe by the time Habuka got his start in architecture. As a wholesaler, the business held large stocks of zelkova lumber used as crosspieces on utility poles. Since lumber used in architecture was probably closely related to its harvestland, he must have found his identity somewhere along the continuum of places between Takada and Kawagoe. A site near the Tokigawa River was selected as the place for his guesthouse, not far from Kawagoe, and ingenuity was layered to make this place precious.

The building is diametrically opposed to the aims of modern architecture. The architecture is for experiencing the place, and not spatial composition. The moment a visitor enters the interior from the entrance, he or she will feel with their entire body the aura of a place opening up and facing a slope. Everything, including the materials and finishing, is exploited to create a special place. Relaxing inside the guesthouse, we are called to reconsider the meaning and potency of the base materials that make up this building, and the meaning and potency of the craftsmanship that processed those base materials. Then, we become aware that every effort has been expended to provide a feel for the meaning and potency of the place.

Although the Tokigawa guesthouse is not very far from central Tokyo, the visitor will definitely feel the experience of another place unlike central Tokyo. Architecture enables the manifestation of meaning and potency for a place. In that aspect, the architecture of Von Jour Caux and the architecture of Takao Habuka maintain a strong connection.

The most famous work of Takao Habuka is probably *Ginza Kyubey Annex* (Fig. 5, p.141), a sushi restaurant located in Ginza, Tokyo. Here again, every effort appears to have been expended in developing new Japanese-style architecture, and creating a unique place found nowhere else. The aim, in my assessment, was not a general solution of space for contemporary cuisine, but instead a permissible special solution, a desire to show a finish only available at Kyubey, a place that *is* Kyubey. Further, that thinking included the expression that "This place is Ginza." Such creative invention made a bet on peculiarity over universality, and is thought to represent an attitude aiming for place rather than space.

From Material to Base Material

In the manifestation of siting characteristics, the architecture of Von Jour Caux and the architecture of Takao Habuka possess common aspects. Moreover, their exploitation of potency in base material to impose character on architecture is another common aspect. With respect to materials that make up the construction, for both basic structural members and finishing members in the architecture, the two architects push us to ponder the stories that the architecture tells through the base materials.

Von Jour Caux talks about the remodeling work for a small house that was his maiden project in the following text. He converses with the master carpenter who built the house and considers how to reduce the materials constituting the architecture to base materials filled with individual character.

The framing used no structural joining metal like nails or braces at all. As a general rule, posts had penetrating beams and penetrating crosspieces with wedging or male-female end interlocking. Lining planks and decorative lattices were embedded and fixed like fine wood-strip craft when the house frame was erected. This was a labor of love with a limited budget. We reused old roof tiles, lay cobblestones over the earthen entry floor, made lining planks out of scaffold boards, made charred ceiling planks out of cypress bracing crosspieces, and spent time with abandon in devising the work.

The ceiling planks in the hallway were made from ripped ditch boards given to us by a fine-lumber shop. The warp-grained planks had knots about 15 centimeters in diameter and were polished by traditional scrubbing. Chestnut groundsill lumber that was twisted and no longer usable was roughly finished into pieces with an adze, applied to the

exterior alternating-member finishing, and cored and keyed to hold fast. I believe the master carpenter's message was the conscientious finishing of a building, which was brought to life through the spirits of the material, not the technology leveraging the base material to construct the building.

Although 30 years had already elapsed, late in the day when I visited for reporting purposes, the weathered glass illustrations in the light fixtures with carved wooden crosspieces made by the master carpenter were replaced with handmade stained glass that I had brought. After a long span of darkness, a small light of new transference had been lit. [3]

By further working and re-finishing general building materials, Von reduces materials to their origins. The revealed products are not commercial building materials like industrial products and standardized materials, but genuine base materials exuding a presence with substance. His architecture outfitted in base materials becomes an innate existence.

The residential complex built in Waseda has mosaic tiles applied to the walls, stone-laid mosaic finishing on the floors, fine metalwork on the hand rails and doors, as well as stained glass and murals. The entire building is an assemblage of bewilderingly colorful base materials. The workmanship is to the credit of numerous artists and craftsmen who answered the call empathetically to Von Jour Caux's projects. He lets their talent loose, and lets them mutually compete to even rambunctious heights.

The work contains many elements, ornamentation, distinctiveness, "one time only"-ness, etc., that modern architecture threw away or denied. The methodology appears to lack universality; however, his attitude brings forth many collaborators, and raises empathy among clients and tenants. Of course, this method is unlikely to attain the mainstream among contemporary creative methods for architecture, but he doesn't think of becoming the mainstream. Recognition of his presence and empathy toward his work are what matter. That is Von Jour Caux and his Troupe. Like a humble band of traveling play actors, the troupe improvises the story of a script or pace of a production to arrange the stage according to the audience's ambience of a single night, and continues their endless travels by living off of the tips from an empathetic audience.

Takao Habuka, a colleague of Von Jour Caux, also maintains extremely deep discernment of base materials. In Habuka's case, his experience with lumber, the family business, runs particularly deep. As noted earlier, he became well acquainted with zelkova, used as crosspieces for utility poles, and began stocking a lot of base material of this kind. The tremendous change in saw mill methods after World War II had made an impression on him.

Before machinery prevailed, lumber production involved workmen drawing large saws by hand. The workmen would simply gaze at the piles of wood, and not do anything for two or three days. Then they would start sharpening the saw blades and get their tools ready, and finally start sawing the timber into pieces. Sawed wood in this fashion has the remnants of the sawtooth impressions, and the breathing of the wood is seemingly retained. Instead of an industrial building product called lumber, the wood pieces themselves harbor an existence as base materials. In the latter 1950s, the chainsaw experienced broad application in cutting down timber, and lumber manufacturing became mechanized with band saws. Habuka's style is to, nonetheless, continue to find a sense of existence for lumber as base material.

As one effort, Takao Habuka consistently selects wood as solid, naturally dried lumber, and uses the material appropriately, according to its original tree-standing characteristic. He once took pains over the joint in a purlin that was 10.2 meters long, and employed a cotter and tail-wedged joint, to which a round peg was impaled to further reinforce the center, as a variant of the oblique scarf—a joint fabrication method conventionally applied to a pillar toward the base.

In addition to lumber, through craftsmen of fine metalwork, *washi* (handmade traditional Japanese paper), and joinery, Habuka takes the base materials constituting the architecture back to their roots. The presence of base materials appear in his architecture to a loquacious degree. A solid zelkova board with astonishing width, pillars formed octagonally, base materials of cypress, pear and sooted bamboo, as well as glass blocks made with lens glass are some examples.

Starting in 1976, Habuka created a group called Look East within his own design office. This gathering was composed of artisans and craftsmen engaged in forging, casting, glasswork, marble mosaic, *washi*, carpentry, and plaster. Members polished their skills and encouraged one another. Through the forum, a diversity of base materials was incorporated into architecture with the appropriate technology.

Habuka takes the base materials under his control, and combines them to generate an elaborate, full picture. In this respect, the method contrasts with Von, who lets the talent of the artists and craftsmen loose. Styles in their buildings are not common, and neither are their fabrication methods. The two cannot be categorized as architects merely pursuing the expression of new Japanese-style architecture. Von Jour Caux is Von Jour Caux after all, and Takao Habuka is Takao Habuka.

From Production to Handwork

In the way lumber manufacturing has changed over time from workmen sawing manually, materials in architecture are becoming industrialized. In reality, the industrialization is about base materials and their manufacture processes. Building materials are made of chemical base materials, and are produced by mechanical and industrial processes. Mortar and plaster, which make up walls, are being replaced by chemical products with cement systems, while wooden boards and solid wood are mostly gone, replaced by wood-based plywood, or metal panels.

Architecture that employs industrialized construction materials changes construction methods from wet processes to dry processes, and is erected through the assembly of parts. Plasterwork where materials are kneaded with water or stewed over heat is disfavored and replaced with combinations of completed pieces. Through these changes, architecture has become industrialized, and closely resembles manufacturing where process supervision is easy to accomplish. Although the implementation of architecture is construction work, it now becomes the assembly of parts and pieces. Process management rather than technical skill is at the heart of this construction technology.

These kinds of changes have enabled architecture to become modernized construction work, but we have lost certain things. Individual character, distinctiveness, and "one time only"-ness have been lost, and architecture resembles catalogue products like automobiles and electrical appliances. Nevertheless, architecture must still be built one at a time in individual places. Since the places physically differ, no architecture, strictly speaking, built in an individual place can exist identically. Not even two are alike. The people who use the architecture, again, are respectively different, whether it be a residence, office, or storefront. Architecture ties into the precious lives of people as a uniquely different existence.

The architecture of Von Jour Caux and his Troupe succeeds through the emphasis of the "one time only"-ness and distinctiveness belonging to architecture, and is situated at the opposite extreme of a catalogue product. The process of creation, therefore, involves much handwork in providing distinctiveness to base materials. As manifested typically in the foilwork and paper marbling, the work of the craftsmen evident at *Ginza Kyubey Annex* in Tokyo is finely detailed yet impactful in its irregularity and chance randomness. Unlike machine accuracy, the precision of technical talent controls the chance variations moment to moment, and results in fine detail that retains lifelike breathing. In the same way, the work of the joinery master carpenter is detailed to the extreme in rigor. Even as the work becomes detailed to such a level like a machine's effort, we can feel the handwork, the product of long years of devotion, rather than machine production. The meticulous fine work overpowers us, and we further appreciate the astonishing detail. (Figs. 8&9, p.143)

The array of techniques and materials implemented by Von

Jour Caux and Takao Habuka depends on the existence of people with the craft to fully utilize them. Their architecture frequently contains devices in which different metals are combined or metal and wood are arranged. Mindful of each other, the craftsmen and artists at times call for harmony and at times aim to surpass others.

The arrangement and conflict among mutually dissimilar material and talent generate human tension. We no longer see that in industrialized, standardized architecture of a modernized industry. The precision, fine detail, and numerous transcendental techniques pushed to the limit are the human product of impassioned handwork, not mechanical details.

Meaning Belonging to Ornamentation

Employing diverse materials and techniques to instill human expression, the architecture built through handwork rather than machine turns the construction work by Von Jour Caux and his Troupe into a kind of modern architecture criticism.

They aim for architecture with distinctiveness and singular installation instead of commitment to function. Attempts to categorize their architecture through artform or style as "neo Japanese style" or "neo expressionism" would probably fail to include everything.

The architecture of Von Jour Caux and his Troupe holds no common aspect in expression. But the attitude toward base material, the attitude toward technology, and the attitude toward function are common. Their architecture, therefore, should not be classified as a styled school.

The architecture of Von Jour Caux is interspersed with handwork possessing late-century or romanticist anecdotes, while the architecture of Takao Habuka affords detailed designs with abstraction and subtle Japanese-style motifs. These are interspersed to the extent allowed by a tempered spirit of crafted transcendental techniques. But the artform motifs and stylistic tendencies of the two clearly have differences. How can we reconcile the substance of expression felt commonly between their architecture?

The vital elements in their architecture are the special proprietary elements that support architectural expression—which is not functional expression found generally in modern architecture. As repeatedly executed, their architecture does not seek universal expression through function. Their expression is a class of ornamentation, rather than function. But here again, misunderstanding must be avoided. The ornaments employed are not ordinary decorations, but possess elements that convey meaning.

Von and Habuka employ ornaments like paintings with a story or gorgeous patterns supported by sophisticated technologies. But they are not mere decorations. They retain a character like the chorus in an ancient Greek tragedy and express the singular occurrence of the architecture.

The chorus appearing in Von Jour Caux's architecture develops storied motifs one after another. Many are motifs of practiced images of women, plants, or animals, for example. Von Jour Caux lets the artists who create the motifs to freely exercise their talent at each station. The scene is just like the chorus leaving the conductor's direction and improvising in song.

In contrast, Takao Habuka calls for a chorus of meticulously marshaled talent. Thus, ornamental techniques are thus brought into architecture from both extremes, the nature of such ornaments also differs between their architecture, and yet their architecture, in fact, is commonly outfitted with expression transcending function.

Even though the base material is different, the genre of ornament is different, and the ways of working for the craftsmen and artists are different, their architecture commonly seeks expression that transcends functionality of the architecture. In that expression, a transcendental illustrative concept high above their individual building architecture has been present, as if connecting up to immortality. That illustrative concept has resulted in creation of the ornamentation common to their architecture.

We are drawn to their architecture, because of a vision aimed at a distance beyond ordinary daily function. That vision is attainable through late-century expression or expression invoking neo Japanese style.

Von Jour Caux and Takao Habuka flesh out architecture in their own ways. Naturally, the character of ornaments incorporated and the process of creation are respectively different. Even though the pathways have differed, they both have held a common aspect in seeking expression that transcended the ordinary.

Previously, Von Jour Caux described a lineage of architects that he considered his ideal, including the names of Antoni Gaudi, Frank Lloyd Wright, Julia Morgan, Greene and Greene, as well as Seiichi Shirai, Kenji Imai, and Togo Murano.[4]

Takao Habuka sought these architects through Von Jour Caux and also researched Otto Wagner. To this base he overlaid a world of Japanese style from his upbringing. The two thus pursued their ideals and sought transcendence—that is where their relationship lies. Even though expression, technique, or motif may differ, they possess a common ideal that can be called Von Jour Caux and his Troupe.

(Architectural Historian)

[1] Titles of architectural works in this writing were aligned to the book, but the older titles were left in brackets.
[2] Hiroyuki Suzuki, *Kenchiku*, 1977.
[3] "Sumai ni Tsuite," *Jutaku Kenchiku*, October 1981.
[4] "Shinpi Jissen no Seikatsusha," *Jun Itami Kenchiku to Toshi* (Shufunotomosha), 2008.

Von Jour Caux
梵寿綱

ある寿舞

日本建築の源流とガウディのイデアの複合

私の処女作は小住宅、「ある寿舞」片切家寿舞）の玄関周りの改装でした。私の建築美学の師で『建築とヒューマニティ』（1954年、早稲田大学出版部）の著者の今井兼次教授が、釘で地面にスケッチを描き、職人に仕事を説明していたと棟梁は私に話しました。今井教授は大学の講義の中で、イメージメディアも始どない時代に、バルセロナのアントニ・ガウディや、ゲーテアヌムの神智学者ルドルフ・シュタイナーや、ストックホルム市庁舎のラグナル・エストベリ達の仕事を、私達に熱く語り伝えていました。私はこの拙い処女作の写真を今井教授にお送り、アメリカ留学中の1963年に、シカゴから東京三宅坂・国立劇場競技設計に単身応募し佳作入選の折には、お祝いの葉書を頂きました。私は学生時代には全く指導を受けていませんが、卒業後の悩みの中で今井教授は私の心の導師となりました。卒業後の悩みを経て私を導師として入所した羽深隆雄も、自立後の悩みを経て私を導師として、その志を継ぐ意思を固めました。こうして、今井導師が導いた建築への志が、私を導師とする羽深隆雄へと受け継がれてゆくことになりました。

1959
Family Home of Esotericism

Origin of Japanese architecture
Combination of Gaudi's ideas

My maiden work was the remodeling of the entrance to a small home celebrating the Katagiri family. The Meister of the carpenter told me about Professor Kenji Imai, who became my mentor for architectural aesthetics and is the author of *Building and Humanity*.

Professor Imai of Waseda University passionately lectured to us with no images or photographs regarding the works and thought of architect Antoni Gaudi of the Sigrid Familial Cathedral in Barcelona, Spain, as well as Rudolf Steiner, a philosopher, architect and esotericism, and architectural visionary of the Goetheanums. He also lectured about Ragner Ostberg of the Stockholm City Hall in Sweden.

I sent a photograph of my fledgling maiden work to my mentor sent me his encouragement. While studying abroad in Chicago in the United States in 1963, I applied for the National Theater Competition Design in Tokyo, Japan. I happened to win upon which my mentor sent me a postcard of Japan 26 Saint Memory Church of Confucius, the construction spot, in celebration.

I was not good student in my school days, but Professor Imai became the mentor of my heart after the graduation of Takao Habuka, a good assistant in my architectural studio. After successful independence, he announced being successor of my will by oneself. Thus, the will and the dream of Professor Imai will be inherited in this way by Takao Habuka through Von Jour Caux.

1968
Touch of Culture

インディアナの家

文化の違いを超えた寿舞

1962年から64年にかけて、私はシカゴ芸術大学に留学して絵画・彫刻・工芸等を学んでいました。芸大教授のビルと親友のベーシルの共同の寿舞は、インディアナ・デューンズ州立公園に隣接する広大な自然林のなかに建てられています。古い住宅の地下室と煙突を残して、その上にそっくり新しい建物を造る計画でした。

相談に乗るという程度の話から始まったことですが、帰国間際に提出した計画案は、彼等の心を捉えたようでした。

ほとんど基本構想のままの実施設計ができあがりましたが、経済的理由等で延期され、1968年にようやく着工の運びとなりました。しかし、無造作な職人等の仕事ぶりに業をにやした彼等は契約を解除して、トレーラーに住みつき、勤務のかたわら自力で工事を始めることになります。訪日した友人等から、彼等の意見の対立は激しくなるばかりで、このままでは完成はあやぶまれるという声が出たのもこの頃のことです。

その後、1970年、72年、76年と訪米の度に、インディアナに立ち寄り、意見を交換しつつ、ゆっくりとですが確実に工夫が重ねられてゆきました。わずか2枚の基本図面が、文化の

相違にもかかわらず合意され、彼等の人生の目的と生き甲斐を左右するに至ったという経験から、私は、貴重な示唆を得ました。人間としての相互理解の重要さと、文化の深層にある、人間としての共通感覚の普遍性を確証することができたということです。

1977年にビルは20数年ぶりに訪日しました。かつて横須賀の基地に勤務し、休日には鎌倉や江ノ島周辺を散策し、日本人の人情に触れ、日本の文化に目覚めた原体験の跡をたどることが目的でした。しかし、彼が憧憬してやまなかった日本の伝統的文化は、私達日本人にとってさえも遠い過去のものとなっていました。そして、失われた文化の心情はチェコ系アメリカ人の思い出の中に育てられ、遠く米国の片田舎に「寿舞」として生き続けているのです。

Von Jour Caux 157

American completed across the difference in culture by oneself

I studied abroad at the School of Art Institute of Chicago from 1962 to 1964. There, I learned about paintings, sculptures, and industrial design. This Family Home was for close friend in William Brinka, a professor at the school, and for Basil Croses, an antique dealer of the Marshall Field department. It was built close to nature in a forest adjacent to a park in Indiana. Leaving the basement and chimney of the old house intact, the new house was rebuild while adjusting to fit the old foundation. This plan began with simple idea, but the image that I submitted just before my returning to my home country seemed to move their hearts.

The practical design based on my idea was completed by an architect friend of theirs, but actual construction was postponed for economic reasons until 1968 when construction finally began. However, they cancelled the contract due to the performance of the craftsmen, and instead began construction by themselves. From the common acquaintance who visited Japan, the completion is anxious about appeared because of they always discussing all about the opposition of their opinion becomes just intense.

In 1970, 1972, and 1976, I stopped by Indiana while visiting the United States. Their invention was repeated slowly afterwards. Despite differences in climate and culture, two rough sketches were agreed upon during this time; this became the main focus in their life, and through this experience, I received a valuable suggestion.. I was able to confirm the universality of common sense and the importance of mutual understanding as a human being in the depths of the culture. In 1977, William Brinka visited Japan for the first time in 20 years since having worked at the base camp in Yokosuka. While there he took a walk through Kamakura and around Enoshima on a holiday, and was touched by Japanese hospitality, or omotenashi. The purpose of the walk was to trace the prototypical experience that woke in Japanese culture. However, the traditional Japanese culture that he couldn't help but admire was confined to the distant past even for the Japanese. The limitless admiration of the lost culture of Japan are brought up in a Czech American memory, and continue to grow in the Celebrated Family Home in Indiana.

ある美瑠(びる)

実体の現実

人々は疑うことなく、現在生きている状況を「実体の現実」と考えています。

ヒトは太古の時代から厳しい自然と直面することを避け、自然との緩衝帯に信仰や文化や技術という疑似自然の枠組みを育ててきました。人間は本質的に、自然から切り離された生物なのです。従って、日常性が必然的に「実体の実現」と「虚構の実現」の二重性を持つのは、人間存在の宿命であり、日常性と非日常性は相反する概念ではなくて、連鎖する「実体の現実」なのです。

実体と虚構の領界が益々曖昧となり日常性が衰弱した現在、非日常性の復権こそが日常性に活力を復活する唯一の手段となる理由がここに在るのです。

「ある美瑠」(竣工当時の名称は「塚田美瑠」)は事務所という機能を持つ社会的な建物ですが、一方そこで働く人々は、一度限りの人生の働き盛りの時期を、事務労務に拘束されて給与を得ています。

それ故、事務所ビルには、事務作業空間としての機能以上に、働く人々の貴重な生命を預かり、社会活動の実践を通じて精神の豊かな成長を助けるという、祈りを捧げる宗教建築を超える働きが求められるのです。

「ある美瑠」に、このような理念を建築化するために、真言密教の胎蔵・金剛の両界曼荼羅構成が持つ、「本質を会得する」という深い体験世界の意味を希求する世界像と、それを心の中に実現する為の技法の実践的側面を援用しようと模索しました。

厳しい建築の佇まいは、日常に対する非日常世界を象徴し、人々は入口に設えた「座すことを拒否する御影石のベンチ」、方位を示さない49個の磁石からなる壁付き照明器具、重厚な把手の扉、無限遠の視点からしか像を結ばぬように部分を三重のアクリル板に刻まれた照明器具とその光源に反射して仄かに輝く天空のシャンデリアのホール吹抜階段を経て、曲を奏でる天女の図柄のエレベーターから曼荼羅図柄の扉を開けて事務所に至ります。

この暗示的な空間体験の日常の繰り返しによって、人々が無意識のうちに日常的労務の実践を通じて、非日常的世界の現実を会得することで、自己の内奥を豊かに育て得ればと願っています。

曼荼羅は人々に、生き生きした生命の活力を経験させる技術の実践的な方法であり、特殊な空間体験の日常的な繰り返しのなかで、人々が非日常世界の内奥の豊穣さを会得できることで、現実の世界に新しい意味を与えるのです。

1967
Practice of Mandala

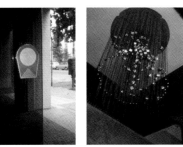

Precious Reality for the Office Building

People are thinking about the present living conditions that without they would doubt the "reality of substance."

To avoiding facing the harsh nature of the past, humans created a fictional nature such as faith, the culture and technology which used to be a promised middle-zone with nature.

A human being is essentially a creature that is separated from nature. It is the fate of the human existence that everyday life consist of two phases, the phase of the "reality of substance" and the "reality of fiction."

In our subconscious, our daily life represents the two phases of the Mandela systematic hierarchies, and any section of the phases are woven into holographic order.

It is not the general idea which opposes it, but daily life of consciousness and non-daily life of our subconscious make up the chain that is the "reality of the substance."

The world of substance and fiction becomes vague all the more at present, and daily life grows weak.

The awakening of the power of imprecate order, dreams and fantasy, is the only means by which the energy of vitality pours into the weakened people in daily life.

This Precious Reality was built as an office building, but on the other hand, for the people working there, it is only for the office worker's labor and their salary.

That is the reason why this space has to protect the valuable life of working people, rather than function as an office. It needs to help enrich the growth of the mind through the practice of demanding social activity, more so than focusing on the religion aspect of the architecture for prayer.

I searched for the practical techniques needed in order to realize the idea of the mystic and to obtain a deep understanding of the meaning, "to understand essence." I traced the idea of the two worlds of Mandala of the Esoteric Buddhism in a heart.

The appearance of the severe architecture symbolizes the world of non-daily life for the daily life.

Upon entering, people will see "the bench of the granite refusing to sit" and the lighting fixture on the wall consisting of the magnets that do not show direction. Next, after opening a heavy door with a solid handle, they will enter a small dark colonnade hall with lighting fixtures consisting of triple-lye acrylic, curved plates, set up in consecutive cubes portreying the viewpoint infinity, and finally a chandelier giving off a faint reflection the light source. After taking a staircase to reach the elevator hall, they will see an elevator door with a design consisting of the celestial maiden angels playing music in the beautifulness of the heavens. Finally, they will reach the Mandala designed office door.

Such is the daily repetition of this suggestive space, the people unconsciously pray through their daily labor when they can bring forth their innermost self-wealth by understanding the non-daily reality of this world.

Mandala's two worlds give the meaning of the real world by composing the existence affirmatively around one's self, and Mandala is the practical way of trying to taste a charming life as a privilege of one's active life.

The word of Mandala Sanskrit consists of Manda, which has the meaning of true nature, essence, charm of life, the world of the all in one, and of the meaning of ownership and accomplishment.

It means the world of the deep experience of "True nature is learned."

Von Jour Caux 161

樹下美人図考
（じゅかびじんずこう）

1968-73
Beauty under the Tree

生命の豊穣

樹下美人図は、豊穣と多産、生命の誕生と維持という人類根元の祈願にもとづく、古来伝承されてきた呪術的図柄である。この典型的な一連の心象や形姿は、伝統のなかに蓄積され継承されてゆく生命の記号の痕跡である。普遍的な無時間性を獲得した形姿、理念的な象徴性に到達した形象は、個人非個人的なものの間、意識無意識の間をつなぐ架構となる。

丹い玉（あかいたま）
1968
Bola roja

ゲーテ『詩と真実』より

「人のすべての喜びは、所在するものたちの規則的な回帰の確信にもとづいている。昼と夜、四季、開花と結実の繰り返し、あるいは巡りくる季節に享受し享楽すべきものこそ、地上の生活の深秘なる源泉である。これらの喜びに広く心をひらけば、われわれはより深く幸福を経験する」

エスト・エスペランサ
1969
Est Esperanza

From Poetry and Truth by Goethe

"All joy of the people is based on the conviction of the regular regression of who shall be located.
Day and night, the four seasons, flowering and the repeat of fruit, or precisely what you should enjoy in the coming season, a deep secret becomes the source of earthly life. If you open your heart to these joys, you will experience a deeper happiness."

Fertility if the Life

A beauty under a tree is a magical pattern that has been handed down since ancient times, based on fertility, fecundity, and the birth of life, praying for the root of mankind. This series of typical symbolic style is a trace of the accumulated form of the inheritance of traditional signage.
This timeless traditional style reached the ideological symbolism, is to shape the bridge over the individual and the whole, the consciousness and the unconscious.

Von Jour Caux 163

ポッゾ・ビアンカ

1970
Pozzo Bianca

プチ・エタン
1973
Petit Etang

From *Poetry and Truth* by Goethe

"All joy of the people is based on the conviction of the regular regression of who shall be located.
Day and night, the four seasons, flowering and the repeat of fruit, or precisely what you should enjoy in the coming season, a deep secret becomes the source of earthly life. If you open your heart to these joys, you will experience a deeper happiness."

Fertility if the Life

A beauty under a tree is a magical pattern that has been handed down since ancient times, based on fertility, fecundity, and the birth of life, praying for the root of mankind. This series of typical symbolic style is a trace of the accumulated form of the inheritance of traditional signage.

This timeless traditional style reached the ideological symbolism, is to shape the bridge over the individual and the whole, the consciousness and the unconscious.

アート・コンプレックス運動について

いつの時代にも建築は永遠の実在への人々の信仰と信念とを
象徴する文化的装置として創造されていました。
そして決して、社会や経済の要求の為にではなく
文化性や社会性や想像性を表現するものとして築かれていました。
今日、国際建築の中にこの様な想像力を見出すことは極めて困難な事態となっています。

この失われた時代の中で梵寿綱は夢と神話を象徴し
芸術と工芸を総合する手段としてArt Complex Movementを組織しました。
我々にとって生活の便宜でしかない筈の社会システムによって
我々の日常生活は予め与えられた役割を果たす為に制御され、
階級付けられ、義務づけられています。
社会的、経済的、政治的構造の中で我々全員が抑圧され
不安定な存在として精神的にも感情的にも疎外されています。

この様な状況が避けられないとの認識に基づいて梵寿綱と仲間たちは
日常の不完全な世俗から非日常の究極の清浄を求める巡礼の語り部の道を選びました。
人間の特質の一つは自我の目覚めです。
しかし自我は他者や状況との関連の中で一時的に位置づけられるもので
本質的なものではありません。
我々自身安定を得るには、日常の生活環境への
帰属の意味を問いただすか超越的な存在を心の中に作り上げて
我々自身の生活の中に確からしさを追求しなければなりません。
しかしながら我々の宿命的な命について考えてみると
昔も今もやがて死を迎える身体に囚われている囚人でありそれでも尚、
一人ひとり生き、それぞれの夢を追いつづけています。
この事実に文化的伝承の存在意味が由来しています。
表層と深層、意識と潜在意識存在と超越、現実性と超現実性、
此岸と彼岸などこれらは相対立するのではなくて全体を相補的に働いているのです。

アート・コンプレックス運動が目指すものは失われた職人の技術を復興して
様々な表現手段を建築の中に取り戻し豊かなオーナメントやディテールによって
再び生命の響きを建築空間の中に再興し後世の人々に
我々が生きた時代の喜びや生きる勇気と生命の尊さを且つて私たちの先達が
私たちに残してくれたように語り伝えることなのです。

梵 寿 綱

Art Complex Movement

In every era, architectural creation served as a culture device symbolizing the
faith and belief in people of physical permanence. Architecture expressed cultural,
social, and imaginative sensibilities, and was not built to the demands of society or economy.
But today, identifying such imaginativeness in international architecture
becomes a considerably more difficult matter.

Amidst this modern void, Von Jour Caux organized the Art Complex Movement
as a means to comprehensively bring together fine art and
craftwork that symbolized vision and legend.
Systems in society that should be no more than conveniences to our lives control, rank, and
obligate us to fulfill our imposed roles. The social, economic, and political
structures oppress all of us, and shun us mentally and emotionally into an unstable existence.

Realizing that this condition would be inevitable, Von Jour Caux and his Troupe chose to
walk the path of itinerant storytellers, and to seek the ultimate,
extraordinary virtue from the imperfect, secular, day-to-day world.
Human beings have an essential characteristic; they gain awareness of themselves (ego).
But the ego is merely positioned temporarily in association with other persons and
circumstances, and not innate.
In order to obtain self-contained stability, we must either question the meaning of
belonging to our daily living environment, or build a transcendental existence within our
hearts and pursue confirmatory efforts within own lives.
A reflection of our destiny in life reveals that—regardless of past or present—
we remain prisoners of our physical bodies that face death. Nonetheless,
each and every person continues to live and pursue his or her dreams.
The existential significance of cultural transference originates in this fact.
Whether surface or depth, whether conscious, subconscious or transcendental,
whether real or surreal, whether mortal life or spiritual afterlife,
these positions are not in mutual conflict, but working complementarily as a whole.

The Art Complex Movement aims to restore the technologies of lost craftsmanship,
recapture various means of expression in architecture, reactivate life's reverberations in
architectural space through ornamentation and detailing, and tell the stories of our times about
joy, courage to live, and nobility of life to future generations as our predecessors did for us.

Von Jour Caux, 1992

Art Complex I

阿維智
あいち

**1975
Gladiator's Nest**

彼岸への誘い
ひがん　　いざな
Invitation far Beyond

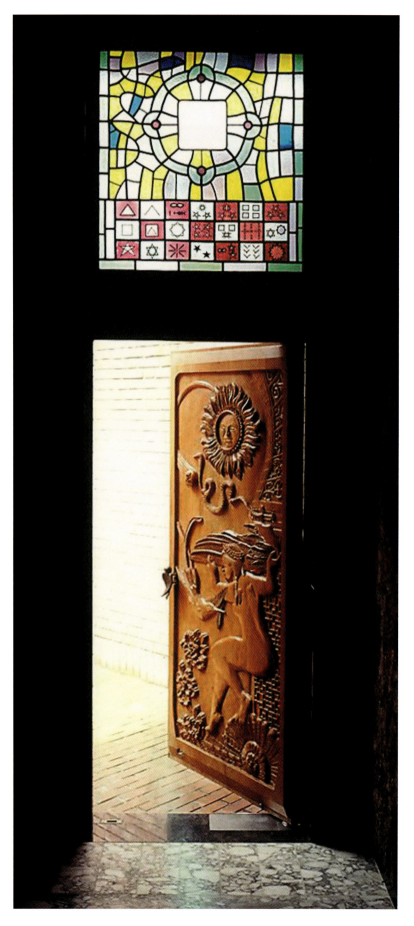

彼岸への誘い

私たちは経験的に、日常の不完全な俗世界から非日常の絶対の聖に思いを馳せ、日常の世界から脱却して非日常の世界に至り、再び日常の世界に立ち戻る、「巡礼」という文化的儀礼を育て、伝承してきました。

ところが現代では個別的な自己実現の時代を迎えて、宗教に基づく巡礼は形骸化してしまいました。しかし本来、人間にとっての巡礼的発心は個別的かつ根源的なものであり、個人的日常生活の延長として、観光の旅や週末の遊び、別荘での生活に反映されています。巡礼空間は、日常を否定するものではなく、活性化するための智慧であり、日常的空間と継続的に接し、綾のように織られているのです。

この現代の巡礼的発心に沿うべく、夢や古代神話の原型によって空間の核を設定し、象徴的言語を組み上げながら、民間企業の社員保養施設である山荘として、宮城県の蔵王山麓の分譲別荘地内に計画されたのが「阿維智」です。

この建築では、密教的な曼荼羅世界の構成を下敷きに、建築の内部にさらに深い疑似自然を築き上げ、自然の中にさらに深い疑似自然を築き上げ、聖地巡礼のような遍路空間の趣を取り入れる試みがなされました。

企業戦士として働くという現実は、極めて非現実的なものであり、その迷妄からの覚醒を衝撃的なまでに促すという意図のもとつくられた阿維智は、文化的装置としての建築をいかに再建するかという課題に取り組んだ試みなのです。

Invitation far Beyond

In the age for realization of self-identity, the Idea of pilgrimage based on individual faith and the religion became merely a name and custom. But, originally pilgrimage which is spiritual awakening for the human being is an individual intend and an impulsive root. Then, pilgrimage is reflected directly as an extension of the personal daily life on the trip for sightseeing, relaxing on weekend in cottage and the life in resort spot.

Pilgrimage space is not denied daily life, but which is a device being activated and twilled the present and the beyond. The space structure of the pilgrimage system consists of "sacred sanctuary" and "spiritual journey"

"A-I-Chi" as a villa was planned to meet such people's intention in present age. It was a certain trail for recreating architecture as acultural device again to settle the center of the space by the archetype of the dream and the ancient myth, and the circumference by symbolic language of the suggestive and significant things.

Resort house sponsored by some company in Mt. Zao, Miyagi Pref. It is nothing but undependable virtual reality as the matter of fact that is the reality of business warrior. This project was proposed for awakening from darkness of those contradictions. The trial was build virtual nature. It is human culture has been down under-covering iconographic composition of esoteric mandala world and woven one circum stance of a route of pilgrimage for sacred places in interior space.

Art Complex II

秘羅檍
(ひらき)

**1977
Hiraki**

鎮守の杜
(ちんじゅのもり)
Woods of Guardian

Von Jour Caux 175

鎮守の杜

かつて伝統的な共同体では、日常の生活空間における聖地として、鎮守の杜と社があり、歳時の祭りや折節の儀式の場としての働きを担ってきました。そしてそれらは、厳しい自然と人間の社会との間の仲立ちの役割を果たしていました。季節の変わり目は、共同体の新しい生活のリズムの始まりを、人々の新しい成熟の段階の始まりを予感させます。この変化期の不安を乗り越え、連帯を固め、心構えを鼓舞するために、通過儀礼と呼ばれる祝祭や儀礼が行われ、森の佇まいとともに独自の文化的景観を育ててきたのです。

この「秘羅樒」は、板橋区の高島平団地の近くに計画された住宅金融公庫融資の賃貸アパートです。この計画では、荒廃した都市生活の積み上げられた箱の中で成長する子供たちのために、擬似的な故郷の「鎮守の杜」の趣を再構築する試みがなされました。そのために外部は深い森の佇まいを、内部は子供たちが、伝統的な集団の成長儀礼の構造に見られる、試練と克服の過程を体験できるように構成されました。

Von Jour Caux　177

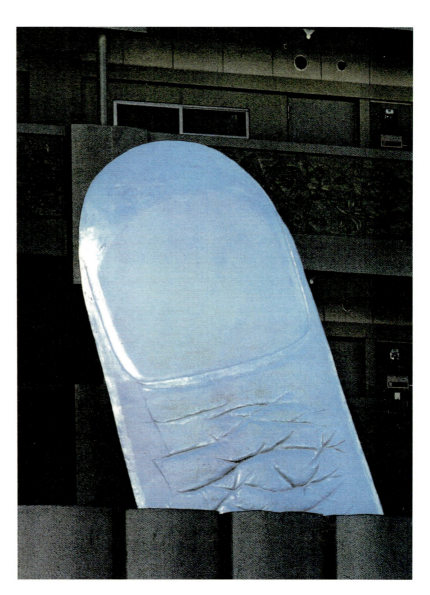

Woods of Guardian

Once in the traditional community, the village shrine and guardian forest were whereabouts as a sacred sanctuary in daily life space, and where is held seasonable festival and initiation ceremony. And these spaces were to be assigned to mediate between the human societies and severe nature.

The change of season predominate a certain rhythm for new beginning of life in the community, and occasion of the life gives an initiation for new beginning of maturity.

This building is rental apartment by the Housing Financial Division in Itabasi-ku, Tokyo, near the Takashimadaira Housing Developing Project. In this project Guardian of Forest Ah where is everyone heart-full home countries, was proposed to reconstruct for growing children living in stacking box housing of vast virtual city life. Feature of façade appearance is to be the deep forest, interior inside is planned like that those children are able to experience of trial and conquest which is shown in construction of cultural initiation ceremony in natural tribes.

Art Complex III

斐醴祈(ひらき)
1979
Condo Hiraki

賢者(けんじゃ)の石(いし)
Wiseman's
Stone

Von Jour Caux 181

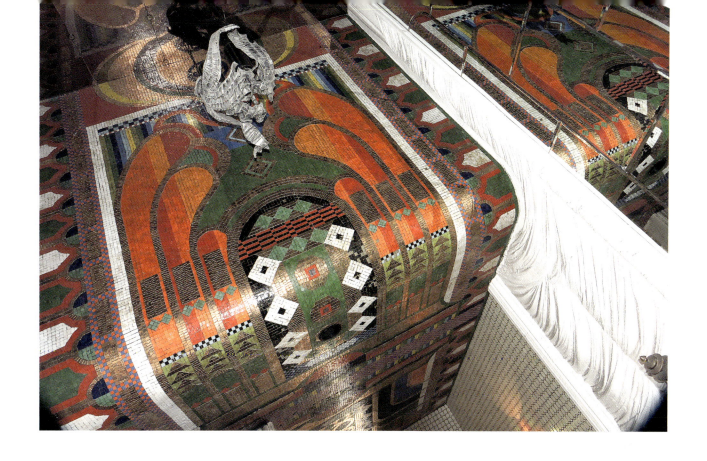

賢者の石

　表層と深層、意識と無意識、実存と超越、現実と超現実、彼岸と此岸、日常と非日常などは、対立するものではなくて、相補的に物事の全体像を形づくっています。そして両者の架け橋として、宗教的な発心や、祝祭や、儀礼とともに、呪術的な媒介者や、夢想的な創造者や、啓示的な思索者たちがあり、これらの強烈なビジョンが直接働きかけ、人々を空間的価値転換の特異な体験に導きます。

　それらの深層の世界から引き出された象徴の断片は、現実と関連を持たず、異様で不可解な雑音として意識の片隅に記憶されますが、やがて人々の無意識と響応して、突如実態の認識を根底から変革する、潜在的な力を秘めているのです。対立的で相補的な関係を、一挙に全体像に結ばせる効用を持つ神秘的な媒体の概念は、錬金術の用語で「賢者の石」と呼ばれています。

　「斐醴祈」は、豊島区池袋の繁華な市街地の片隅にある、住宅金融公庫融資の賃貸アパートを含む複合ビルです。ここでは、シュールレアリスムの手法（ブリコラージュ・モンタージュ・トロンブルイユ・ディペイズマンなど）を駆使して価値の転換を図りました。現実は今、急速に非日常性を増して、両者の領域はますます曖昧になってきており、その中で、実在の身体に包まれた自我は、捉えどころのない影のように漂っています。日常の常識を一気に転換させるシュールレアリスムの表現手法を建築の空間表現に取り入れることで、人々の生活の価値観を「鉛」から「金」に変化させる錬金術が企図されたのです。

Wiseman's Stone

Then, the way of skill for reading the sign of the mysterious indication in the sight of usual and daily familiar things and conditions was discovered, and developed moreover to change reality to another.

The trial to make a bridge for the surreal world was practiced in this project by using developed skill of surrealism with its being based persistently in the daily life.

The general idea of the mysterious medium which solves at once conflicting effect and complementary relations to the whole, is being called a "Wise man's stone" by the alchemy. "Hi-Ra-Ki" project is the trial for changing structure of the various everyday matters by using the most of surrealism of technique, like Bricolage, montage, trompe-l'oeil, diapause man and etcetera. Stimulating people's creative power and setting up a very realistic fantasy, this trial has been done in the space device "Hi-Ra-Ki" as "Wiseman's stone".

This is a complex and rental apartment building by the Housing Financial Division in Ikebukuro, Toshima-ku. Now what reality is becoming vaguely increasing border of non-reality. In this situation human ego caught in mortal physical body is drifting between them like thin shadow. This project based on method of the alchemy changing led to gold, using surrealistic technical that changes daily common sense to beyond at once.

Art Complex IV

和世陀(わせだ)

1983
Waseda el Dorado

幻想の響き(げんそうのひびき)
Rhythms of Vision

幻想の響き

個としての人間は、根源的生命衝動にまで遡行するとき、いつの時代にも、滅びる肉体の内に閉ざされながらも、自己完成を希求しつつ、命を伝承しているという、動かしがたい事実に行き当たります。すべての文化的多様性に見られる数々の試行錯誤は、この事実の回答を模索する永遠の試みなのです。

する空想の舞台装置を、極めて社会的要求の厳しい建築物の中に構築することによって、人々の深層の記憶を揺さぶり、それぞれの幻想物語へ誘う、機縁となることを企図して計画されました。

私たちの願いは、虚構化された現実を神話的世界の「夢見る力」で再生することでした。仲間たちとの協動作業を意識した最初の建物で、引き渡しの前に、仲間たちの合同展として内部を10日間公開しました。この期間中に数千人の予想を超えた来訪者を迎えて、私たちの試みが現代に強い文化的な衝撃を与え、大きな反響を生み出したのです。

「和世陀」は、早稲田大学正門ほど近く、大学通りの並木に沿った、敷地面積200平米、延べ床面積1000平米、1階部分店舗の6階建て集合住宅です。現実生活を通じての自己完成の体験が困難な現代に、演劇的経験を可能と

Rhythms of Vision

The reason why the modern crisis of human nature resides, in what people are not able to find the way of the self establishment and the reorganization of reality at all. But, it goes to the fact that individual human life is handed down with hoping self-completion inside of the body. Which falls in age as well when it goes back to original impulse of the root. Trial and error of which seen in the cultural variety is the trial of searching for the answer of this fact in the eternity.
Assembling of attaining the purpose of the growth by the spiritual awakening in the trial experience appears repeatedly from the beginning in folk tale and fantasy.
A hero wanders about loophole between the life and the death while its being thrown in the super-natural conditions and its being forced to solve riddle puzzle in mystery and trial beyond the imagination
This is a condominium apartment building which site area only 200 UF and total floor area less than 1000 UF , near the Waseda University on Univ. street where row of tree in Sinnjuku-ku. We hope to reconstruct present virtualized reality to suprime reality by Force of Dream in mythology world. This task also is the first intentional project of collaboration with our troupe, and we planned open house groupe exposition for 10 days before handing over this building to our client. This event gave rise unexpectedly to successful vibration supported by several thousand visitors because of deep culture impact.

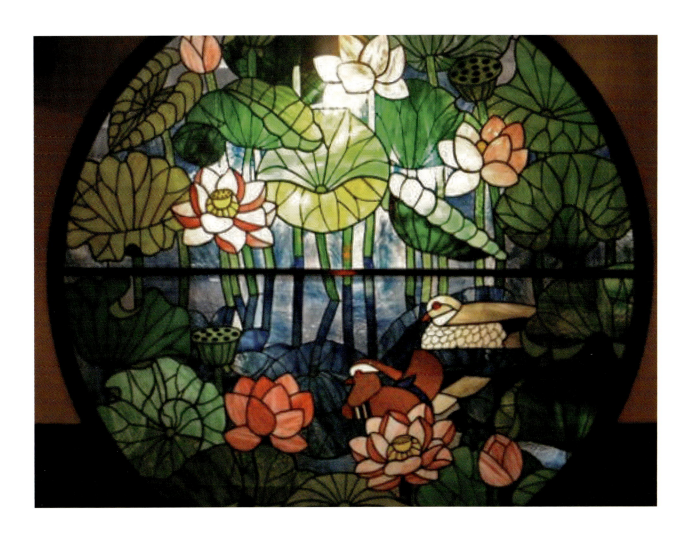

Von Jour Caux 191

Art Complex V

無量寿舞
むりょうすまい

1985
Eternal Home

生命潮流
せいめいちょうりゅう
Life-tide

生命潮流

人間の「老いと死」という永遠の主題に、建築空間を通じてどのように応え得るかが課題でした。現世の夢をほとんど喪失して介護を必要とする老人達が、僅かな記憶を頼り意匠を手がかりにして、自力で命の記憶を織り成し、再び命の輝きを取り戻せる工夫が模索されました。

「無量寿舞」は、絶対の救済と永遠の生命を意味する無量寿と、祝福された生命が喜びを舞う思いを寿舞（住まい）にかけて考えたものです。季節や事象の初源的印象を、象徴的意匠として散りばめ、図像や象徴の森を経て浄土に至るという、遍路空間の仕掛けが巡らされました。

Life-tide

This is a nursing home for the aged by public finance in Higashiyanato city, located in the suburbs of Tokyo. We were strongly encouraged by the results of previously successful event. The theme this time was to create a message pertaining to the eternal dilemma of aging and death by weaving working elements into the architectural space. We searched for a way of recalling the memory of life itself for those who had lost their present dream and needed help with their physical life, by conjuring up what few memories remain in their minds with suggestive designs offered by our hands. To help return brightness to their life, we set up images inside this space that portrayed a complex network of iconology and symbols to help pass through a maze-like forest on a pilgrimage to a spiritual paradise.

Art Complex VI

精霊の館
せいれい やかた

1984
Mundi Animus

存在の証明
そんざい しょうめい
Presence to be

Von Jour Caux 199

存在の証明

「集合的無意識」は、神話や伝説や民話やおとぎ話、古代建造物や造形意匠、装飾模様に共通する象徴や図像の表現を借りて、繰り返し現れます。スイスの精神医学者カール・グスタフ・ユングは、このような類型的な理解の傾向をもたらすものを「原型」と呼びました。豊島区の巣鴨駅に程近い寂れた商店街の奥に建つ、施主の住宅と事務所を含む賃貸住宅「精霊の館」は、ユングの「原型」と「集合的無意識」の空間化と曼荼羅世界が主題となりました。この原型の概念は、我々の建築の仕事の根幹に当初から深く関わっているのです。

事物には霊的な存在が関与していて、現実に起こる様々な現象はその働きに起因するという世界観は、「アニミズム」と呼ばれますが、ユングは原型の現われの一つとして、男性の心にある無意識的な女性的傾向をアニマと名づけ、女性の心にある無意識的な男性的傾向をアニムスと名づけ、彼の分析心理学の重要な手がかりとしました。

この建築では、両界曼荼羅の金剛界と胎蔵界をアニマとアニムスに対応して捉え、これらの象徴を日常生活の営みに直接反映することで、「日常の世界」そのものを「聖なる世界」に反転させ得る文化的な装置の創造が意図されたのです。

Presence to be

This is a nursing home for the aged by public finance in Higashiyanato city, located in the suburbs of Tokyo. The unconsciousness appears repeatedly through the expression of symbolism and iconography, which is common in myths, legends, folklore, fairy tales, ancient monumental space, and in styling mold designs and decorative patterns. Jung is called an "archetype," something that brings understanding. The world view of life that spiritual existence originates in objects, and that the various phenomena that happen in our reality are caused by that mechanism, is known as animism.

An unconscious feminine tendency in the male heart was named anima, and an unconscious masculine tendency in the female heart was named animus; Jung made the important clue of his analysis the theme of this project, which was to create an actual building space realizing the universal archetype.

Psychology is one of the manifestations of the archetype.

This is a rental apartment building with owner's house on desolate shopping street near JR Sugamo Station in the Toshima ward.

The main theme of this project was to create a space of universal archetype and meta-unconsciousness which is known as the Mandala world, constructed of the worlds of Kongoukai and Taizoukai corresponding with Gustav Jung's Anima and Animus. Reflecting on the effects of the union of those symbols with regards to daily life, we tried to create architecture as a cultural device for changing the present, real world into the hidden paradise beyond.

Art Complex VII

和泉(いずみ)の扉(とびら)

1989
Door to Fountain

地霊(ちれい)の浄化(じょうか)
Genius loci

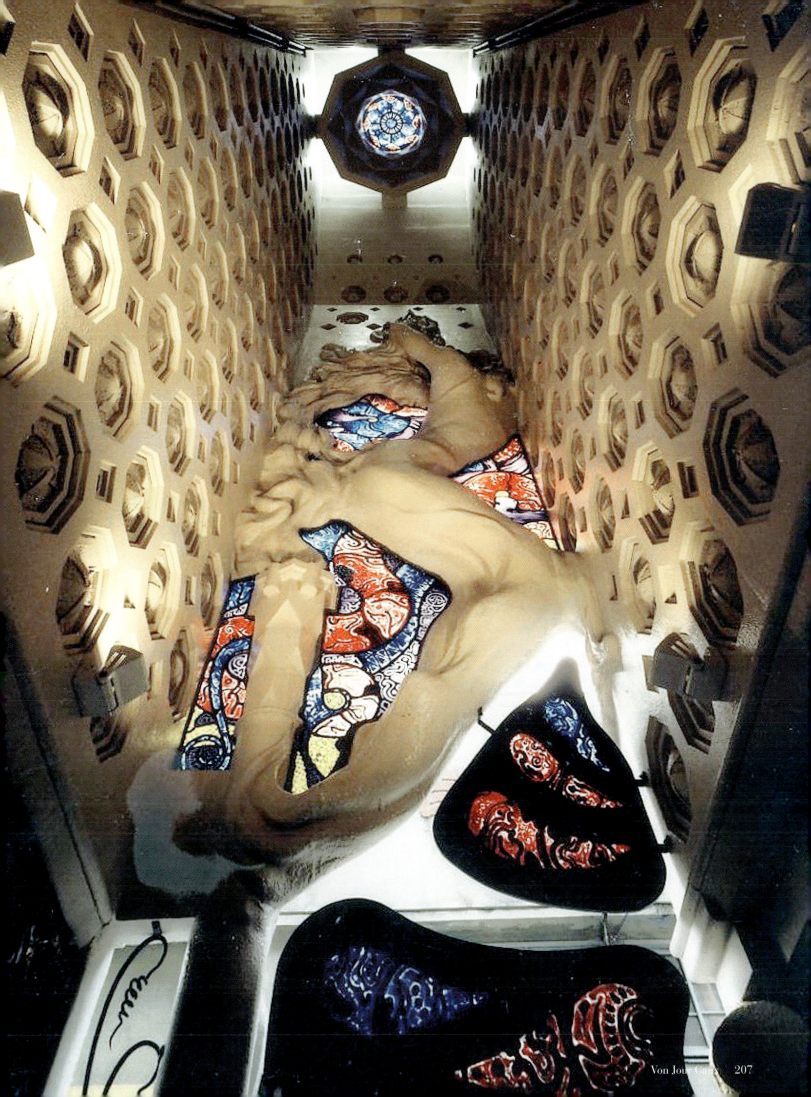

Genius loci

Shintoism has succeeded in becoming the training method for increasing the body censoring o "Iyashirochi" and "Kekarechi" out of the necessity to search for signs of the sacred ground in nature since the old days. Iyashirochi means vital land, where healing power for impurities brought on by human being occupation exist. Kekarechi refers to land ridden with sickness, where the vital force of the original ground was lost and defiled. Then, a shrine is built in the chosen Iyashirochi, and the "Torii," or monumental gate, that serves as the boundary between the sacred area and daily life is erected for people engrossed in everyday sensitivity, in order to let know the meaning of its existence.

This is a rental apartment building, with the owner's house on narrow pathway on Kousyu-Kaidou Av. near Daitabashi Big Crossing in Tokyo's Suginami ward. It is located near the entrance of peaceful residential area that sits in the middle of a metropolitan area. The theme for this building was to create a Gate of Fountain, which means district name Izumi, an architectural imaging device to help recall deep human unconsciousness. Since this building site is spiritless due to being built on what was once a swamp, and because of the high voltage electric wire netting, we decided to mold a Pegasas rushing high in from the sky for encouragement.

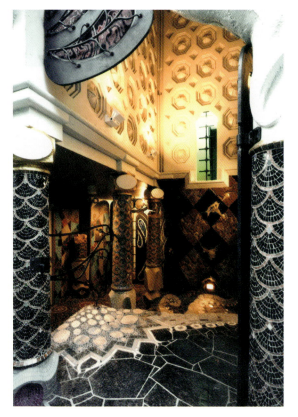

地霊の浄化

神道では古くから、聖地の気配を自然の中に探る必要性から、「イヤシロチ」と「ケカレチ」を身体的に感知する修行が受け継がれてきました。「イヤシロチ」は人間の営みの穢れを癒す力を持っている土地を、「ケカレチ」は本来の大地の生命力を失った穢れた土地を意味します。そして選ばれた「イヤシロチ」に社が建てられ、日常の生活圏との境界に結界を示す「鳥居」が建てられ、日常的な感性に埋もれた人々にも、その存在が理解できるようになっているのです。

「和泉の扉」は、杉並区の代田橋交差点近く、甲州街道から奥に入り和泉町を経て街道に抜ける狭い道筋に建つ、施主の住宅を含む賃貸住宅です。この辺りは大通りの喧噪から住宅街の静寂への境界で、和泉町界隈への入り口にあたるので、日常と非日常の境にある「門」のイメージを重ね合わせて、根源の記憶を喚起する仕掛けを試みました。昔、沼地だった所で上部には高圧電線が低く走るという全く生気のない敷地なので、天空を駆けるペガサスの彫刻を施し、元気を与えました。

Art Complex VIII

きらめく器(うつわ)

1990
Royal Vessel

幻想(げんそう)の祝祭(しゅくさい)
Mirage of
Illusion

幻想の祝祭

虹は大気と太陽と雨（水）の合作で、人々の生活の中で自然の神秘性を表わす最も端的で最も美しいものです。その美しく儚い現象ゆえに、虹はしばしば天上界と地上、現世と彼岸をつなぐ重要な意味を持つようになりました。色彩は光の本質であり、光は生命の本質です。「生命は色彩が表わすように、「生命は色彩」なのです。

荒廃した都市の砂漠の中に、大気と水と光の豊かな恵みを象徴する虹、現世と彼岸をつなぐ虹の蜃気楼を再現することは、決して無意味な試みではありません。豊島区池袋の「斐禮祈」のちょうど筋向かいに建つこの建物は、施主の住宅を含む非常に間口の狭い小さな商業ビルです。

華麗な彫金細工の置物の佇まいを持つ外観は、90センチ角の銀色のアルキャスト・パネルに玉虫色に輝くステンドグラスをはめ込んだもので、陰陽二種類の構成パネルを回転させて多様な構成を生み出し、それに偶然選ばれた彩色ガラスを配することで、抽象的な曼荼羅図像を表現しています。この小建築は、街並みに面したファサードの限られた立面に、虹の「色彩曼荼羅」を提案したものなのです。

Mirage of Celebration for Illusion

The sun, and rain water, are the most straightforward when portraying natural mystery and appear most beautiful in the people's lives. Because of transient and beautiful phenomena, a rainbow had the meaning of a mysterious bridge between this world and the heavenly world. Color is the true nature of light and light is the true nature of life. The phrase, "Life is colored," can be interpreted as, "Life is a color." Color has a big influence on the person's heart, their body, and the light in their life. Though light and color are usually perceived through sight, it is known that it can also be recognized physically by a dermal sense of touch.

This is a small, narrow commercial building with owner's house on the opposite side of same street as Art Complex O Wiseman's Stone in Ikebukuro, Toshima ward. Bright silver jewelry work comprised of 90cm square aluminum casting panels placed on iridescent colored stained glass, which has been laid out according to the principles of Yin and Yang. These represent Mandala in abstract form.

Art Complex IX

性源寺(しょうげんじ)

**1992
Cradle Temple**

彼方(かなた)から彼方(かなた)へ
From Beyond to Far Beyond

修行の基本は、ひたすら座禅すること「只管打坐」と、日常の作業に努める「作務」にあります。しかし教条主義的な生き方を強いる類の信仰は、個人主義に教育された現代人には支持されず、檀家も衰退の一途をたどっています。信仰の究極にあるものは、人間として完成された自己の姿です。私たちは敢えて宗派の教義を超えて、現代に通じる極彩色の浄土世界を提案しました。

彼方から彼方へ

「色即是空」には二つの側面があります。一つは「色彩は光である」という知的な認識であり、もう一つは色と光の関係の喩えから「存在するものの本質は無である」という身体的な会得です。前者は現象として認知できますが、後者は身体的な実感として個人的な体験を通じて会得する性質なので、その理解を助ける手段として修行が必要となります。

存在の本質が無であるならば、自分の生命も無なのだから、無の身体に閉ざされた自我もまた無になります。所詮無である自我に出来る悩み事にとらわれて、振り回されるのは全く無意味なことになります。「発心」とは、この現実を頭脳ではなく身体的に納得する時点を意味し、この段階に到達して初めて仏教の求める世界が現れてくるのです。

「性源寺」は、福島県いわき市に建つ、曹洞宗の鶴見総持寺系寺院の本堂で、手がけたのは付属する庫裏及び客殿です。曹洞宗は禅の修行の厳しさで知られる質素を旨とする宗派で、その

Von Jour Caux 217

From Beyond to Far Beyond

The basis of the Sodo Buddhism School training comprises, "sit earnestly in religious contemplation," "strict duty," and "for the daily work." There are two sides in "color be in vain," that is the fundamental idea of Buddhism. One is the intellectual recognition of, "A color is light," and the other is the physical comprehension of, "The true nature of what exists is nothing," according to a metaphor of color and light. Though the former can be recognized as a phenomenon, the latter goes through the personal experience as a physical feeling and therefore training becomes necessary to gain a masterful understanding.

If the true nature of existence is nothingness, then life in a body is also nothing, and the self that is locked in the body also becomes nothing. Being swayed and swung by the troubles of worrying, anything originating in the self becomes meaningless if the self is nothing after all. "Spiritual awakening" is understanding that which is not mental but physical, and reaching out at the moment the world which looks for Buddhism appears in this reality.

This is a guest and priest house attached to a Buddhist temple of the Sodo Buddhist School, which is known for having the most severe ascetic Zen practices in Iwaki City in Fukushima Prefecture. However, today, only the dogmatic doctrine of forcing a way of life unilaterally could not be understood by modern people who are educated based on individualism, as members of parishioner have been decreasing. The purpose of deep belief is to search the world for one's perfect self. We daringly proposed realizing an actual paradise for today, beyond many schools' concepts.

Von Jour Caux 219

Art Complex X

舞都和亜
まいんどわあ

1992
Trip to Carnival

心魂の響応
しんこん きょうおう
Vibration of the Human Soul

心魂の響応

我々は、人間の生きることの営みの根底の願いを文化的装置の中に再建し、それに携わる語り部としての職人達の技芸を復活させようと活動してきました。選ばれた素材自体と素材の組み合わせから生まれる波動的効果や、空間構成と装飾意匠の案配によって、波動をより理想的な状態に変化させる技術を謙虚に追究する姿勢が、真に建築家を志す者に求められます。

これらの経緯を踏まえての確信の第一歩となる「舞都和亜」の主題は、「健全な身体に健全な精神が宿らんことを」か〝A sound mind in a sound body〟から、「身体的な空間と人間の心が響きあう建築」と決定されました。この仕事を通じて今まで無意識のうちに導かれてきた様々な試みの方向が、一つの明確な意味の姿を現し始めたような気がします。

舞都和亜は、杉並区の「和泉の扉」の道筋の奥に建つ、住宅都市整備公団による民間賃貸住宅です。一流施工会社の企画部長である施主はガウディの熱烈なファンで、「和泉の扉」を何度も訪れ「和世陀」を見て、設計を依頼してくれました。人のできないことを成したとの思い出を持ちたいと、予算を超えない範囲で私たちに全能力の全てを傾けてほしいというのが唯一の条件で、表現の全てを任されました。私たちはこの仕事が「梵寿綱と仲間たち」運動の前半の総決算であると自負しています。

Vibration of the Human Soul

Our activities have been aimed at rekindling the deep desire we humans have for architecture as cultural device, and to revive the art of craftsmanship. However, from now on, we must search for a spatial method which aids in healing people's body and mind amongst this ever worsening society. It is expected of a genuine architect to modestly investigate the changing ideal conditions through technology, including the vibration effect which is derived from the combination of the materials used. The main theme of the "Sound of the Mind," becomes the first step of the conviction based on these particulars, indicated in the phrase, "A sound mind in a sound body," indicating that the architecture, sound, physical space, and the affected human affected each other. The direction the various trials took us through unconsciously led us to the premonition of beginning to seem to have come to the sight of one definite meaning.

This is a condominium apartment building by the Housing Development Division on the same street as the Art Complex O La Porta Izumi in the Suginami ward. The client, a planning manager for a renowned general contracting company, is also an avid fan of Antonio Gaudi. He came to us about this project after visiting the Art Complex Oc Rhythms of Vision and Art Complex O La Porta Izumi many times. He wanted to produce the best memory of life, having done incredible tasks that were only previously dreamt about. His only request as a client was for us to complete the project under a strict budget. We are proud of this work as it is the first period sentimental monument of Von Jour Caux and his TroupAf's movement.

論考2

頭と手の邂逅──梵 寿綱・羽深隆雄論
倉方俊輔

はじめに
梵と羽深の現代性

『生命の讃歌』という本書のタイトルが象徴している通り、梵寿綱と羽深隆雄は半世紀以上にわたり一貫して、すべての事物を交換可能なものに変えていく近代社会において、「生命」という掛け替えることのできない本質を、建築によって讃える方策を探してきた。

梵・羽深の活動が刺激的なのは、それが物づくりから場所性が失われ、施設の費用対効果が強く意識されるといった工業化・経済化の動向に向き合い、それを逆手にとる形でなされているからだ。

このような現代性は、作品を一見しただけでは見出しづらいかもしれない。神話を語り、技芸を解説する本人の言葉からは一層、読み取りづらいだろう。私が強調したいのは、梵・羽深が単純に「反時代」的な存在ではないことだ。だからこそ、今、語るべき意味が出てくる。私たちが工業化と経済化の中で戦う上でも、有用なのだ。その仕組みを解明することが、本稿の目的である。

梵 寿綱の頭
1959年の早稲田モダニズム

時計の針を、東京タワーが完成した翌年の1959年に戻したい。梵寿綱の処女作「ある寿舞〔片切家寿舞〕」から話を始めたいのだ（fig. 1）。これは梵寿綱を名乗るはるか以前の作品である。正確に記せば、設計者は本名の田中俊郎ということになる。「寿舞」というネーミングも梵時代になってからだから、「片切家住宅の改修設計」と呼んだ方が適切かもしれない。

何よりも汲み取り便所の臭突が目を引く。門扉の脇にあって、さまざまのモザイクタイルの小片で彩られている。小片は四角く囲われた領域をも乗り越えて、外へと逸脱しようとしている。東京都23区でも下水道の普及率はまだ約2割という当時における、この大正時代の住宅の改修には、近代化に邁進する時代性とも、背後の木造住宅とも直接には無関連に、概念に囲い込まれることを拒否した生命の力が感じられる。

類似したデザインを探すと、色とりどりの瀬戸物の破片でコンクリートの壁を覆った大多喜町役場庁舎に行き着く。同年に千葉県に完成し、1959年の日本建築学会賞を受賞した。設計したのは今井兼次で、アントニ・ガウディを日本に紹介した人物として知られる。1895年に東京に生まれた今井は、早稲田大学建築学科を第7期生として1919年に卒業し、同年から1965年に名誉教授となるまで教鞭をとって、早稲田大学の建築学科の傾向に影響を与えた。まだ一般には知られていなかったガウディの意義を、写真もほとんど示さないままに語る今井の情熱を今も思い出すと、梵は語っている。

fig.1 「ある寿舞」外観。
Exterior of *Family Home of Esotericism*.

今井自身、ガウディ的と称される造形を本格的に展開したのは、大多喜町役場庁舎の後である。また、高度成長の前半期というこの1959年の時点で、明解な反「近代建築」の態度や、ましてポストモダニズムの考えがあったはずはない。したがって、この2つの作品の類似は、表層的なデザインの模倣ではない。さらに息が長く、近代とそこにおける建築をどう捉えるかという、早稲田大学の建築学科の傾向に由来するだろう。

進歩主義・普遍主義・理性主義に強く根ざした建築を、仮に「近代建築」と定義すると、2作品とも「近代建築」にはあたらない。それでも「近代」的な建築でないとまでは言えないだろう。なぜなら、どちらも伝統や場所性の拘束から解き放たれた自由を謳歌し、創造としての造形を現実に構築することで、さらに遠くまで人間の可能性を切り開こうとしているとみなせるからだ。人間の自由を拡張しようと望む「近代」性は、むしろ「近代建築」よりも強い。

1910年に始まった早稲田大学の建築学科の傾向の一つは、このようなロマンティシズムとヒューマニズムを特徴とする「早稲田モダニズム」であり、創作者としての梵の起点にはそれがある。すべての語るべき建築家がそうであるように、時代に無関係な根無し草ではなく、現在の年表的な事実の上に浮いているのでもない。彼にとっての主観的常識から世界を捉えて、考え始めているのである。

生まれ育ちの演劇性

梵は、特に1983年の「和世陀」以降、「日本のガウディ」として有名になった。1959年の最初から「ガウディ風」であることは、初志貫徹してそうした造形に心酔した建築家だということを意味するのだろうか。いや、そうではない。その間の紆余曲折を追うことが、建築家の理解のためには必要である。

キーワードの一つが「演劇性」だ。梵寿綱（本名、田中俊郎）は1934年、大衆演劇の街として知られる東京の浅草に生まれた。梵が幼い頃に没した母は、前進座創設時の女優だったという。父は大衆演劇の脚本や演出を生業としていた。息子の演劇への関心は、早稲田大学高等学院への入学でさらに熱を帯びた。同校が早稲田大学の付属高校であり、受験の必要がないのをいいことに「年間四百回程の映画鑑賞を始めとして、新劇、歌劇、演奏会、能や文楽や歌舞伎から松竹や日劇のレビュー、更には新橋芸者の東踊りや京都の都踊り等、学業をサボって暇を作っては三昧に

明け暮れる毎日をおくった」*1 ことを、梵は述懐している。

就業の必要がないほどに裕福なわけではない家で、演劇に傾倒するというのは、どういうことだろうか。それは「主観的」には何にでもなれる可能性を保持したがりながらも、「客観的」には何かのスペシャリストとして独り立ちしなければいけないという二律背反の立場に自分が置かれていることを、強く意識させるにちがいない。

1952年の大学進学で梵が理工系に進んだのは、将来の生計に配慮したためだった。その中で建築学科を選んだのは「もっとも評価が曖昧」と考えたからだという。1956年の卒業時は、中堅ゼネコンの中野組（現・ナカノフドー建設）に現場監督として就職した。1959年には中野組を退社し、建築設計事務所を開いた。だが、先に述べた片切家住宅の改修設計以外に大した仕事もなかった。

先に「主観的」と表現したのは「自分が決める世界のありよう」であり、「客観的」は「世界に決められる自分のありよう」と言い換えられる。両者はいかに調停可能なのか？解答を出す素材を与えたのは、アメリカだった。梵を捉える上で最重要なのは、これまで語られてきたようなガウディのヨーロッパなどではなく、アメリカだ。しかも、戦後日本の建築界が整理した形で受け入れたそれではなく、世界をつかみ取るべく、自らがもがいて獲得したアメリカである。何とか工面した金をもとに、梵が最安値の貨物船でロサンゼルスに上陸したのは1962年初頭だった。

ここまでは梵の模索期と言える。当時の経験がその後、無駄になったわけではない。後で詳しく述べるが、中野組で得た現場体験と人脈は、帰国後の建築人生を支えることになった。加えて、大学卒業後に、前川國男建築設計事務所や坂倉準三建築研究所といった当時の設計エリートが勤める類の建築設計事務所に行かなかった——行けなかった——からこそ、設計者と職人の距離を近く感じ、梵寿綱を名乗るようになってからのコラボレーションが生まれたことも指摘できる。ただ、この28歳の時点で、以後の道筋は何も固まっていなかった。彼は建築的な素地のない家に生まれた。師と呼べる建築設計者も持たなかった。梵は、例えば今井兼次との関係がそうであるような人との出会いや経験した事実を基に、建築とは何かということを自らで組み立てた人物である。この点で、新潟県上越市で木材を扱う家に生まれ、梵と出会うことから建築人生をスタートさせた羽深隆雄とは好対照をなしている。

もう一点、次に進む前に指摘したいのは、第二次世界大

戦から復興しつつある大都市で演劇に親しんだ梵の特権である。それは仮想の楽しみに溢れた中で、時に演劇的なキャラを使い分けながら、客観と主観の二律背反を生きざるを得ないという現在の私たちの経験を、この時代の人間にしては先取りしていると言える。1934年に生まれ、東京で育たなければ、そうはならなかっただろう。この結果的な先駆性が、物質的には日本が豊かになった1970〜80年代に至ってから、梵が頭角を現した遠因だと考えられる。

様式のアメリカとの出逢い

梵がアメリカを目指した理由には、1960年前後の雰囲気が現れている。1959年に来日したバックミンスター・フラーの講演会に啓発されて宇宙時代の建築家像を模索し、ミース・ファン・デル・ローエの仕事に惹かれた。それでミースが建築を教えていたイリノイ工科大学への留学を希望したというのだから。ここまでは戦後日本の建築界が捉えた、典型的なアメリカ像の範疇に収まる話である。

違うのは、実際につかみ取った対象だ。当初は1962年3月からイリノイ工科大学への入学を希望していたのだが、それが許可されなかった。半年間が空いてしまい、金銭的にも苦しくなった梵は、すぐにシカゴにある大手出版社コンデナスト社の「HOUSE AND GARDEN」誌デザインセンターで働き始めた。肩書きは「キッチン・バスルーム・スペシャリスト」。アメリカ各地のディーラーやクライアントからシートが届く。そこには項目に沿って、それぞれの好みの雰囲気や色彩が書き込まれている。その希望に見合った様式でキッチンやバスルームをデザインし、図面とパース、仕様と商品カタログ一式を整えて、次々と送り返す仕事だった。

近代化が進行したにもかかわらず、いや、それだからこそ、様式という感情に訴えるだけの要素が残存し、それらが個別に、システマティックに取り扱われる。梵が捉えたのは、進歩主義・普遍主義・理性主義に従って「近代建築」を先導しているといったような、戦後日本の建築家の大部分が信じていたものとは、異なるアメリカの姿だった。この仕事における、様式をシステムとして処理する考え方を彼は拒否しなかった。後年の回想を記したい。

「画一化された日本のキッチンと異なり、10数万種のスタイルを組合せから選択するだけで様々なデザインが生み出せて、モダン・ランチウエスタン・中国風・日本風・バロック・ロココ・ルイ16世などの多様で趣味的なクライアントの要求に自動的に応えられる仕組みができあがって

いたのです。〈中略〉ハウス・アンド・ガーデンの6か月で学んだことは、現代は世界の過去から現代までの文化情報を共有できているので、教条主義的な現代のトレンドも、所詮は様式の歴史を構成する一つの情報に過ぎないということでした」[2]。

梵以外の人間であれば、別の認識に達していたはずだ。このような理解に至ったのは、単にイリノイ工科大学にすぐに入学できず、代わりにインテリアの仕事に就いたからではない。海を渡って「世界に決められる自分のありよう」を脱し、「自分が決める世界のありよう」に近づきたいという若い情熱が後押ししただろう。そして、つかみ取った内容が〈様式の思想〉と〈システムの思考〉の併存だったのは、その融合が生来の演劇性と建築を近づける鍵だったからだと考えられる。しかし、先を急ぎすぎてはいけない。こうしたロジックを当時の梵が深く自覚してはいなかったことが、その後の仕事の幅の広さから分かるからだ。時の流れを追って、それが開花するプロセスを見ていきたい。

システム思考による最初の成果

梵のミース熱は半年のうちに冷めた。1962年9月に入学したのは、シカゴ芸術大学の絵画彫刻専攻だった。結局、二人の接点は、梵がミースの中に現実を突き抜ける存在を一瞬、垣間見るという、いかにも〈早稲田モダニズム〉らしいロマンティシズムだけだったのだろうか。

そうでもなさそうだ。梵は1963年2月末に締め切られた国立劇場コンペで、応募307案の中の佳作を得て、建築界に初めてその名を刻んだ（fig. 2）。案は厳格な柱で屋根スラブを支えたもので、ミースのベルリンの「新国立ギャラリー」（1968年）を彷彿とさせる。その原型であり、不実施に終わったバカルディ社ビル案（1957年）を下敷きにしたことは明白だろう。正方形平面の内部は、グリッドに従った直線によって大ホールから小部屋までに分割され、図面はまるで図式のように見える。

同じ頃から翌年にかけて、梵が手がけた抽象絵画は、Chicago Artist CompetitionやChicago Art Festivalなどに次々と入選を果たした。抽象絵画自体が、アメリカに渡って初めて制作したものだという。その内容は後に「システムデザインプログラム手法で、大威張りで手抜きができる曼荼羅的な抽象画でありながら、鑑賞者の記憶の奥底にある普遍的な象徴や隠喩の記憶と饗応して感情移入を誘うような表現」[3]と説明されている。

フラーやミースに対する関心は、機能的・工学的な側面を大事に考える梵の心理に由来する。それを入り口に、両者の中に、プロジェクトの全体を構造をもったシステムとして捉え、一つ上の立場から問題の解決を図る〈システム思考〉を見出したと考えられる。それが有効だという意識は、シカゴ芸術大学時代にレミントン・ランドの図書館企画室で図書館のインテリア設計に携わり、スペース・プランニングを学んだことで、より高まっただろう。1961年、ソ連による史上初の有人宇宙飛行を目の当たりにしたジョン・F・ケネディ大統領が、今後10年以内に人類初の月への有人宇宙飛行を成功させると宣言し、壮大なアポロ計画を達成するためのシステムに注目が集まっていた当時のアメリカの空気も、後押ししていたに違いない。すなわち、国立劇場コンペ案や抽象絵画は、まず前提として、そのようなシステムの表現なのである。多くの「近代建築」がそうであったような、スタイリッシュなデザインの問題ではない。当時も以後も──現在の一般的な認識とは異なり、実際には──梵は制作の上で機能的・工学的な側面を重視している。ただし、それは必要条件である。十分条件ではない。前述した言葉で言えば「世界に決められる自分のありよう」つまり物事の「客観的」な部分を満たした上で、もう一方の要素が魂だと考えているのである。

　梵が工学系の大学でなく、シカゴ芸術大学に入学して良かったのは、幅広い制作技法や芸術史を学べたことだ。それによって、もう一方の「主観的」な部分つまり「自分が決める世界のありよう」が必要という意識も高揚した。理論面で重要なのは、独特の感情移入論である。梵は美術制作の実践とドイツの美術史家ヴィルヘルム・ヴォリンガーの『抽象と感情移入』の再読を通して、同書がテオドール・リップスの心理学的美学から引き継いだ「感情移入衝動」と、それだけでは古典主義的な美以外が解釈できないとして別に提唱した「抽象衝動」を混ぜ合わせて、抽象的な形態を通じて情感が伝達できるとした。先に梵が自らの抽象絵画を、システム思考に基づいて感情移入を誘う作品と説明していたのは、このことである。国立劇場コンペ案についても「ミース的な鉄とガラスの抽象的構成の中に江戸桃山文化の華麗な情緒を感じさせる応募作」*4と後に解説している。

　独特の感情移入の理論を打ち立てることで、梵は主観的には、「客観的」な〈システム思考〉に基づきながら、生命の持つ「主観的」な部分、すなわち人間の記憶や感情、欲望や願望に位置を与えることができたことになる。

　ただ、別人の立場から眺めると、疑問がないではない。生まれる疑問は2つあって、一つは「様式」の問題はどこへ行ったのかということ。もう一つは、それは制作者の「主観的」な部分を伝達すると言っているから、作り手の「自分の決める世界のありよう」の権利は保証されているが、受け手それぞれの「自分の決める世界のありよう」が認められるような説明になっていないのではないかということである。

　それにしても、この時点での梵の論が、抽象的な表現を前提に、制作した個人が価値を決定するものに聞こえるからと言って、文句を付けるのは筋違いだろう。何せまだ1962年、近代主義の真っ最中だ。1970年代後半から80年代に一世を風靡したいわゆるポストモダニズムにしても、前半の「抽象的な表現」という枠を外した程度で、後半の建築家幻想は温存されている場合が多かったのだから。

アメリカ遊学で得た7要素と未成の2要素

　こうしてみると、1962〜63年のアメリカ遊学の意味は、本当に大きかったのが分かる。梵が獲得したものを列挙すれば、〈システム思考〉、〈様式の是認〉、〈感情移入の理論〉、〈幅広い制作技法〉、〈芸術史の理解〉、〈戦略性〉、これらの前提としての現代が〈大衆社会であるという認識〉と、全

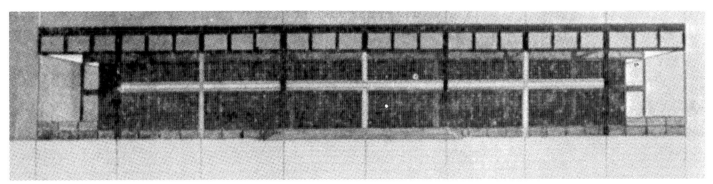

fig.2 梵寿綱「国立劇場」競技設計案。
Von Jour Caux's design proposal of the *National Theatre* competition.

部で7つもある。もちろん、それまでの育ちや大学や中野組での経験の中に種子は存在しただろう。しかし、それが開花したのは、厳格に定められた目的を持たない「遊学」を通じてである。7つすべてが、国内の通常の建築教育や建築修業で出会うことがほぼ期待できないものであることを考えると、アドバンテージはなおさらである。

例えば20年後の「和世陀」（1983年）も、先の7つの組み合わせでできている。つまり、〈システム思考〉に基づいて機能的・工学的に無理のない枠組みを作った上で、他の建築家なら踏み込まないほどの〈様式の是認〉を行い、〈幅広い制作技法〉を理解しているがゆえに「仲間たち」に仕事を任せ、〈大衆社会であるという認識〉に根ざしたアピールで、人々の持つ〈感情移入の理論〉に訴え、建築家らしく〈芸術史の理解〉でも説明するという〈戦略性〉を持っているから、今でも語られる存在としてある。

その一方で、前節の最後でまとめたように、1962〜63年の時点では、それは個人の抽象的な表現だった。それに対して「和世陀」は、みんなによる具象的な表現である。この時点では、〈様式の是認〉を全面展開した〈具象的な表現〉と、〈集団創作〉の2つの要素が見られない。

本章を終える前に、この2つの要素を育む重要な出来事も、アメリカ遊学に存在したことを付け加えたい。帰国を決めた梵は、シカゴ芸術大学で出会った妻との新婚旅行を兼ねて、アメリカで初めての旅行に出た。東海岸からメキシコに飛んで西海岸にまわり、ルート66号を北上してシカゴに戻るというコースだった。

その時に1955年に開園していたディズニーランドを訪れた。「はりぼてでキッチュな雰囲気の中に、現実的ではないが、妙に真実味のある確かな手ごたえを体験した」*5と記している。梵寿綱を名乗る以前の1972年のことである。額面通りに受け止めて良いだろう。他にもディズニーランドに触れた梵の言葉は、「HOUSE AND GARDEN」誌に関してと同様に、否定的なものではない。建築家には珍しく、背後の合理的なシステムの上で様式がコントロールされ、思い思いに人々が楽しんでいるという事実を、偏見なく受け止めている。ただし、それが〈様式の是認〉を全面展開した具象的な表現として建築化するのには、1974年以降の梵時代を待たなくてはならない。

この旅行の最中、梵は二人の男性が共同生活を行う「インディアナの家」のスケッチを描いていた。出来上がった基本設計に基づいた住宅は、着工が1968年にずれ込み、4年がかりのセルフビルドで1972年に完成した。同年に訪問した梵は「実際の建物は工期中の変更を通じて、その印象はますます基本案に近づいていた。〈中略〉私の果たした役割はきわめて不十分なものであったが、結果として私の他のいくつかの作品といちじるしく共通の雰囲気を持っていることを」*6認めている。ここには建築が作り手の強い統合の下にないことが、受け手にとって幸せだという理念がある。こちらは帰国後の梵が時間をかけて育んでいったもう一つの要素である〈集団創作〉へと発展する。

1960年代後半の活動と「ある美瑠(ビル)」

1964年12月、東京オリンピックを成功裏に終えて2か月後の日本に帰国した梵は〈システム思考〉を武器にした。高度成長期の後半の日本は、物量の大小から、それらが織り成すシステムへと関心を推移させていった。時代が求めていたものを提供して、まず梵は建築界で足場を固めていった。

初めて教鞭をとった授業の名が「建築システム論」だった。梵はその講師として招かれた。講義を聴講していた学生の中に、2年生になったばかりの同学科第一期生・羽深隆雄の姿もあった。梵の冷静な造形論は、新潟県上越市から上京した若者にとって、想像すらしなかったものだったろう。羽深は知性の洗礼を受け、彼を生涯の師と仰ぐことになる。

1965年の9月からは、北野建設の設計部次長に就任した。1年後には日産建設（現・りんかい日産建設）に技術研究室を設立し、主任研究員として、耐震性能の高いパネル式プレハブ技術であるカミュ工法の特許を持つフランスのレイモン・カミュ社との合弁会社設立に貢献した。1967年からは都市開発中央研究所の主任企画員に就いて、安田火災海上保険の各支社の営繕を後見し、後の1976年に新宿副都心に建設されることになる「安田火災海上本社ビル」（現・損保ジャパン日本興亜本社ビル）の初期調査やアメリカへの視察をアレンジするなどした。

日中こうして働いた梵は、夜になると事務所に顔を出した。帰国して間もなく、中野組からの縁で東京都・日本橋に建つビルを手がけることになり、集まってきたメンバーと設計を始めたのだった。1967年1月に竣工した「ある美瑠〔塚田美瑠〕」の一室を借りて、1968年10月には正式に「株式会社 梵 設計作務室」が発足した。大学を卒業した羽深も所員に加わった。

1969年は、梵が建築ジャーナリズム界にデビューした年だ。『新建築』4月号に「最高裁判所」のコンペで最終20

fig.3 梵寿綱「最高裁判所庁舎」設計競技応募案。
Von Jour Caux's design proposal of the *Supreme Court Hall* competition.

作品に残った案が掲載され、山口文象、圓堂政嘉、槇文彦、出江寛、川崎清ら、年長の建築家たちと肩を並べた（fig. 3）。11月号には「ある美瑠」が紹介されている。12月号では、建築評論家の村松貞次郎が、梵を次世代を担う「第3の建築家」に位置づけた。冒頭の文章はこうだ。

「最高裁コンペ応募作品展をご覧になった方は、記憶されているかもしれない。南蛮屏風のようなパース、はるかに庁舎があって、手前にオランダのカピタンや白衣の僧侶が描かれていたあれである。また本誌先月（11月）号に発表された風変わりなインテリアを持った「塚田美瑠」、仏画風のレリーフがあって抹香くさいし、ロココ調の家具もある。この"風変わり"な建築家が梵（所員5名）を主宰する田中俊郎である。まだ若い。35歳。長身白皙の好男子。早口でよく話す」*7。

しかし、写真をご覧いただければ分かるように、「ある美瑠」は「早口でよく話」してはいない。もし今も建っていて、何も知らずに遭遇したら、梵の作品と気づかないのではないか。情熱的にモザイクタイルを使ったアメリカ留学以前の「ある寿舞」とも、梵のスタイル以外の何物でもない1970年代以降の建築とも違う。鉄筋コンクリート造6階建ての建物の外観を一見しても、そこにあるのは円と直線のみである。

それでも、この寡黙さは普通ではない。一体いつの時代の建物なのだろうか？　眺めているうちに、不思議な感覚に襲われてくる。左右対称のファサードで、ガラスブロックや丸窓をあしらった姿は、モダニズム初期の例えばオーギュスト・ペレの作品のようにも、有名建築家が設計していない高度成長期の街場のビルのようにも、フォルマリスティックな最新の建築のようにも感じられる。これといった装飾は無く、窓は窓で、壁は壁らしい。それでは形態は機能に従っているかと言うと、わずかに屈折した壁面や微妙に貼り分けた壁面タイル、ガラスブロックの文様などに気付いて、それも怪しくなってくる。

「ある美瑠」は単純に反時代的だったり、反機能的だったりするのではない。さまざまな形態操作によって、時代にも機能にも意味付けられない存在を目指している。皆が同じように認識する事実から出発し、人間は進歩していく。そんな近代主義に異を唱えている。

こうした「ある美瑠」の存在の目的は、装飾性が顕著になる内部でも変わらない。装飾の数々を、1974年以降の梵時代などと関連させながら挙げてみよう。

229

最も具象的なものが、エレベーターや6階サロンのドアに施された仏教図案のエッチング（fig. 4）で、建物のホール部分に注ぐ後の情熱の萌芽が読み取れる。サロンの内部では、ロココ調の長椅子に仏教図案の布地を用いて、室内の兜からアンティーク家具までを横断した空間が形作られている。施主の意向に沿った形で、建築界では俗っぽいとして毛嫌いされがちな日本近現代の住まいの和洋折衷を臆面もなく推し進めている。この延長上に、後の独立住宅のシリーズ「寿舞」がある。他方で、入り口の「座れない」長椅子や、無限遠から見た時に意味の現れる図像といった無用の用は、その後の梵にはあまり見られないものだ。

　内部には、外観には大っぴらに現れていない装飾性がある。とはいえ、それは外観と同じく、単純に反時代的だったり、反機能的だったりするのではない。別の言い方をすれば、ここにあるのは今井兼次のデザインからは遠い。しかし、今井の姿勢は引き継いでいる。すなわち、何かから建築ができるのではなく、建築から何かができるかということ。取り替えの利かないこの人間の時間にいかに貢献できるのかという真っ当な思いが根底にある。梵はこう語る。

「そこで働く人々は、一度限りの人生の働き盛りの時期の貴重な時間を、事務労務に拘束されて給与を得ています。／それ故、事務所ビルには、事務作業空間としての機能以上に、働く人々の貴重な生命を預かり、社会活動の実践を通じて精神の豊かな成長を助けるという、祈りを捧げる宗教建築を超える働きが求められているのです」[*8]。

　非機能的なものは、平準化に回収されない。それこそが生命の時間につながる。こうした真に合理的な考え方が「ある美瑠」には流れている。オフィスビルという経済の真っ只中にあるのにもかかわらず、それに回収されないものを形で組み立てている。オフィスも「生命」の時間の一部だからにほかならない。

「梵 寿綱」前夜のマンションの意味

　田中俊郎が梵寿綱を名乗るようになったのは、1974年6月とされる。事務所名の「梵」を新たな名乗りとし、同時に事務所を解散して、「梵寿綱と仲間たち」を結成した。自身は、この1974年を境に梵以前の「第二期」と現在までの「第三期」とに分割している。創作者の自覚としては納得がいく。

　ただし、作品そのもので捉えると、事態は異なる。「ある美瑠」と同じ施主からの依頼で1969年に竣工した「リドー住吉」——梵の事務所もここにあった——と、後述する1974年の「カーサ中目黒」とでは、同じ集合住宅でも違いは大きい。むしろ後者は「阿維智」以降の梵作品のデザインに連なる。切れ目はむしろ梵以前、1970年代前半にある。梵寿綱の個性が建築表現として確定するに至った契機に、一連のマンションの設計があることは興味深い。それは孤立して捉えられがちだった梵の仕事を、これも従来の建築史では看過されていたマンション（民間集合住宅）史と結びつけて解釈できるからだ。

　日本におけるマンションのデザインは大雑把に言って、(1) 擬ホテル→(2) 擬邸宅→(3) 擬ホテルと推移してきた。(3) は1990年代以降のタワーマンション中心のあり方である。装飾と生活感の少ない外観と、広いロビーを特徴とする。(1) と (3) は装飾性が少なく直線的であり、その間に「マンション」とは——「団地」に代表される公団住宅・公営住宅・公社住宅とは違って——曲線的な装飾性を有したものとして一般に認知されていた (2) の時代がある。(1) から (2) への転換を象徴するものこそ、建築家の芦原義信が設計し、1964年に竣工した「秀和青山レジデンス」と、自社設計の1967年に竣工した「秀和外苑レジデンス」の違いである。青山の方は、1962年に区分所有法が制定され、民間集

fig.4 仏教図案のエッチング。
Buddhist design by etching.

合住宅の法的位置付けが明確化されたことを背景に生まれた高級路線の第1次マンションブーム（1963～64年）、「ビラ・ビアンカ」（1964年）や「コープオリンピア」（1965年）。それに対して、外苑の方は、大衆化路線をとった第2次マンションブーム（1968～69年）以降、大京のライオンズマンションシリーズなどに至って、いわゆる建築家の名が急速に消える。

大多数の建築設計者と同様に、民間で食っていくしかない梵は、まず大蔵屋からの依頼によるマンションを手がける。羽深が担当した同年竣工の「シャンボール目黒」（1969年）、「シャンボール松濤」（1969年）、など一連のシャンボールマンションがある。

しかし、秀和を超える建築的な試みとして記憶にとどめたいのは、カーサシリーズのほうだ。中堅ゼネコンの中野組が第2次マンションブームを受け、1968年に不動産事業に進出して展開したマンション群である。第1号として1969年に竣工したのが「カーサ池尻」（東京都世田谷区）である。白い塗り壁や曲線が用いられたバルコニーの手すりを見ると、秀和のマンションが1960年代後半から採用した「南欧風」を踏襲していることが分かる。壁のレンガタイルやアーチの使用など、よりキャラクターを打ち出そうとしていると言えるものの。

中野組は梵が最初に勤めた会社だったから、マンション会社としては後発組としての個性化に声がかかるのは自然なことだった。そうして1972年に竣工した「和泉の扉」（東京都杉並区）では、路線をさらに推し進めている。曲線を組み合わせた入口、様式的な左右の照明や飾り格子、白い外壁から一転して包み込まれる雰囲気の煉瓦貼りのエントランスなどには、アメリカで学んだ様式と、建築家らしい空間構成が生きている。男女をあしらったタイル装飾もある。梵寿綱を名乗ってからの作品に特徴的な具象的なイメージは、このマンションで初めて本格的に登場するのである。

翌年竣工した「カーサ相生」（東京都中央区）も、梵の面目躍如である。中央のエレベーターコアの部分や妻面の外壁などは、黄色とオレンジの花柄模様の繰り返しである。「様式の是認」だけでなく、アメリカで学んだ「システム思考」もここには導入されている。15階建ての建物はHPC工法の採用によって合理化されている。計画上も総戸数290戸、25平米でワンルームマンションの先駆と言える。低コストで大衆のための集合住宅を提供し、渋谷区や港区を中心に展開した秀和レジデンスの枠組みを脱したと評価できよう。

さらに翌年の「カーサ中目黒」（東京都目黒区）になると、梵寿綱の作品と言ってよいものになっている。こちらは住宅街に建つ、小規模な複合メゾネット型の集合住宅だ。奇妙な装飾が垂れた塀の上をよく見ると、カタツムリの彫刻が這っている。1980年の倶会櫻聴院の妻面の日時計に通じる、天使の日時計に迎えられて上がる細い階段の先には、大きなタイル壁画。謎めいた図像の中で、描かれた魔法陣が梵自身の作品であることを示している。その先の洞窟のような暗がりも、「和世陀」のような後年の作品と共通する。

秀和のマンションについて、梵は次のように述べている。

「戦後の共同住宅を総括するなら〈中略〉青い屋根に白い壁に象徴される秀和レジデンスが大衆の夢を組み上げる形で浮かび上がってきた経緯の方を、もっと評価するべきだと以前提案したことがあります〈中略〉秀和レジデンスは限られた高い金利の資金でマンションを建設していて大衆が自分の夢に近いと確認した上で積極的に買い求めることで事業が成り立っているわけです。ですからもし、建築家が自分の時代の夢の象徴を再構築する役割を担っていると少しでも認識しているなら、この事実に対してもっと謙虚にならなければいけないと思うのですが」[9]。

カーサシリーズにおいて、アメリカで発見した「システム思考」と「様式の是認」は高度に融合し、ディズニーランドに触発された生まれ育ち以来の演劇性が「ある美瑠」と異なった形で開花し始めた。マンションという当時大衆化しつつあった存在によって、〈システム思考〉、〈様式の是認〉、〈感情移入の理論〉、〈制作技法の知識〉、〈芸術史の理解〉、〈戦略の重視〉、これらの前提としての現代が〈大衆社会であるという認識〉が融合しはじめた。

そして、もう一段、いわば「非作家としての作家」とでもいうべき思想が、「梵」という名乗りを生むのである。これも経済の真っ只中で遂行された過程だ。

「頭」による「手」のプロジェクト

1974年6月から、梵寿綱という名の下に作品が発表される。作品群は、大きく次の3つに分かれる。

一つは、1975年竣工のI「阿維智」から1992年のX「舞都和亜」までの10作品からなる「Art Complex」である。一般的な建物種別で言うと、Iが会社の別荘、Vが老人ホーム、IXが仏教寺院で、残りが共同住宅である。・時を共同で暮らす場という点に共通点が見出せる。

二つ目は、1976年の「エスト・エスペランサ」から1986

年の「プチ・エタン」までの数棟における「樹下美人図考」の名称で発表された。どれも商業的なビルである。

3つ目が、1976年の「小山家寿舞」(小山家住宅)以降の「寿舞」で、「すまい」の言葉通り、基本的には独立住宅である。

以上のようにシリーズ名を冠し、アーティスト(工人)との協働を進めていった。梵寿綱とは、こうしたプロジェクトとしての自覚を持った際の人格に与えられた名前である。そのことは、1974年以降も、雑誌発表の際には本名である田中俊郎の名で、より客観的な解説の併記が見られる点からも明らかだろう。

「阿維智」は巡礼をテーマに、動線上にそれまでに類を見ないほどの造形が各所にほどこされ、心の中に像を結ぶ「全体」が追求されている (fig.5)こうした造形の意図について、1979年の「斐醴祈」(ルボア平喜池袋)を語る梵の言葉を引用しよう。

「対立的で相補的な関係を、一挙に全体像に結ばれる効用をもつ神秘的な媒体の概念は、錬金術の用語で「賢者の石」と呼ばれています。「斐醴祈」は、さまざまな日常的事象をシュールリアリズムの手法を駆使して転換させ、人びとの創造力を刺激し、超現実的幻想を惹き起こす媒体の働きを持つ、賢者の石としての空間的装置を企図して計画されました」*10。

先に述べた3つのシリーズとも、近代建築の理性的、統一的、進歩的な建築のあり方に対して、感性的、分裂的、懐古も許容する無時間的なスタイルを提示している。大きな役割を果たしているのが、工人たちの仕事である。3つのシリーズにおけるその姿と働きは、共通性を持ちながらも、それぞれに区別されている。

「Art Complex」のそれは最も分裂的と言える。これは資金面での融通性と同時に、共同で暮らす場において、個々人の幻想が胚胎しながら一段上の共同の状態を構築することが重要だという判断があろう。「樹下美人図考」では、商業ビルに要求される装飾性を加速させ、単に自らの物件が目立つだけの目的を超えるものが創出されている。「寿舞」は思い出が堆積する場としての個人住宅への要求を取り入り、擬様式的な意匠で応えたものだ。このような、それぞれが社会的に置かれたポジションの利用に、梵の冷静な判断とジャッジメントが表れている。〈システム思考〉と〈様式の思想〉が確認できるのである。

つかみ取った内容が〈様式の思想〉と〈システムの思想〉の併存だったのは、その融合が生来の「演劇性」と建築を近づける鍵だった。梵は頭によって手を使っている。最初にあった自らの「手」を捨てて、正反合の道のりを、経済社会の中で辿っている。その結果、建築にしかできないことを、生命の讃美として行っているのだ。

梵の都市性

梵の作品にはバラバラに楽しめる豊かさがある。強烈な造形的個性というよりは、梵の確かな思想に基づいて、工人たちにそれぞれの個性を発揮させているのだ。今井兼次が職人を使ったのに対して、梵寿綱は「アーティスト」を援用していると言えよう。アーティストには、個人のエゴがある。その上に個を超えたものが現れると梵は見る。それを司るのが建築家であると。

最後に指摘しておきたいのは、梵に色濃い〈都市性〉である。アーティストにしても、都市の産物だ。これと関連する梵の作品の性格については、1977年の鈴木博之の文章以上のものはないだろう。梵の作品の全体性が、単体の建物に限定されていないと指摘し、それが街歩きの人々によって発見されていると述べる。それは「固有性を備えた唯一

fig.5 「阿維智」内観。
Interior of *Gladiator's Nest*.

fig.6 「四季彩一力」内観。
Interior of *Shikisai Ichiriki Hotel*.

無二の場所をつくりだそうとする」というのとは、少し異なるだろう。もっと軽やかな、後年の梵寿綱の言葉で言えば、「『日常の世界』そのものを『聖なる世界』に反転させ得る文化的な装置の創造」(「ムンディ・アニムス」解説文)である。非固定的で、言ってみればゲリラ的な梵の作品が、だからこそ強靭な革命であることを、まだ30代前半の建築史家が、当時の空気の中で確かに捉えていたことに驚かされる。それは現在でも梵寿綱の作品が再発見され、人気があるという事実と共鳴している。

羽深隆雄の手
動作空間としての「四季彩一力」

羽深隆雄は最も成功した梵寿綱の同志である。しかし、作風は大きく異なる。「和風」や「伝統」といった一般的に梵には使われない言葉で形容されがちであることは、その違いを代表している。けれど、こうした言葉だけでは収まらない創造性が羽深にはある。

福島県・磐梯熱海の「四季彩一力」は、1918年に創業した老舗旅館だ。国内外の要人の来訪も多い。2015年にもイギリスのウィリアム王子が外国の要人として初めて東日本大震災後の福島に一泊し、東京から駆けつけた安倍首相が歓迎夕食会を開催したことで話題となった (fig. 6)。

同じルートでわれわれも入ろう。羽深が設計した増築部(1994年)はダイナミックである。エントランスアプローチの空間は左右対称で軸性が強く、視線は自ず上方に向かう。通常の和風旅館のイメージからはほど遠い。キリスト教の教会でいえばステンドグラスの位置に配されているのは、特殊手漉き和紙。素材を透過した外光と、下部に仕掛けられたシーリングライトの光が融合して、天井の江戸墨流し和紙を照らす。床は石やタイルによる模様。正面の木製建具の向こうに、彫塑的なコンクリート壁が透けて見える。ここは多様な素材を、一目に収められる場なのだ。歩を進めるにつれ、何一つとして機械的な対称性が存在しない和紙の模様、刻一刻と変化する光といった繊細さが浮かび上がる。その要素はあまりに多いので、見る人によって、あるいは時間や気候や気分によって、前面に突出する印象は異なるに違いない。建物の外部の成り立ちに甘えず、どっちつかずの曖昧さも無い、むしろ西洋的と言える空間性が、細部の繊細さを保証している。訪問者は建築が作り出す世界に巻き込まれるのである。

エントランスアプローチを抜けた先のフロント、ロビー、売店、ラウンジはすべてひとつながりの空間で、ラウンジから庭に張り出した半円形の部分は総ガラス張りになっている。

こう書くと、よくある単純な、ガラス張りの、勇気がなく、曖昧なワンルームの空間と同様に思える。しかし、現実の印象はまったく異なる。天井や床の仕上げの違いが空間を分節し、人間の動きと寄り添う。遠くからも目に止まるコンクリート先付アートフォーム工法レリーフは、近づくにつれて細部が見えていき、椅子に腰掛けた際の目の喜びになる。何度か往復するうち、例えば欅の柱（fig. 7）に具象的な動物の彫刻を発見して、まるで江戸時代の寺院建築の人懐っこい装飾に大工や左官のサービス精神を見たときのように、頬が緩む。繊細な仕掛けが、内部のそれぞれの場所を性格付けている。平面図や立面図に現れづらい部分が設計されているのだ。図面は良いものを生むための一手段であって、図面を書き切るのが設計の目的ではないから、本来は当たり前の話だが。

人の動きに伴って展開する、もてなしの仕掛けは、食の空間で最高潮に達する。吹き抜けに咲いた大ぶりの和紙の花、宙に浮いた土壁の円環、そして、赤い根のようなオブジェ……これらをどのような点で「和風」や「伝統」と呼ぼ

うか、少し悩むかもしれない。光によって素材は映え、その奥が見たくなる。心を高揚させる機能と、日常を離れてわざわざ訪ねるという旅館の目的とが一致している。万人の身体に対応した機能だけでない。一見して分かる視覚的な面白さだけでもない。心と身体を動かす動作空間がここにある。

旅館の主要部と思われる客室はどうだろうか。天井に工夫を凝らして視線を上方に誘い、意匠が変化に富んで、間延びしていないのは他と同様だが、ここは対照的に静的である。「泊まる」は「止まる」に通じる。ここでは滞在という動作が空間として設計されている。「四季彩一力」は、旅館というものが決して単純な機能で成り立っていないという当然の事実に気付かせる。羽深は専門家ぶった漢語や外来語を超えて、大和言葉の本質へと到達する。その言葉は梵と違って、易しい。しかし、深い。

合理性も押さえながら、既往のビルディングタイプ（施設類型）の適用で事足れりとしない。こう書くと、梵と同じに思える。だが、異なる。それぞれの人間の行動に応じながら、それは緩急が付き、また時に弦楽器が時に管楽器が雰囲気を作るオーケストラの一作品のようなもので、全体を貫くテイストは統合されている。梵はもっと離散的である。この〈統合性〉こそが、全体の構成法における大きな差異と言えるだろう。

施主との信頼関係も見逃せない。羽深は、それ以前の1985年にも一力の増改築を手掛けている。そこからの客室増築の相談を受けたのに対して、大規模な増改築による全体の平面計画の合理化を提案し、猪苗代湖からの流れが注ぐ名園「水月園」を取り込む構成として実現させた。「四季彩一力」のひとつながりになった設計は、そこにしかない場所と人間に寄り添う羽深の性格を映し出している。

師の影響からの自立

だが、人間の個性が建築の特質に至るまでには、時間が必要だった。「四季彩一力」の1985年の増改築時の貴賓室を訪ねると、当時40歳だったとは思えない成熟ぶりに感心する一方、ある種の感慨にかられる。テーマは明らかに和洋の混淆である。窓辺のステンドグラスの脇から蔓のような柱が立ち上がり、中央で花肘木状の形態を描く。日本の「洋館」の意図的な継承と言える。洋装の伝統継承者である昭和天皇もお泊まりになった「貴賓室」としての機能を高度に昇華したとみなせるが、同様にアール・ヌーヴォーを思わせる工芸的なデザインは「N.S.P.日本精版印刷」（1983年）や「壺

fig.7 「四季彩一力」柱。
The pillar of *Shikisai Ichiriki Hotel*.

の家」（1984年）にも使われているので、それだけに帰すことはできない。「壺の家」の鍛造の床柱などを制作した倉田光太郎は、前年に完成した梵寿綱の「和世陀」の手摺扉も手掛けている。

羽深は、1945年に新潟県上越市の木材を扱う家に生まれた。1967年に大学を卒業した後、梵の事務所に勤め、1975年に柿工房設計事務所を設立した。独立以降も梵との仲は親密だ。今も「田中さん」と尊敬と親しみを込めて呼ぶ。梵寿綱を名乗るのは1974年からだから、正確には羽深が知るのは、梵以前の田中俊郎である。羽深は梵が必要とした職人を何人も紹介した。「斐醴祈」（1979年）では、羽深が玄関ホール天井の金磁モザイクを制作した。羽深が「N.S.P.日本精版印刷」を、梵が「和世陀」を始めた頃には、一緒にイタリアとスペインに赴き、共にガウディを改めて学んだ。羽深にとって、田中俊郎が建築の唯一の師であり、田中が梵寿綱になることを助けた。10歳しか歳が違わない二人は師弟であり、同志のようである。

だが、それだけに、稀に見る「頭」を備えた梵からスタートしてしまった困難さは想像に難くない。例えば、若くして世に出、最後まで世界を自分流に解釈したフランク・ロイド・ライトを弟子が乗り越えるとしたら、どれだけ大変だろうか。

しかし、羽深はそこから自らの場所を見つけた。1994年に完成した「四季彩一力」は、技術の適用においても、全体の構成法に関しても、背後の思想についても、羽深のスタイルと呼べるものになっている。その成功は「仙寿庵」（1997年）、「貴祥庵」（1999年、現・星野リゾート 界 松本）、「大和の湯」（2005年）といった作品を生むことになる。

素材・意匠・空間の変化

羽深のスタイル（様式）とは何か。さらに見ていくために、「湧雲の望楼」を訪れることにしよう。秩父の山々が見渡せる埼玉県・都幾川に設計したゲストハウスである。

スケールの大きな自然に対峙するダイナミックな設計は、ここでも健在である。鍛造の引手に触れ、欅による高さ3m幅90cmの大扉の重さを感じながら引くと、装飾性に溢れた吹き抜けの空間が迎える。見上げながら、来訪者は知るだろう。ここでは単に目の前の光景をこちら側から眺める場ではなく、あちら側からこちら側へと風景を迎え入れ、共に暮らすための空間が設計されているのだと。

この吹き抜けのホールを中心に、内部には流動的な立体空間がある。ギャラリー、和室、ゲストルームといった各室

fig.8 「湧雲の望楼」内観。
Interior of *Wakigumo no Boroh*.

がそれぞれに独自の居場所として設えられながら、その間の関係性に気づかせる仕掛けが施されている。空気が抜けるような雰囲気が感じられる。それが自然と外部につながっている（fig. 8）。

同じルートを今度は素材で追っていこう。背の高い扉は60年以上前に伐採された欅の一枚板だ。繊細で大胆な三重格子の彫り込みが、無垢の肌合いを際立たせている。鍛造の引き手は、これと全く異なる素材である。だが、捩じ曲げるという人為を通じて、天然の賜物を感じられるのは同様だ。二つは建設という行為を通じて合一し、扉となった。それを推す時の重く、しっかりとした感触が、入るという動作に物語性を加える。二度目からのそれは、目にしただけで、身体感覚を想起させるものになるだろう。この家における素材は、加工する身体と、それに触る身体という二重の身体性をまとっている（fig. 9）。

しかし、そうだとしても、人はなぜここで、有限の物質や人間から醸させる重苦しさではなく、空気が抜けるような雰囲気を感じるのだろう。一つの理由は、先に述べたような空間の設えである。もう一つ効いているのは、そこかしこに施された羽深自身の意匠だろう。上方に続く扉にそそのかされて見上げれば、藤の花弁をデザインしたシルクスクリーンによる文様が軒裏に花開いている。淡い色彩のそれは、普通に日本建築の「伝統」を継承しようとしたら出てこない羽深独特の類のものである。直接の機能とは無関係であり、秋田杉柾板の素材に拘束されてもいない。純粋な目の楽しみである。

障子組子のデザインにも、同様の浮遊感が感じ取れないだろうか。それは抽象画のように重力を感じさせず、技術に

fig.9 1951年に伐採された欅材。彫り込みは三重格子のデザイン。
Carved in the felling has been zelkova in 1951 the design of triple lattice.

縛られず、意味に束縛されていない。社会的基盤からの構築を、技術という背景を、形態の意味を理解しているからこそ、それらを意識しながら、羽深の手は舞う。こうした重力感の無さも、羽深のデザインと凡百の「和風」や「伝統」の意匠との大きな違いの一つだ。

身体を自由にする空間、技術によって引き出された素材性、目を楽しませる意匠。仮にこう３つにまとめた時、それは実際の羽深の建築において重なって存在しているものを、理性の言葉で析出したに過ぎない。人間が経験するたびに、そのいずれかが突出するだろう。内部に招き入れられた自然が、さらにタイミングによる違いを増加させる。こうした建築の多層性においても、「四季彩一力」と立地や用途の違いを超えて共通性が見られる。これを独自のスタイル（様式）と呼ばずして、何をそう言うのか。

先の３つを結ぶものは「変化(へんげ)」だと思われる。大事なのは素材そのものではなく、素材の変化なのだ。人の技による変容である。外壁が最も顕著だが、羽深は職人に敬意を抱きながら、新たなチャレンジをさせている。人間の手と素材の可能性を、ひっぱり出している。これは職人と材料に囲まれた環境でなければ、いわば「手」を持って生まれなければ極めて困難である。羽深自身の手による無重力の意匠と共通したものを、具体的な素材を通じて追求しているのだ。

それは、ここではないどこかへ、というロマンティシズムとみなせる。それが解放された感触を見る者に与えるのである。

羽深の建築では、まるで材料に生命があるかのように、人間の生命が感じることができる。何かを作るための建材や素材というよりも、自然そのものに接した感覚である。そこから地球そのものの「造化の妙」を知ることができる。ここに梵とは明らかに違う形で、梵の大きなベクトルが受け注がれている。木材を扱う家という生まれを利用した、こうしたスタイルが成就したのが「四季彩一力」と「湧雲の望楼」だった。

飲食の小空間における技巧

羽深の作品は社会の中で成り立っている。もっと率直に、経済活動の中で成り立っていると言ってもよい。これは重要なことだ。

冒頭に挙げた「四季彩一力」もさることながら、ここでは「銀座久兵衛 別館」（2006年）を見ていきたい。東京・銀座の本店の斜向かいに羽深が設計した別館は、やはり十分に独創的である。それが世界的にも著名な寿司の名店として、さらりと受け入れられているわけだが。

寿司を食する時間、人は動かない。数十センチの距離に作り手と食べ手が対峙し、その間に言葉と非言語的コミュニケーションが往還しながら、時が過ぎ行く。寿司は凝視する

ような小ささである。身体的に繊細である。一瞬の内に一皿の味覚がある。通常のスケールの時間、そして空間が変容する体験だと言える。

であるとしたら、寿司屋で人は動かない代わりに、感じることの密度を増すことができる。この店での金春通りから座席までの距離は実際には至近だが、奥へと誘惑する意匠が、そう感じさせない。通りに面した石材の狭間、狭く豊かなエントランスの空間、図と地が交錯する組子障子の間。材と材との間隔を巧みに空けることも、羽深のデザインの特徴である。「空」は感じ取れるが、それだけで自立しては存在しえない。つかんだと思った瞬間に、するりと逃げる。羽深は空隙がロマンティックであることを知っているのだろう。

たどり着いた席で、腰が落ち着いた頃には、存外に多様な素材が小空間に投入されていることに気づく。至近距離にいるからこそ、素材の肌合いまで感じ取れる。杉柾透彫、截金（fig.10）、鍛造の床柱といった技も次第に浮かび上がる。一手間をかけることで変化する素材が、時間と空間を芳醇にしている。

極小の空間を設計する技巧は、次いで手掛けた「銀座久兵衛 京王プラザホテル店」にも横溢している。御影石やガラス、檜や漆といった素材の取り合わせの巧さはもちろんだが、ここでは平面計画に注目したい。ビル内の通路から4.3mの奥行きしかないという厳しい与条件を感じさせない。人体寸法を熟知しながら、必要な裏動線まで巧みにとられている。客にとって、ここが自分の場所だと感じるという余裕まで生まれている。このような贅沢さと軽やかさの両立は、皿に盛られ、奥から出され、カトラリーを使って食するというのとは異なった、寿司における贅沢さと軽やかさの美学と同一である。

自由を与える「手」

「銀座久兵衛」の2店舗や「四季彩一力」から分かるのは、経済活動の中で成り立つ空間を、心を動かす手わざで生み出す羽深の技だ。クライアントに利益を与える設計ができるから、仕事が仕事を呼んで、成功したのである。建築家の仕事は形を決定することだから、王道と言える。

なぜ、羽深の設計が人の心を動かすかというと、素材も意匠も空間構成も、既存の「～らしさ」という決まりごとを逃れているからだ。建築の中の素材は、その本性を捨てて全体の構築にただ奉仕したり、イメージを表現するだけの材料に貶められていない。しかし、だからといって、既存の「木らしさ」や「土らしさ」、「鉄らしさ」に留まっているのでもない。羽深の建築における素材は、手を加えられることで変化し、新しい個性を発揮している。だから、訪れる者はハッとする。

意匠についても同じだ。羽深のデザインは「旅館らしさ」や「和風らしさ」といったイメージに拘束されていない。和の基本を踏まえた上で、大胆に操作されている。訪問者はそれまで見知っていながらも、どこか入り込みづらかった意匠が自分の側に来た気がして、軽やかな楽しみを覚える。

建築の空間構成も、「旅館」や「寿司屋」といった約束事に縛られていない。原理に立ち返り、建物内のそれぞれの場所が、機能的、心理的にどうあるべきかを考えて、設計されている。それら複数の場が人間を軸に統合され、心と身体を動かす動作空間が仕上がっている。

羽深は今どき珍しいくらいに断固として、形を決定しているのだ。だがそれは、こうあれと強要された素材や、こう理解しろと強制する意匠、こうしろと拘束する空間を生み出すのとはまったく異なる。新しい自由の領域が、形の決定を通して確保されている。それが人の心を正直に動かす。だから、人間世界の原理である経済活動の中で成立するという仕組

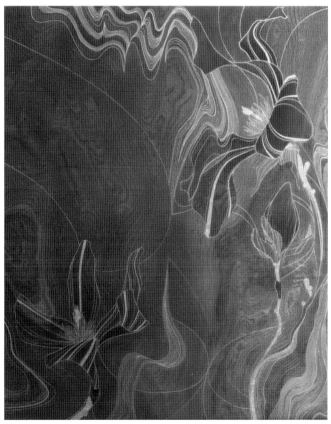

fig.10 欅の如鱗杢に施された截金。P.087にカラー図版。
"Kirigane" cut gold leaf that has been subjected to the Zelkova wood grain, such as fish scales. Color is posted on p.87.

みだ。

建築家としては革新的なタイプである。その上で、和風を主たる対象にしているところが巧い。それが「伝統」と呼ばれ、小難しく、重苦しいといった先入観を持たれがちであるだけに、素材や意匠や空間構成に手を加え、そこにしかないものに新たな生命を与えた時の効果は大きい。羽深は固形化しがちな伝統の重さを、逆手に取って乗り越えている。

文字通りに、逆手に取るのに必要なのは「手」である。羽深にはそれがある。和の空間を肌で知り、精緻なデザイン力を持ち、それを実現させるための職人と素材に対する知識とつながりを備えている。これは新潟県上越市の木材を扱う家に生を受け、その後も生家とのつながりを保ちながら、意匠の技巧を磨いてきた生まれ育ちのなせるわざである。

羽深の作品に一貫して私は、大地に芽吹いたものが重力の拘束を逃れ、天上を目指すようなロマンティシズムを感じる。素材も意匠も空間構成も、そのようにそれぞれの出自を失わないまま、ここまで行けるのだということを証明している。それを可能にしているのは、手の技術だ。以上の形容を作品だけでなく、その経歴に向けることも許されるだろう。建築が、すべての素材や観念やビルディングタイプ、あるいは場所や人間が交換可能なのではないことを証明している。「生命の讃歌」が歌われている。

では、羽深は物事をマクロに捉えないのか。そんなことはない。プロジェクトの全体を構造をもったシステムとして把握し、一つ上の立場から問題の解決を図るような思考が、経営面まで踏み込んだ「四季彩一力」の提案にも、既存の建物内での「銀座久兵衛」の解決にも見て取れる。梵が生来、得意としていた〈システム思考〉は、これらの中にもあるのだ。

羽深の出発点は「手」である。それが「頭」を獲得していった。そんな決まりごとを脱する手わざとシステム思考の融合が、いかに経済社会の中で求められ、建築が人間に生命力を与えているか。最新作の「会津中央病院」は、その現時点での達成である。

「会津中央病院」という総合

「会津中央病院」の第1期工事として、地下1階地上7階建の新棟WEST 2が2009年に完成した。翌年、これに接続する地下1階地上8階建の既存棟に対する免震レトロフィットと内装リニューアル工事が終了した。2015年5月末には第2期増築工事として、地上8階建のEAST CENTERが竣工する。以上を合わせると約35000平方メートルに及ぶ。

しかも、専門性を要する総合病院建築だ。これまでに見てきたような遊興の空間ではない。羽深の手わざは、どのように発揮されているのだろうか。

WEST 2の1階に大きな水槽が設けられている。水族館のようで、子どもが笑いながらお母さんに話しかけていた。吹き抜けのまわりではピアノの生演奏も行われ、カフェやショップなどが明るい雰囲気を作り出している。

WEST 2の上階も既存棟も、同じデザインの温度感で統一されていた。それが広いロビーや個別の相談室といった機能に応じて変奏されているのが見て取れる。人間を中心に統合された空間を築く羽深の個性は健在で、そのコンセプトは「病院らしくない病院」、まさに「病院らしさ」をさらりと逃れている。病院という「施設」を模倣してはいないし、それを隠蔽しようともしていない。人々が訪れ、留まり、それぞれの目的を果たす動作空間を設えている。旅館や飲食店と同じように。ただし、より静かに。

羽深はおそらく、病院を特殊なものではなく、生活空間の一部とみなしているのだろう。「健常者」と「患者」は地続きである。どこまでが健康でどこからがそうでないのか、一線を引くことができそうもない。ある日、一転することだってある。そうは思いたくはないから、人は病院を特殊な場とみなして、視界の外に置こうとするのかもしれない。頭では行かなくてはと分かっている時でも、足を遠ざけがちだ。しかし、こうした作りであれば、普段から出入りしたい気分になるだろう。心を動かす意匠が、身体を動かす。予防措置としてのデザインだ。生命というものに一線を引かない。老いも若きも等しく有しているそれが、最後の瞬間まで尊重されるべきであるという思想が横たわっている。

それは病院の合理性にもつながっている。WEST 2ではナースステーションの配置を工夫して、各室へのスムーズなアプローチを可能にし、WEST 2とEAST CENTERは共にスパンを15m確保したPC・PCa構造として耐震壁を無くし、将来的な平面の変更に対応可能となっている。緊急時の備えにも多大な力が注がれている。耐震性の高い基礎免震構造や、ガスディーゼルエンジンによる発電設備などを完備しているわけだが、設備を機械的に採用しているだけでなく、災害時の搬送やトリアージに十分なスペースが救命救急のエントランス部分には設けられている（fig.11）。実際に使う場面が想像されているのだ。医師の動線と患者の動線の分離も同じだ。衛生的で、どちらにも負担がかからない、共に人間として扱う平面計画となっている。巨大な病院

fig.11 「会津中央病院」救命救急用エントランス。
The emergency preparedness of *Aidu Chuo Hospital*.

と極小の銀座久兵衛が、同じ設計者によるものだと思えてくる。そして、確かに同じ設計者なのだ。

だから、人間の生命と共に素材の生命が生かされているのも驚くに値しない。EAST CENTERで人々を迎えるのは、羽深の手が描き出した3枚の意匠パネルだ。繊細なミラーガラスエッチングとステンレスエッチング、日本のモザイク作家の第一人者である喜井豊治による大理石モザイク画を取り合わせ、「宇宙」「地球」「生命」を表現している。意味に束縛された表面上の意匠ではない。想像を刺激し、素材そのものが見せる変化の妙が人を勇気づける。

外壁には地元の窯元による1枚1枚、色を調整しながら焼き上げた約19000枚もの陶板タイルが打ち込まれている。遠目にも明快なパターンとして親しく認知されながら、近くに寄ると1枚1枚の違った表情が現れる。それは既存棟からガラス越しに眺められて、インテリアを改めたのと同じ効果を発揮する。中間にある庭には、石や玉砂利が文様を描いて敷き詰められ、光を映すガラスのオブジェと風にそよぐ水が共鳴する。たっぷり取られた空間で、一目に収まる多様な素材が讃歌を歌っている。

贅沢すぎるだろうか。ここまで触れてきたグレードの高い技術も芸術性も、民間の医療機関としての将来を見込んだものであることは疑いない。経済の真っ只中で建築にしかできないことが遂行されている。それは梵も行ってきたことだ。

羽深は理事長の信頼を得て、第1期、第2期、今後に計画されている第3期と、敷地全体を見据えて、病棟などの構成を再編している。先を読んだシステム思考、病院内のさまざまな立場の人間に寄り添う力と、施工者を掌握する能力が、このキャラクターを有した大規模施設を現実のものとしている。頭と手を兼ね備えた建築家は、クライアントの替え難いパートナーである。

「会津中央病院」から思い出されるのは、過去の羽深の作品に留まらない。梵の「無量寿舞」(社会福祉法人向台老人ホーム、1984年)にも、視覚だけでなく身体的な感覚に訴え、健常者とそうでない者、あるいは生と死といった近代的な分別を超えて、最後まで生命を讃えようという意志がみなぎっていた。システム思考とエッチングのような細部、新しいビルディングタイプを任せられる施主からの信頼という点では、羽深の出発点である梵の「ある美瑠」や1970年代のマンションのありようが蘇る。あるいはガウディと同時代を生きた建築家、リュイス・ドメネク・イ・ムンタネーによるサン・パウ病院のように地域性・工芸性と普遍性・合理性とが結びつき、地域に果たす病院の役割を想起させる。

急速に進化している医療に対し「会津中央病院」は施設の費用対効果が強く意識されるような工業化・経済化の動向を単純に敵とせず、本来、建築家がそうであるように、社会の状況を逆手にとる形で、交換不可能な「生命」の本質を建築を通して讃えている。脈々と受け継がれてきた系譜の最新作だといえる。

邂逅の讃歌

梵と羽深の違いを端的に言えば、それは「頭」と「手」の違いである。

「頭」とは、事業の目標を明確にし、それを実現するための要素を構成するシステム思考の能力である。梵の中心はそこにある。もちろん、梵が人間力やデザイン力を具有しないわけではない。その逆であることは、まわりに多くの協働者が集った事実が証明している。それでも、梵が時流を泳ぎながら、一人の人間としての存在感を発揮できた鍵は、生まれついての素質を、努力で研磨して製作された武器であるところの「頭」だ。

とはいえ、これだけでは一人の武勇伝で終わるだろう。そうではなく、梵が生み出した建築が語るべき質を有し、その過程が解明されるべきなのは、武器の使い方を正しく制御しているからだ。梵は「頭」を〈哲学〉によってジャッジしているのだ。

「手」は逆に、具体的である。羽深の特筆すべき具有はこの「手」、すなわち、自らが精緻なデザイン力を持ち、それを実現させるための職人と素材に対する知識とつながりを備えていることである。それが細部に耽溺するようなものではなく、この生来の環境を正しく伸ばした結果として、梵とは異なるスタイルが生まれた。

とはいえ、これだけでは一人の努力の物語に終わるだろう。梵における〈哲学〉に相当するものは、何だろうか。地域と場所を超えて、個々人の間に共感を生むようなものは、羽深において〈美〉だと捉えられる。羽深は「手」を〈美〉によってジャッジしているのだ。「美」を基準にした時、自分の仕事と他人の仕事との間の根本的な分別は消え去るだろう。人間の営みと自然の営みが同一の地平で考えられるに違いない。具体的な建設から始まり、人間の生命を通じて、最終的に世界そのものの成り立ちを垣間見せる。こうした回路は梵と共通である。

生命体の中で、人間だけが頭と手を発達させた。ちょうど人間の生命を代表するものが、この両者だとしても、頭と手

とでは、ずいぶん違う。梵は「頭」が先にあり、羽深は「手」が先にある。

梵と羽深は、似ていない。むしろ、ほど遠い。だからこそ、「頭」は「手」を尊敬してそれを求め、「手」は「頭」に憧れてそれを希求する。二人の建築家は、生まれから来る資質において、実に対照的だ。同型の対になっている。だからこそ、互いが必要であり、同じものを追求する幅が生まれ、建築の〈生命〉とは何かを考える上で有用である。そもそも、二つの個性が並び立って多くを語る、あまり無いような本書の成り立ちも、梵と羽深の同志的な関係なくしてありえなかったろう。

梵と羽深の共通点は〈建築による生命の讃歌〉である。それが具体的にどのような手法によってなされ、いかなる射程を持つか、ここまで論述してきた。

最後に指摘したいのは、梵と羽深こそが〈建築家〉である点である。施主に託されて、建設を総合指揮し、時代に残るものを創る。だから、文化の一部となって親しまれる。我々の生をより豊かにし、ここではない場所に一回一回繋いでくれることで、掛け替えのない生の本質を讃えてくれる。このようなものが建築ではないか。

梵・羽深は正統ではないルートを辿っているかもしれない。しかし、異端ではない。極めて正統なアーキテクトの可能性を示していることを理解してもいい時だろう。本稿がそれに微力でも貢献できたら幸いである。

（建築史家、大阪市立大学工学研究科准教授）

*1 梵寿綱談
*2 梵寿綱談
*3 梵寿綱談
*4 「座談会：戦後の陶壁画をめぐって（1978年2月10日）」『装飾タイル研究』第4巻、1978年
*5 田中俊郎「インディアナの家」『新建築』1972年8月号、p.277
*6 前掲5、p.278
*7 村松貞次郎「第3の建築家」『新建築』1969年12月号、p.241
*8 梵寿綱談
*9 前掲4
*10 梵寿綱「斐醴祈」『建築文化』1987年5月号、p.85

Essay 2
Happenstance of Head and Hand:
Treatise on Von Jour Caux and Takao Habuka
Dr. Shunsuke Kurakata

Introduction
Modernism of Von and Habuka

Exactly as the book's title *Praise for the Life* symbolizes, Von Jour Caux and Takao Habuka, for across and beyond a half-century, have faithfully explored through architecture the means to praise the precious essence of life, irreplaceable amidst our modern society where everything has become replaceable.

Von-Habuka work is stimulating, because it recognizes the trends of industrialization and economization, such as intensely conscious cost versus benefit and the removal of siting characteristics, and counters these trends to advantage.

The modernism described here may be difficult to discover through initial examination of the works, and even more difficult to comprehend from the masters' own words that recount fables and comment on the technique and art. Allow me to emphasize that Von and Habuka are not merely in opposition to their era. In fact, we now have an invaluable moment to hold a meaningful conversation, which is also useful in our battle amidst industrialization and economization. The purpose of this treatise is to elucidate their mechanisms.

Von Jour Caux's Head
Waseda Modernism of 1959

Let us turn the clock back to 1959, the year after Tokyo Tower was completed. Our exploration starts here with *Family Home of Esotericism* the maiden project of Von Jour Caux, long before the architect adopted this name (fig.1, p.224). To state matters accurately, the architect's real name was Toshiro Tanaka, and the word "*Sumai*" (pronunciation in Japanese meaning "family home") in the Japanese title was established later during the "Von" period, so this project at the time might be more appropriately described as remodeling the Katagiri home.

The most prominent feature is the vent stack for the waste-tank toilet. Back then, the installation rate of sewer lines even in central Tokyo was about 20%. Next to the entrance, this stack is adorned with tile fragments in a mosaic that seemingly want to hop over their enclosed square space and stray outward. The remodeled Taisho Era house exudes vitality that rejects being boxed into any concept, disconnected from that time period of charging ahead toward modernization, and from the wooden dwellings in the background.

A search for similar designwork leads to the Otaki Town Hall, whose concrete walls are covered with shards of colorful porcelain. This structure built in Chiba Prefecture was also completed in 1959, and received an Architectural Institute of Japan prize in the same year. The architect was Kenji Imai, known as the first person to introduce Antoni Gaudi's world to Japan. Born in 1895 in Tokyo, Imai was graduated from Waseda University's seventh annual class of the Department of Architecture in 1919. He promptly assumed a teaching position there, and stayed on this track until he became Professor Emeritus in 1965. Throughout his tenure, Imai imposed an influence on the trends at the Department of Architecture at Waseda University. Von has spoken of memories still fresh about Imai, showing very few photos during his passionate talks espousing the significance of Gaudi, who remained largely unknown at the time.

The full development of Imai's own artform described as Gaudi-esque came after Otaki Town Hall. In truth, a clear attitude opposing "modern architecture" or post-Modernist philosophy could not have been possible in 1959, during the first half of post-War rapid economic growth. The similarity of the two works, therefore, was not the superficial resemblance of design, but originated deeper within the trends of the Department of Architecture at Waseda University in how to treat Modernism and modern architecture.

If architecture deeply imbued with progressivism, universalism, and rationalism were defined as "modern architecture," then the two works would not be "modern architecture." Yet they could not be ruled out as "modern-ish" architecture. They both sing proudly of liberation, unfettered by tradition or siting characteristics. By building creative artform into reality, their attempts can be viewed as taking the cutting edge of human potential further. Modernism that desires greater human liberation is more powerful than modern architecture.

One trend of the Department of Architecture that opened in 1910 at Waseda University consisted of Waseda Modernism with characteristics of Romanticism and Humanism. Von's origin as a creator contained this component. Like all architects of mention, he has been neither rootlessly disconnected from his time, nor aloft the chronicling charts of current historical evidence. His thought processes began from analyzing the world by subjective common sense as he saw it.

Theater of Upbringing

Von became particularly well known as "Japan's Gaudi" after *Waseda el Dorado* (1983). Does being Gaudi-styled from the beginning in 1959 mean that he has been an architect ardently obsessed with that type of artform ever since his initial passion? No. We must trace the meanderings in between to understand the architect.

One keyword in this context is "Theater." Von Jour Caux (real name: Toshiro Tanaka) was born in Asakusa, the district in Tokyo known for popular theater (*taishu engeki*). His mother died while Von was still quite young, and was apparently an actress when the *Zenshinza* troupe was founded. His father's livelihood was writing scripts and directing popular theater. Von's interest in the theater heightened considerably after entering Waseda University High School. Since the school was attached to Waseda University and required no examinations to advance into the university, Von reminisces, "Aside from viewing 400 movies in a year, I spent many days skipping classes and finding time otherwise to enjoy Western-style theater (*shingeki*), musicals, concerts, *noh, bunraku, kabuki*, revues by Shochiku and Nichigeki, *azuma* dance by Shimbashi geisha, and even miyako dance of Kyoto." [*1]

In a home not so affluent to obviate the need to have a career, why would Von take such a leaning toward theater? His feelings must have coalesced around the desire to retain the possibility, subjectively, of becoming anything he wanted, but tempered, objectively, with the necessity to stand on his own as some sort of specialist. He was conscious of being in a position of two conflicting but valid sets of rules.

His step toward the sciences in entering university in 1952 considered his attention paid toward a future livelihood, and his selection of the Department of Architecture reflected a belief that the discipline made the vaguest evaluations. Upon graduation in 1956, he took his first job at Nakanogumi, a medium-ranked general contractor — now known as Nakano Corporation—, and worked as a site supervisor. He left Nakanogumi in 1959 and established an architectural design office, but work was minimal except for the remodel of the Katagiri home described above.

The description of "subjective" can be restated as "the arrangement of the world as determined by oneself," while "objective" can be restated as "the arrangement of oneself as determined by the world." How can the two be reconciled? Eventually, the United States supplied the base material for an answer. The most important key to assessing Von is not Gaudi's Europe as discussed over the years, but the United States. Not in the form neatly organized by the architecture industry of post-war Japan, but the United States as acquired through struggles by the architect himself, in an attempt to grasp the world. Somehow arranging for the funds, Von landed in Los Angeles in 1962 via least-costing cargo vessel.

The years until this point could be called Von's exploratory period, since the early experience was not wasted. As described in further detail later, the on-site experience and personal connections obtained at Nakanogumi supported his architectural career after the return to Japan. Moreover, after graduation, not entering (not being able to enter) the architectural firms of Kunio Maekawa or Junzo Sakakura, considered employment for the architectural elite at the time, can be noted as a factor in Von's feel for proximity between architect and craftsman, and in the emergence of collaborations after he took on the name of Von Jour Caux. But at this particular moment in time, nothing in the 28-year-old's future was determined. He was born in a home that had no architectural roots, and he had no architect who could be called a mentor. Von was an individual who put together his definition of architecture based on encounters with people, like his relationship with Kenji Imai, for example, and facts obtained through experiences. In this respect, Takao Habuka, who was born in a lumber trader's household in Joetsu, Niigata Prefecture and had started his architectural career before meeting Von, presents a marked contrast.

As one more item to highlight before moving on, I note Von's privilege of deep enjoyment of theater in a large city that was recovering from World War II. In one sense, he was ahead of his time, taking in the experience of our lives today, where we are compelled to live with two conflicting sets of rules between objectivity and subjectivity, at times choosing among theatrical characters to ride out an environment awash in virtual entertainment. Von could not have had this experience without being born in 1934 and growing up in Tokyo. The consequent early exposure is considered a minor factor in the rise of Von's renown in the 1970-80s, when Japan became materially affluent.

Encounter with US Style

The situation around 1960 relates to the reasons that Von headed for the United States. Enlightened from attending a forum of Buckminster Fuller who came to Japan in 1959, Von explored the image of being a Space Age architect, and was also drawn to the work of Mies van der Rohe. Consequently, he hoped to study at the Illinois Institute of Technology (IIT), where Mies was teaching architecture. This description fits within the typical image of the United States as perceived by the architecture industry of post-war Japan.

What he actually acquired was different. His initial hope was to be admitted to IIT in March 1962, but he was not accepted. Struggling financially now and looking to be idle for a half-year, Von quickly went to work in Chicago at the design center for *House and Garden* published by Conde-Nast. As "Kitchen & Bathroom Specialist," he designed kitchens and bathrooms along the styles requested. Dealers and clients from around the country sent their order sheets, with preferences and colors provided for each section. Von put together the drawings and renderings, hardware specifications, and product catalogues. These packages were shipped out one after another.

Despite modernization, or because of modernization, just the element called style remained to appeal to the emotions, and was individually and systematically handled. Von formed an image of the United States that was different from what the large majority of post-War architects in Japan believed: that the United States was leading "modern architecture" according to progressivism, universalism, and rationalism. And he did not reject the approach of processing styles as systems. His reflection in later years is as follows:

"Unlike the cookie-cutter kitchens of Japan, combinations of several hundred thousand styles could generate all kinds of designs. The system to automatically respond to diverse, avocational client requests like Modern, Ranch Western, Chinese, Japanese, Baroque, Rococo, Louis XVI, etc., was complete. … . In the six months at House and Garden, I learned that doctrinairist contemporary trends were merely one set of information constituting the history of style, since in our contemporary era we were able to share the body of cultural information worldwide from the past until present." *2

Somebody besides Von would have arrived at a different assessment, but not simply because he was denied admission to IIT and took an interior design job. The young, passionate desire to escape "the arrangement of oneself as determined by the world" and move closer to "the arrangement of the world as determined by oneself" was most likely a driver for the man who crossed the ocean. The content he netted was the side-by-side existence of "ideology of style" and "systematic thinking", and their fusion can be considered the key that brought the "theater" in his upbringing closer to architecture. But there is no need for hasty analysis. The breadth of Von's subsequent work shows that he was not deeply cognizant of this logic at the time, as we see the blending process unfold.

Initial Fruits of Systematic Thinking

Von's avid interest in Mies cooled over that half-year. His admission in September 1962 was to the School of the Art Institute of Chicago (SAIC) as a major in picture art and sculpture. Consequently, the connection between the two might have seemed like a glance by Von of strident reality within Mies, an apt sort of romanticism like "Waseda Modernism".
Apparently not. For the national theater contest that closed in February 1963, Von received an honorable mention for his work among 307 applications, and his name landed in the world of architecture for the first time (fig.2, p.226). The plan called for staid pillars that supported a roof slab, and evoked *the New*

National Gallery (1968) of Berlin by Mies. Quite clearly, the Bacardi Building Plan (1957) that ended without construction and was the original construct provided his base sketch. The interior of the square plan is divided by straight lines along a grid into large halls and small chambers. The drawing looks almost like a graph.

Between that time and the following year, Von's abstract picture art received successive mentions at the Chicago Artist Competition and Chicago Art Festival. Yet he had never produced any abstract art until his first efforts after arriving in the United States. The works are later described as "Abstract pieces like mandalas that proudly allowed for cutting corners through system-design programming methods, yet aligning with universal symbols and recollections of metaphor in the deepest reaches of the viewer's memory and inviting their empathy." *3

Von's interest in Fuller and Mies originates from his psyche that attaches importance to functional and technical aspects. From this entry point, through the two men, he apparently discovered "systematic thinking," to solve problems from a position one level higher, by assessing the entire project as a system with structure. The conscious belief in the validity of this approach was probably enhanced during his time at SAIC, while engaged in the interior designs of libraries at Remington Rand's Library Planning Office where he learned about space planning. Undoubtedly, the backdrop of the United States in 1961 moved him as well. John F. Kennedy witnessed the world's first manned space flight, and the president proclaimed that within 10 years humankind would go to the moon for the first time. Subsequently, much attention was focused on the systems that would achieve this ambitious Apollo Program. In short, the national theater competition proposal and the abstract art were both expressions of such systems, and took no issue with stylish design as much modern architecture did. Then and thereafter, Von actually emphasized functional and technical aspects in his creative work which differs from today's general understanding. But that was for the required conditions and not the satisfying conditions. The approach answers the "objective" portion or "the arrangement of oneself as determined by the world," if I use my previous description, of things, and considers the soul as the other element.

Von's fortune of entering SAIC instead of an engineering school meant that he learned broad creative techniques and art history. This journey elevated his consciousness of the necessity for the "subjective" portion, or "the arrangement of the world as determined by oneself." This unique empathism is theoretically important here. Through his creation of fine art and re-reading of *Abstraction and Empathy* by art historian Wilhelm Worringer, Von concluded that abstract forms could convey feelings through mixtures of empathy impulses, which the book inherited from the psychological aesthetics of

Theodor Lipps, and abstract impulses, which were separately proclaimed as necessary or else only classicistic beauty could be interpreted. When Von described his own abstract art as works that invite empathy based on systematic thinking, this is what he meant. He later details his national theater competition proposal as "an entry that evokes emotional feelings of glorious Edo-Momoyama Culture amidst an abstract composition of Mies-ish iron and glass." [*4]

Establishing his own particular empathism, Von was able to — based on "objective" systematic thinking—impose positions on the "subjective" portions held by life, in other words, the memories, emotions, desires, and hopes of people. From the vantage point of another person, however, the theory is not devoid of questions. In fact, two questions arise. The first question: where has the problem of "style" gone? Next, the theory states that the creator's "subjective" portions are conveyed. Thus, the rights belonging to the artist regarding "the arrangement of the world as determined by oneself" are assured, which prompts the second question. Doesn't the explanation fail to enable recognition of "the arrangement of the world as determined by oneself" for each of the viewers?

Although Von's theory at this point in time sounds like the individual who creates the art determines the value on the premise of abstract expression, complaining would be off base. It was still 1962, right in the middle of Modernism. Even post-modernism that carried the day from the latter 1970s to the 1980s merely removed the frame of "abstract expression" from the early 1970s. The architect's fantasies in the latter half were frequently kept intact.

Seven Elements Acquired During US Studies and Two Elements Incomplete

The significance of studying in the US between 1962 and 1963 was truly enormous. Von's acquisitions totaled seven: Systematic Thinking, Endorsement of Style, Empathism, Broad Creative Techniques, Art History Comprehension, Strategism, and Recognition of Populist Society (present day, as premise to the foregoing). Of course, their seeds probably existed in his upbringing and experiences at Waseda or Nakanogumi. They blossomed during the study abroad, when there were no rigorous objectives established. Considering that all seven elements would unlikely be encountered during the ordinary course of education or training for architecture in Japan, we can further appreciate the advantage gained.

For example, *Waseda el Dorado* (1983), produced 20 years later, comprises a combination of these seven. First, a nominally functional and engineered framework was built, based on Systematic Thinking. The Endorsement of Style extended far beyond where any other architect would dare go, while his comprehension of Broad Creative Techniques allowed the work to be delegated to colleagues. With an appeal rooted

in Recognition of Populist Society, the work, which remains in conversation today, enlisted people's Empathism and also retained Strategism that aptly for an architect allowed for a description through Art History Comprehension.

Yet, as concluded in the previous section, the theory was merely a personal, abstract expression around 1962-63. In contrast, *Waseda el Dorado* was a collaborative, practiced expression. At this point, the two elements of Practiced Expression (that fully developed from Endorsement of Style) and Group Creation were absent.

As an addendum to this section, I note that important events did occur during Von's US studies to nurture these last two elements. Having made the decision to return to Japan, Von left for his first trip around America that also served as a honeymoon with his wife, whom he met at SAIC. They flew from the East Coast to Mexico and toured the West Coast, and returned to Chicago northward on Route 66.

The travels included a visit to Disneyland, which had opened in 1955. He wrote, "Amidst a kitsch atmosphere of façade, I experienced a definite, yet surreal impact of peculiar authenticity." [*5] That was in 1972, before he took the name Von Jour Caux. This writing can probably be taken at face value. His other writings about Disneyland, like his regards of *House and Garden*, were not negative. Rare for an architect, he accepted without prejudice the fact that styles were controlled atop a rational system in the background and people were finding their own amusement. Architecture of Practiced Expression as fully developed Endorsement of Style, however, would have to wait for the period of 1974 and later.

During the trip, Von sketched *Touch of Culture*, in which two men live together. Based on the completed basic plans, construction of the house finally started in 1968, and was finished in 1972 as a self-built structure that took four years. Von visited the house that year and admitted, "The actual structure, through changes during the years of construction, came ever closer to the basic plans in my impression. … The role I served was quite inadequate, yet the creation ultimately retained an ambiance shared among several of my other works." [*6] Here we find an idea that architecture not placed under strong governance of the creative hand (original architect) is happiness to the receiving hand (client). Von groomed this idea over time and developed the additional element of Group Creation, after returning to Japan.

Activities of the Latter 1960s and *Practice of Mandala*

Two months after the Tokyo Olympics ended on a high note, Von returned to Japan in December 1964 with Systematic Thinking in his arsenal. Now in the latter half of its period of rapid economic growth, Japan had shifted its interest from the large and small in material quantity to the systems weaved together and created from this large and small. Von first built a solid foundation in the architectural world by providing what this period sought.

The course that he first taught was Architecture System Theory. Von was invited as a lecturer. Among the students attending the lectures was Takao Habuka, a second-year student belonging to the first annual class of the department. Von's cool artform theory was most probably beyond anything imagined by this youth who had come up to Tokyo from Joestu, Niigata Prefecture. Habuka was baptized in the knowledge, revering Von as his lifetime mentor.

In Sepember 1965, Von took the post of deputy manager for the Planning Department of Kitano Construction. One year later, he established the technology research laboratory at Nissan Construction (now Rinkai Nissan) as chief researcher. His efforts contributed to establishing a joint venture with Raymond Camus Company of France, holder of the patented Camus Construction Method of highly seismic resistant, paneled prefab technology. By 1967, he was chief planner at the City Planning Reserch Center. He looked after the building and repairing of the branch offices at Yasuda Fire and Marine Insurance, and worked on the initial survey of *the Yasuda Fire and Marine Headquarters Building* (now *Sompo Japan Nippon Koa Headquarters Building*) that would be built in 1976 as part of the Shinjuku Urban Redevelopment, as well as arrangements for visits to the US.

Von worked at his day jobs, and showed up at his office at night. Shortly after returning to Japan, he had landed a project through his connection with Nakanogumi for a building to be constructed in Nihombashi, Tokyo. Planning on the building began with colleagues at the office. In October 1968 the Brahman Architects Office Co., Ltd., was formally launched, leasing a room in *Practice of Mandala* that was completed in January 1967. Habuka, who had graduated from university, joined the team.

Von's debut in architectural journalism came in 1969. Among the proposals for the Supreme Court competition, the 20 finalists were published in the April issue of *Shinkenchiku*. Von joined the ranks of veteran architects, including Bunzo Yamaguchi, Masayoshi Yendo, Fumihiko Maki, Kan Izue, and Kiyoshi Kawasaki (fig.3, p.228). The November issue introduced *Practice of Mandala*, and the December issue had architectural critic Teijiro Muramatsu place Von as "the third architect" that would assume the next generation. Here is the starting passage:

"Those who have seen the entries to the Supreme Court competition may recall the courthouse lying far ahead of renderings like those of a folding screen, with illustrations in the foreground of Dutch ship captains and Buddhist monks in white. In addition, *Practice of Mandala*, announced last month (November issue), has unusual interiors: Buddhist illustration-like relief give off a stinky incense feel,

and Rococo furniture is appointed. This "unusual" architect is Toshiro Tanaka, sponsor of Von (staffed by five). Still young. Thirty-five years old. A handsome, tall, and light-complexioned man. Fast and ebullient talker." *7

But *Practice of Mandala*, as the photos show, is hardly a "fast and ebullient talker." Still standing today, the building would probably not reveal itself as Von's work to someone who walked by without the knowledge, and differs from *Family Home of Esotericism*, which is passionately adorned with mosaic tiles and pre-United States, and from his indisputable style of architecture in the 1970s and beyond. A scan of the six-story, reinforced concrete building presents just circles and straight lines.

Nonetheless, this reticence is uncommon. What period does the edifice belong to? Further inspection invokes curious sensations. The construction features a symmetrical façade embedded with round windows and glass blocks for a sense of the latest formalistic architecture found in, for example, the early modernist works of Auguste Perret, and urban buildings designed during the period of rapid economic growth by architects without renown. Ornamentation is minimal, windows are like windows, and walls are like walls. The format appears to concede to function, until the observer notices the slightly indented wall facings, the delicately segregated wall tiles, and glass-block patterns, and starts to suspect something.

Practice of Mandala is not simply rebelling against the period or opposing functionality. A variety of manipulations has striven for an existence defined neither by period nor function. Humankind makes progress by embarking from facts generally understood in the same way. But this work contests such modernism.

The significance of *Practice of Mandala* is consistent with its interiors, where ornamentation becomes prominent. Numerous ornaments, in relation to the Von Period of 1974 onward, are noteworthy.

The most practiced are Buddhist-themed etchings installed in the elevator and on the doors of the sixth floor salon(fig.4, p.229). These explain the subsequent buds of passion poured into the hallways of the building. For the salon's interiors, Buddhist-themed upholstery is selected for Rococo-styled benches, and the formed space crosses from the helmet to the antique furniture in the room. The blend of Japanese and Western styles, found in modern and contemporary homes of Japan yet largely spurned by architects as vulgar, is unashamedly prevalent, in line with the client's intentions. Extending from here, Von's *Sumai* series of freestanding homes follows later. In contrast, the entryway bench, unavailable for sitting on, is not seen in Von's later works. Although a meaningful illustration when viewed at infinite distance, it serves no purpose. Such useless utility is rarely observed for Von in later years.

245

The interiors have ornamentation that is not nearly as obvious on the exteriors. Nonetheless, like the exteriors, the interiors neither rebel in the period nor oppose functionality. Stated another way, the result here is remote from Kenji Imai's designs, but inherits Imai's attitude. In other words, architecture doesn't emerge from anything, but something emerges as possible from architecture. A sincere feeling runs deep as to how to contribute to people's time that cannot be replaced. Von comments thus:

"During their peak period of being able to work, those who work there spend their precious time bound to clerical labor in earning salaries. Consequently, beyond the function as office work space, office buildings must work harder than religious architecture where prayer is offered, since they hold the precious lives of working people and aid in prosperous spiritual growth through the practice of social activities."*8

Nonfunctional things cannot be resolved by leveling, which relates to the timespan of life. This truly rational thought runs through *Practice of Mandala*. Although in the midst of an economy called an office building, a tangible shape that cannot be resolved has been assembled, because the office is also part of the time spent in "life."

Significance of Condominiums Before Dawn of Von Jour Caux

Toshiro Tanaka apparently began calling himself Von Jour Caux around June 1974. Assuming the name Von (Brahman) of his office, he unwound his business organization at the same time and formed "Von Jour Caux and His Troupe." Drawing a line at this point in time, Von himself has divided his creative periods as the Second Phase prior to 1974 and the Third Phase that runs to the present, a convincing decision of self-awareness for a creator.

Matters seem a little different, however, in examining the buildings themselves. For instance, *Redeau Sumiyoshi* ordered from the same client as *Practice of Mandala* and completed in 1969 (Von had an office here, too) and *Casa Nakameguro* of 1974 (discussed below) are both condominiums with large differences. The latter connects more with the designs of his buildings like *Gladiator's Nest* and later. The dividing line, therefore, seems a little earlier, early in the 1970s. His design of a series of condominiums is quite interesting in seeing the development and definition of Von Jour Caux's individual character into architectural expression, particularly because Von's buildings, which have tended to be considered in isolation, can be interpreted in connection with the development history of private condominiums, which have previously remained under-appreciated in the annals of architecture.

The design work for private condominiums in Japan has roughly followed a trend of (1) Pseudo-hotel, (2) Pseudo fine-residence, (3) Pseudo-hotel. The condo towers of the 1990s and later represent the period (3), featuring relatively stark appearances in terms of ornamentation and lived-in feel, and large lobbies. Adornment is light and the lines straight for periods (1) and (3), while people generally recognized the private condominiums built during the period (2) to have curved ornamentation, unlike the "towns" or rows of public apartment buildings called *danchi*, developed through public housing corporations and local governments. The differences between *Shuwa Aoyama Residence* completed in 1964 and designed by architect Yoshinobu Ashihara, and *Shuwa Gaien Residence*, internally designed by the developer and completed in 1967, symbolize the transition from Periods (1) to (2). The Section Ownership Law was enacted in 1962, and clarified the legal framework for private residential complexes. Consequently, *Aoyama* rode on the high-class trend of the first condominium boom (1963-64), along with *Villa Bianca* (1964) and *Co-op Olympia* (1965). *Gaien*, on the other hand, followed the popular trend of the second condominium boom (1968-69) along with the Lions Mansion series developed by Daikyo. Credit for architects in this housing segment quickly disappeared.

Like the vast majority of architects in the world, Von had to establish a livelihood in the private sector, and consequently took on condominium projects ordered from Okuraya. For example, the Chambord Mansion series included *Chambord Meguro* (1969) and *Chambord Shoto* (1969) handled by Habuka and completed in the same year.

The Casa series, however, deserves a place in the record as an architectural vision surpassing Shuwa. Seizing the opportunity of the second condominium boom, intermediate general contractor Nakanogumi built this group of condominiums off of its 1968 foray into real estate development. Project No. 1 called *Door to Fountain* (Setagaya-ku, Tokyo) was completed in 1969. The plastered white walls and curved balcony railings followed the Southern European style adopted by Shuwa condos in the latter half of the 1960s, although stronger characteristics are attempted with brick tiles on walls and the appointment of arches.

As the first company Von went to work for and as a late entrant to condominium development, the call from Nakanogumi for assistance in applying character to the projects was natural. *Door to Fountain* (Suginami-ku, Tokyo) was completed in 1972, and drove the trend further. Curvature was combined at the entryways, while styled lighting to the left and right, ornamental lattices, and a bricked entrance with an enclosed feel in contrast to the white exterior walls were testament to styles acquired in the United States and space composition of an architect. Tile ornaments included forms of men and women. Distinctive, practiced imagery found in the buildings after taking on the name Von Jour Caux appeared in full form for the first time with this condominium.

Casa Aioi (Chuo-ku, Tokyo) completed in the following year bolstered his reputation further. The central elevator core and exterior wall ends were floral iterations of yellow and orange. Here we see implemented not only Endorsement of Style but also Systematic Thinking acquired in the United States. Adoption of HPC construction rationalized the 15-story building, which could be considered the pioneer of studio condominiums with 25-square meter plans for 290 residential units in total. In overall assessment, this affordable housing complex for the populace escaped the Shuwa Residence scheme developed mainly in Shibuya-ku and Minato-ku.

The ensuing year's *Casa Nakameguro* (Meguro-ku, Tokyo) is definitely worthy of mention as a Von Jour Caux building. Built in a residential neighborhood, the small-scale complex assumes a maisonette format. The front walls have curious hanging ornamentation; a close examination of the top reveals sculpted snails that crawl along. An angel's sundial (thematically connected to the sundial on the end wall of *Sumai of Encounter* (1980)) greets one at the flight of a narrow staircase, which ascends to a large tiled mural. Among the mysterious figures in the picture, the illustrated magical square signifies the creation as Von's own. Lying further ahead, darkness like a cave is common to later works like *Waseda el Dorado*. Von states the following about the Shuwa condominiums.

"As a summation on post-War residential complexes, I have proposed previously that we should more fully extol the history of how Shuwa Residence condominiums, typified by their blue roofs and white walls, … became prominent in forming the dreams of the populace. … A Shuwa residence condo was built under limited funding at a high interest rate. The business case is successful, because the public actively purchases the units by confirming that the property is close to their own dream. If architects in some small way recognize their role in reenacting representations of the dreams held in their times, they should be more humble regarding this fact."[9]

In the Casa condominium series, Systematic Thinking and Endorsement of Style learned in the United States merged at a level of sophistication, and the theater ever since Von's upbringing stimulated by Disneyland began to blossom in a form different from *Practice of Mandala* through condominiums, which were about to pervade popular society at the time. Systematic Thinking, Endorsement of Style, Empathism, Knowledge of Creative Techniques, Art History Comprehension, Emphasis of Strategy, and Recognition of Populist Society (for the current time, as premise to the foregoing).

And the thinking that might be described as being "a writer who wasn't a writer," brought forth the assumption of the name Von. This was also a process conducted in the midst of the economy.

Projects of the "Hand" by the "Head"

Beginning in June 1974, building announcements began to appear under the name Von Jour Caux. The groupings of the work largely make up the following three sets. The first Art Complex set was ten buildings from I. *Gladiator's Nest* to X. *Trip to Carnival*. General classifications for the building would label I as a resort villa of a company, V as an elderly citizens' home, IX as a Buddhist temple, and the rest as residential complexes. The buildings have a common theme, if considered places where people live together temporarily.

The second set runs from *Est Esperanza* (1976) through *Pettit Etang* (1986), a few buildings with titles belonging to the Beauty under the Tree motif. They are all commercial buildings. The last set is the work on Sumai, basically freestanding homes as the word in Japanese means, for *Sumai of Koyama Family* (1976) and later works.

Von established a title for each set or series, and proceeded in collaboration with artists (craftsmen). Von Jour Caux was the name given to the person that held self-awareness of such projects. Distinct usage of the name is also clear from the fact that his real name Toshiro Tanaka was used in journal announcements written with more objective commentary alongside.

Gladiator's Nest, with literally pilgrimage as the theme, was filled with installation art along the paths of human movement at an unprecedented scale, and pursued a complete scope to connect images within the mind. Regarding the intent of the artwork installed, I cite Von talking about *Condo Hiraki* (1979, fig.5, p.231).

"The concept of a mysterious medium with the efficacy of connecting conflicting and complementary relations into the overall picture in one step is called the 'philosopher's stone' in alchemist terminology. Condo Hiraki was developed in the plan to be a spatial apparatus like a philosopher's stone with the capability of a medium that converts various ordinary phenomena by executing surrealistic methods, stimulates people's creative powers, and produces supernatural illusions."[10]

All three sets of buildings described above present timeless styles that allow sensitivity, disruption, and retrospection over the rational, uniform, and progressive state of modern architecture. The work of the craftsmen serves an enormous role here. Their form and work are common yet distinct among the three sets, of which *Art Complex* is found to be most disruptive. The flexibility of available funding was a likely factor, as well as the probable decision made simultaneously regarding the importance of constructing a communal arrangement one level higher to let individual fantasies germinate in a place where people live together. For the Beauty under the Tree motif, the ornamentation requirement for commercial buildings was accelerated, with creations beyond the purpose of solely providing autonomous visibility to the properties. The *Sumai* series took in the needs of a private residence as a place where memories were accumulated, and responded with pseudo-stylistic designs. Each building shows the calm judgment and discernment of Von in exploiting the position held by each in society. Systematic Thinking and Ideology of Style can be verified.

The mutual presence of Ideology of Style and Systematic Thinking was the content acquired, and their merger was the key to drawing the theater experienced since his upbringing closer to architecture. Von utilized hands with his head. He first disposed of his own "hands" that he originally had, and tracked the thesis, antithesis, and synthesis within an economic society. He has consequently praised life through ways that only architecture is able.

Von's Urban Nature

Von's buildings afford the wealth of enjoying them separately. Instead of an intense artform personality, the craftsmen release their own personalities based on Von's confident thinking. In contrast to Kenji Imai, who employed the craftsman, Von Jour Caux aids the "artist." The artist has an ego. Von saw a product surpassing the individual emerging above that, and the architect as the director in the arrangement.

One last note about Von concerns his strong urban nature. As an artist, he is an urban product. No text speaks more appropriately about the character of Von's buildings in this regard than what Hiroyuki Suzuki put forth in 1977. He noted that the totality of Von's projects was not limited to individual buildings, and being discovered by people walking around the city. That departs somewhat from "The effort to create a unique place furnished with its own characteristics." A lighter description in the words of Von Jour Caux in his later years would be "the creation of a cultural apparatus to invert the actual 'everyday world' into a 'sacred world.'" (Description of *Mundi Animus*) It is astonishing to see an architectural historian still in his early 30's confidently identifying the buildings of Von as not fixed and unexpectedly astounding, an enduring revolution. Suzuki's commentary resonates with the fact Von Jour Caux's works continue to be rediscovered and remain popular today.

Takao Habuka's Hand

Shikisai Ichiriki Hotel as Operating Space

Takao Habuka is Von Jour Caux's colleague who has attained the most success, but the building styles vastly differ. The descriptions of "Japanese style" and "tradition" generally unused for Von represent those differences. The creativity of Habuka does not quite fit within the confines of these words, however.

Located in Bandai Atami, Fukushima Prefecture, *Shikisai Ichiriki* is a *ryokan* (traditional Japanese inn) founded in 1918.

The venerable lodging receives visitors of renown from within and outside of Japan. Last year (2015), Prince William of England spent one night in Fukushima as the first foreign VIP since the East Japan Earthquake occurred. The welcoming dinner hosted by Prime Minister Abe from Tokyo made further news (fig.6, p.233).

Let us enter the property along the same route. The addition (1994) designed by Habuka is enthralling. The approach to the entrance presents a strongly axial, laterally symmetrical space, and the eyes naturally gaze upward. The portrayal is far from an ordinary Japanese *ryokan*. Where stained glass might be empaneled in a Christian church, we find special, handmade Japanese paper (*washi*). The natural outdoor translucence via this material and ceiling lights arranged below blend and illuminate *washi* with ink flow patterns on the ceiling. The floors are patterns made of stone and tile. Beyond wooden fixtures in front, a sculpted concrete wall is visible. A diverse set of materials is compiled into a single view. Each step inward reveals *washi* patterns without any traces of mechanical symmetry and a delicate ambience of light varying continually over time. Depending on the observer or depending on the time of day, season, or mood experienced, the most prominent impression from among the staggering number of elements is likely to be different. The space, more Western styled than not, presents no ambiguity, steers clear of depending on the set-up of the exterior, and assures the subtlety of the details. The visitor is enveloped in a world conjured by the architecture.

The reception area, lobby, kiosk, and lounge that lie beyond the entrance approach are contiguous space, and the semicircle extending towards the garden from the lounge is glass encased. The description may sound similar to a conventionally simple, glass-walled, uninspiring, ambiguous, single chamber. The real impression is actually completely different. Differences in the finish to ceiling and floor divide the space into sections and adhere to human movements. The Precast concrete relief made from foam art catches the eye from a distance. More and more detail reveals itself as one draws near, and becomes a visual delight when one is finally settled in a chair. The delight is compounded through fresh discoveries found walking back and forth, such as practiced animal carvings in a zelkova-wood pillar (fig.7, p.234). These are reminiscent of casual ornamentation found on temple architecture of the Edo Period— "special efforts" made by carpenters or plasterers of the time. Delicate fixtures add character to the respective interior places. The plans include details hard to find on the horizontal and vertical projections. Of course, drawings are merely a means to obtain good results, and the purpose of the plans is not to exhaustively complete the drawings.

The fixtures of hospitality unfold in accompaniment to human activity, and reach their acme in the dining space. Large *washi* flowers bloom in a vault overhead, rings float in space along clay walls, and objet d'art like red roots spread out. These may be perplexing in terms of "Japanese style" and "tradition." Light burnishes the materials and provokes the desire to look further. The features of excitement and purpose of leaving the day-to-day life to visit a *ryokan* align. An operating space tugs at the body and heart here beyond the functions that adapt to the physical dimensions of everybody and the visual entertainment immediately evident.

Let us examine the guest rooms, the principal part of the *ryokan*. Ingenuity worked into the ceilings that invite the gaze upward, richly varied designs, and nothing insipid are the same hallmarks as the other parts, but the rooms, in contrast, are sedate. In Japanese, "to stay overnight" is pronounced the same as "to stop." The operation of staying is designed into the space. *Shikisai Ichiriki Hotel* makes one aware of the obvious fact that a *ryokan* is hardly composed of simple functions. Habuka supplants the Japanese language of professional compound words formed by *kanji* and words of foreign origin, and arrives at the essence of native Japanese *yamato* words, which are gentle, yet deep, and unlike Von.

Rationality is retained, while application of a conventional building type is not considered sufficient. This description sounds the same as Von. But it's not. The theme throughout is unified like an orchestral work that manages various human behaviors and in which the strings or the winds take turns to provide the ambience while tempo varies. While Von is more divergent, this integrity represents a tremendous difference in overall compositional method.

The trusting relationship with the client should not be missed. Habuka handled a previous renovation and expansion at *Ichiriki* in 1985. In response to a consultation request for the expansion of guest rooms, he proposed a rationalization of the entire floor plan through large-scale renovated expansion, and achieved this in a composition that included the renowned *Suigetsuen* garden fed by Inawashiro Lake. The contiguous design of *Shikisai Ichiriki Hotel* reflects the personality of Habuka, who adhered to the place and people found only there.

Independence from Mentor's Influence

Time, however, was necessary for individual human character to mold into particular qualities of architecture. A visit to the VIP room from the renovation of 1985 leaves one impressed with the maturity for a 40 year-old at the time, while certain deep emotion also wells up. The theme is clearly a jumble of Japanese and Western styles. Pillars like vines spring up next to stained glass lining the windows, and draft into forms like sculpted corbels. This is an intentional carryover from early Western-style buildings. The sophisticated elevation in features is seemingly apparent for the VIP room, in which the Showa Emperor, successor in traditions of Western-style apparel, also stayed. But the device represented crafted designs reminiscent

of Art Nouveau and was also used in *Nihon Seihan Printing* (1983) and *Tsubo no Ie* (1984), which means credit as a unique application cannot be given. For instance, Kotaro Kurata, who produced the forged alcove post for *Tsubo no Ie*, also produced the handrail door of Von's *Waseda el Dorado* completed the year before.

Habuka was born in 1945 to a lumber-trading household in Joetsu, Niigata Prefecture. After graduation from university in 1967, he went to work at Von's architect office, and established S.E.N. Architect Associates in 1975. His friendship with Von has remained close since embarking on his own business, and Habuka addresses him "Tanaka-san" with respect and affection even today. Since Von Jour Caux was the name assumed in 1974, Habuka knew the Toshiro Tanaka before Von, to be precise. He introduced many of the craftsmen Von required. Habuka produced the gilded porcelain mosaic of the entrance hall ceiling for *Condo Hiraki* (1979). Around the time Habuka began work on *Nihon Seihan Printing* and Von on *Waseda el Dorado*, they traveled together to Italy and Spain to study Gaudi again. Toshiro Tanaka was Habuka's sole mentor in architecture, and Habuka helped Tanaka to become Von Jour Caux. The two were just ten years apart as master and pupil and also like colleagues.

The difficulty in this association, nonetheless, is not hard to imagine in which Von led with a rare "head." For example, how tough would it be for a student of Frank Lloyd Wright, who got a start in the world at a young age and interpreted the world in his own way until the end, to overtake his teacher?

Habuka, nevertheless, found his own place. *Shikisai Ichiriki Hotel* completed in 1994 comprises Habuka's style with respect to the application of technology, overall compositional method, and thinking in the background. The success led to *Senjuan Hotel* (1997), *Kishyoan* (1999, now Hoshino Resort Kai Matsumoto), and *Yamato no Yu* (2005).

Metamorphosis of Material, Design, Space

What is Habuka's style? For closer inspection, we visit *Wakigumo no Boroh*, a guesthouse set in Tokigawa, Saitama Prefecture, with vistas of the Chichibu Mountains.

Dynamic plans square off with nature's big scale and thrive in the environment again. Clasping the forged handle, the visitor tugs the massive zelkova door, 3 meters high and 90 centimeters wide, and is greeted with a vaulted space filled with ornamentation. An upward gaze yields the explanation. This spot is not merely to look at the scene in front of the eyes, but a designed space for living together with the scenery welcomed in from the outer side to the inner side (fig.8, p.235). The interior has fluid, vertical space, centered on this vaulted hallway. The gallery, traditional Japanese room, guestroom, etc., are set in their own places, while certain devices make one

249

aware of the relations between them. The ambience seems like air is being released, and connects naturally to the exterior.

We can examine the base material along the same route. The tall door is a solid board, made from a zelkova tree cut down 60 years or more ago. A delicate, yet bold carving of a triple lattice accents the solid-wood feel. The forged handle presents a completely different material, but the crafted twisting renders its feel into a similar gift of nature. The act of construction has unified the two into a door. The weighty, mighty touch adds a story to the motion of opening and entering. Merely looking at the door should invoke a physical sensation from the second time onward. The base material in this house is dressed with a dual physique, one that is processed and one that makes contact (fig.9, p.235).

If the above seems to be the case, why do people sense an air-releasing ambience, rather than a burdensome weight that effuses from people and substances with limits? One reason is the space planning, as noted above. The other working element is Habuka's own designs installed here and there. Tricked into gazing upward by a towering door, one sees blossom patterns under the eaves made by silk-screened designs of wisteria petals. The pale hues are Habuka's own, a class that would never appear under ordinary attempts to carry on with traditions in Japanese architecture. These have no relation to the direct function and are not constrained by the vertical-grained Akita cypress boards. It is pure eye candy.

A similar floating feel seems to rise from the design of the mullions in the *shoji* (papered sliding doors): Weightless like an abstract picture, unconstrained by technology, and unbridled by meaning. Because he comprehends structure wrought from social fabric, the backdrop defined by technology, and the meaning of format, Habuka's hands dance with conscious intent. Weightlessness is another large difference between Habuka's designwork and the numerous other designs categorized as Japanese style or tradition.

Space to liberate the body, material quality revealed through technology, and designwork entertaining to the eyes: even if I were to provisionally compile the creation along these three categories, the actual Habuka architecture would contain things that overlap and be artificially extracted by these reasoned terms. Each time people take in the experience a different category will probably have prominence. Nature invited into the interior increases the differences that arise from timing. In this multi-layering of architecture as well, common aspects with *Shikisai Ichirki Hotel* are evident, despite differences in location and application. These aspects are none other than Habuka's own style.

The connection among the three categories above is believed to be "Metamorphosis." The importance is not the material, but morphing of the material through artisanship. The exterior walls are the most obvious in this regard. Habuka regards

the craftsmen highly, but also poses fresh challenges to gain the potential of both the human hand and base material. This direction is quite difficult to provide unless one is born with the so-called "hand," or raised in an environment of craftsmen and materials. Specific materials are the medium for pursuing a common identity to Habuka's own designwork of weightlessness, which can be considered the romanticism of going somewhere else that isn't here. That provides a releasing feel to the viewer.

Human life can be felt in Habuka's architecture, as if the materials had life. The sensation is more like direct contact with true nature, rather than construction material or base material used to build something. From there, we can learn about the mystery of transformation of the earth itself. A large vector from Von is paid forward, but clearly in a different form than Von. The style that exploited being born in a lumber trader's household fully matured in *Shikisai Ichiriki Hotel* and *Wakigumo no Boroh*.

Techniques in Small Dining Spaces

Habuka's works succeed in society. To be frank, they succeed amidst economic activity. This is an important point.

Shikisai Ichiriki Hotel, described at the beginning, is also a case, but here, let us examine *Ginza Kyubey Annex* (2006). Habuka designed the Annex diagonally across from the Main Restaurant in Ginza, Tokyo, with ample individual creativity. The place was nonetheless accepted smoothly as a globally renowned sushi restaurant.

People don't move while eating sushi. The preparer and eater face each other at a distance of a few dozen centimeters. Time passes while words and non-verbal communication go back and forth. The sushi is small enough to stare at, and physically delicate. The taste of one plate lasts for an instant. The experience alters the ordinary scale of time and space.

Instead of people moving around in a sushi restaurant, the density of sensations can be increased. The distance from Kanaharu-dori Street to a seat in the restaurant is actually quite close, but the design that beckons to the back doesn't provide that sensation. The narrow spacing of stonework facing the street, the narrow but plentiful entrance space, and spacing between the shoji mullions intersecting illustration and base represent Habuka's design characteristic of deftly vacated intervals between materials. "Openness" can be felt, but is unable to exist on its own. The moment you think you have it, it slips through your fingers. Habuka knows the romantic quality of gaps.

By the time the guest has reached a seat and sat down, the surprisingly diverse materials loaded into the small space are recognized. The immediacy permits detection of the materials' feel. Openwork of vertical-grained cedar, metallic foilwork "Kirigane" (fig.10, p.237), and a forged alcove pillar gradually reveal themselves. Material transformed through workmanship enriches time and space.

The techniques for planning extremely small space are abundant in the successive *Ginza Kyubey Keio Plaza Hotel Tokyo*. The skillful selection of material, such as marble, glass, Japanese cedar, and lacquer is evident, but the horizontal projection is especially noteworthy. Although the allowance is just 4.3 meters of depth from the corridor in the building, this dire restriction is not pronounced. A seasoned knowledge of human physical dimensions enables a skillful measurement of the necessary pathways in back. The customer even gains a margin of comfort, a sense that the place is his or her own. The dual enablement of luxury and lightness in this way is identical to the aesthetics of luxury and lightness in sushi, unlike an arranged dish brought out from the back and partaken with cutlery.

Freedom Provided by the Hand

The two *Ginza Kyubey* restaurants and *Shikisai Ichiriki Hotel* show how successful space amidst economic activity was created with inspiring workmanship as a result of Habuka's artful technique. His ability to offer profitable designs to clients meant that projects resulted in subsequent projects, which led to his success. Since the job of an architect is to define the shapes, in that sense he traveled the royal road.

Habuka's plans stir the heart, because material, design and spatial composition avoid the rules of conventional likeness. For instance, material within the architecture is not rid of its true nature and cast to voluntarily serve the entire structure or to express imagery. Yet the material does not remain "like wood," "like earth," or "like iron." Material in Habuka architecture metamorphoses through workmanship, and unleashes fresh character. The visitor, consequently, is surprised.

The same holds for designwork. Habuka's designs are not constrained by illustrative concepts of "*ryokan*-like" or "Japanese style-like." The fundamentals of Japanese tradition are addressed and boldly manipulated. The visitor, seeing such effort before that was hard to appreciate, feels like design has come over to his or her side, and recognizes a gentle delight.

Spatial composition of the architecture is not strapped to promises of a ryokan or sushi restaurant. The plans step back to principles, and thought through functionally and psychologically as to how the places should belong within the building. Those multiple places are integrated around the human being, and are finished into an operating space that stirs the heart and body.

Almost rare for the present day, Habuka is obstinate about deciding the shapes. But that insistence is completely different from material forced to be thus, design forced to specific comprehension, and space constrained to be thus. Determination of the shapes secures fresh, free domains that

honestly move people's hearts. The mechanism rightly succeeds amidst economic activity, which is a principle of the human world.

An innovative type as an architect, Habuka has adroitly found his major subject to be Japanese style, called "tradition" and prejudiced as tortuous and burdensome. Yet workmanship that is applied to material, design, and spatial composition of this subject and breathes new life into what is uniquely present delivers a tremendous impact. Habuka takes the weight of "tradition" that tends to be monolithic, exploits it to advantage, and outdoes it.

Exploiting to advantage, incidentally, requires the "hand," which Habuka possesses. He has a visceral sense of traditional Japanese space, refined designing capacity, and knowledge and connections of craftsmen and material to execute the designwork. The skill set relates to his upbringing: born in a lumber-trading household of Joetsu, Niigata Prefecture, maintaining his ties later to his birthright, and committed to the artful skill of designwork.

I sense consistency in Habuka's work, a romanticism where the things that sprout on the ground escape the confinement of gravity and reach for the heavens. Material, design, and spatial composition attest to the distance they can go without losing their origins. The work of the hand enables that. This description is permitted not just for the buildings, but the career as well. The architecture is a witness to the fact that not all materials, concepts, building types, or for that matter, places or people are replaceable. The *Praise of Life* is being sung.

Does Habuka refrain from a macro assessment? Certainly not. The thinking to solve problems from a higher perspective is evident in the proposal for *Shikisai Ichiriki Hotel* that extended into business matters, and in the solution for *Ginza Kyubey* within an existing building, where the entire project is assessed as a system. Systematic Thinking, Von's native forte, also lives within these.

The starting point for Habuka was the "hand," which acquired the "head." The merger of artisanship that voided rules and Systematic Thinking is apparently needed amidst our economic society, and architecture has apparently provided a life force to humans. Habuka's latest project *Aidu Chuo Hospital* marks his achievement of the present day.

Comprehensiveness of *Aidu Chuo Hospital*

Phase I of *Aidu Chuo Hospital* was completed in 2009 as the new wing called West 2, seven floors high and one level underground. In the following year, seismic base-isolation retrofitting and interior renovation work were finished for the existing main wing, eight floors high and one level underground. The Phase II expansion concluded in May 2015 with the completion of East Center, eight floors high. The aggregate floor space is 35,000 square meters. The architectural work of a full-service hospital requires specialist knowledge. This is neither leisure nor entertainment space discussed previously. How does Habuka perform his artisanship?

The ground floor of West 2 houses a large fish tank like an aquarium. A child is smiling and talking to his mother. Around a vaulted space, live piano concerts are held, while the café and shops produce a vibrant ambiance.

The upper floors of West 2 and the main wing were unified with the same design warmth, though modified according to function, such as a spacious lobby and individual consultation rooms. The human-centric, integrated space architected by Habuka shows that his individual character is thriving, with the concept being "a hospital unlike a hospital." "Hospital-likeness" is smoothly avoided. There is no modeling of a facility like a hospital, but no evasion of being a hospital either. The plans provide an operating space to fulfill the various purposes of the people who visit and stay, just like a *ryokan* or restaurant, but more quietly.

Habuka probably envisioned the hospital as part of our living space and not an extraordinary place. The continuum between a healthy person and infirm patient is uninterrupted; permanent lines cannot be drawn to mark off the healthy zone. Anybody's health can turn suddenly, but nobody wants to think about that. This train of thought causes hospitals to be considered extraordinary places and to be moved outside the field of view. We tend to avoid going to a hospital, even if our heads tell us we should go. The presented architecture here, however, encourages us to visit regularly. The designwork that moves the heart, also moves the feet. In essence, design provides a preventative measure. Life is not categorized; young and old equally possess life. The notion that life should be respected until the last moment is prevalent.

This thinking leads to judicious logic in the hospital. In West 2, the nurses' stations are inventively arranged to enable smooth approaches to patient rooms. West 2 and East Center have spans of 15 meters owing to their PC/PCa construction that eliminates quake-resistant walls and supports future changes in the layout. Much effort went into emergency preparedness(fig.11, p.239). For instance, the buildings are highly quake-resistant with seismic isolation for the foundation and equipped with electric power generators with gas and diesel engines. Plant and equipment were not selected perfunctorily; the sites of actual usage were contemplated. Ample space for transport and triage in a disaster is arranged at the emergency ward entrance. The separation of traffic between physicians and patients is likewise accounted for. Each flow is sanitary and unencumbered by the other, and contained in a horizontal plan that allows both groups to be treated like people. This feature encourages the belief that the enormous hospital and miniature *Ginza Kyubey* were of the same architect. Of course, they were.

Thus, the life of materials is supported unsurprisingly along with human life. People are greeted at East Center with three designed panels drafted by Habuka's hand. They respectively express Space, Earth, and Life, a selection of delicate mirror-glass etching, stainless steel etching, and marble mosaic created by Japan's most renowned mosaic artist Toyoharu Kii. Instead of being superficially restricted in meaning, the design stimulates the imagination, and the mystery of metamorphosis of the materials themselves lends encouragement to people.

On the exterior walls, 19,000 outdoor tiles fired by a local ceramic foundry are embedded. The distinct pattern from a distance is friendly and recognizable, while each tile emerges with a different expression up close. The art can be viewed beyond the glass of the main wing, and delivers the same effect as the revamped interiors. The garden in between has beds of stone and round gravel laid in patterns that resonate with glass objet d'art projecting light and water waving in the breeze. The generously appointed space lets diverse materials fit into one picture to sing praise.

Is it too luxurious? The high-grade engineering and artistic refinement described so far clearly foresees the future of a private medical institution. The project performs only what architecture can do amidst the economy. Von has also performed in this way.

Having obtained the trust of the hospital director, Habuka has restructured the buildings through Phase I, Phase II, and Phase III planned next, taking stock of the entire property. Systematic Thinking that incorporates the future, capacity to relate to people at various positions within the hospital, and competence to direct the contractors have made a large-scale facility possessing this character a reality. The architect blessed with head and hands is an indispensable partner of the client.

Aidu Chuo Hospital leads to recollections beyond Habuka's own past work. Von's *Eternal Home* (elderly citizens' home, Mukoudai Social welfare corporation, 1984) appealed to not just visual but physical senses, and was filled with the strong will to praise life until the end by overcoming modern distinctions between people healthy and infirm, or between life and death. The Systematic Thinking, details like etchings, and the client's entrustment of a new building type bring back Habuka's starting point at Von's *Practice of Mandala* and 1970s condominiums. Like the Hospital de Sant Pau by Lluís Domènech i Montaner, who lived in the same period as Gaudi, regionality and craftsmanship connect with universality and rationality, and cause the role of a hospital in community to be envisioned.

With respect to the rapid advances being made in medical care, *Aidu Chuo Hospital* does not simply consider industrializing and economizing trends to be adversarial where cost-versus-benefit of a facility is scrutinized. Instead, by taking advantage of conditions in society, the architect, as he or she inherently should, praises the essence of irreplaceable life through architecture. This is the latest work of a lineage continuously passed on.

Praise for Happenstance

An audacious description of the difference between Von and Habuka would be the difference between "head" and "hand." "Head" refers to the competence of Systematic Thinking that clarifies the business goals and arranges the elements to achieve the goals. Von's core is here. Of course, Von is not devoid of human and design competence. The gathering of many collaborators around him proves the opposite, in fact. Nonetheless, the key that enabled Von to release his existence as an individual was the "head," the weapon produced from his natural genius through polished effort.

This summation alone would end like a hero's story here. The reason Von's architectural creations possess the qualities worth mentioning and should have their processes revealed is because he correctly controls how to use his weapons. Von judges the "head" with "philosophy."

The "hand," in contrast, is specific. Habuka's noteworthy tooling is this "hand," his own refined designing capacity, and knowledge and connections of craftsmen and material to achieve the designwork. This competence is not an addiction to detail, but the result of a proper extension of his inherited environment. A style different from Von's was born.

This summation alone would end like the endeavors of an individual. What constitutes "philosophy" for Von? The quality that produced empathy among people regardless of community or place can be assessed as "beauty" for Habuka. Habuka judges the "hand" with "beauty." When "beauty" is the yardstick, any fundamental division between one's own work and another's work should disappear. Human activity and nature's activity are conceivable on the same continuum. Specific construction provides the start, and ultimately glimpses of the makeup of the world are observed through human life. This cycle is shared with Von.

Among life bodies, humans alone advanced with respect to head (intelligence) and hand (craft). Both significantly represent human life, but "head" and "hand" are considerably different. Von first has the "head," and Habuka first had the "hand."

Von and Habuka are dissimilar, and actually, distant. For this reason, the "head" respects and desires the "hand," while the "hand" longs for and desires the "head." Natural genius definitely contrasts the two architects. They form a pair of the same type. That is why they need each other, and why breadth emerges in their pursuit of the same. The contrast is useful in pondering what life means for architecture. Without the relationship of Von and Habuka as colleagues, this somewhat

uncommon book to discuss two personalities at length would probably not have come into existence.

The intersection of Von and Habuka allows the praise of life through architecture. The specific methodology involved and range held have been presented thus far.

Finally, I should stress that Von and Habuka remain architects. Entrusted by the client, they supply comprehensive direction to the construction and complete lasting creations of an era. Their work becomes endearing as part of our culture, enriches our lives, praises the essence of precious life through a connection each time to a different place. In short, that is architecture.

Von and Habuka may not be tracing an orthodox trajectory, but they are certainly not nonconformist. We must carefully comprehend the signs of highly orthodox architecting potential. If this narrative has accordingly served as a contribution in a small way, the author will be pleased.

(Architectural historian, Associate Professor of
Faculty of Engineering at Osaka City University)

*1 Von Jour Caux talked.
*2 Von Jour Caux talked.
*3 Von Jour Caux talked.
*4 Round-table discussion: About Pottery mural after WW2,
  Sosyoku Tail Kenkyu (1978)
*5 Toshiro Tanaka, "Indiana no ie," *Shinkenchiku* (Aug. 1972), p. 277
*6 *Ibid.*, 5 p. 278
*7 Sadajiro Muramatsu, "Daisan no Kenchikuka,"
  Shinkenchiku (Dec. 1969), p. 241
*8 Von Jour Caux talked.
*9 *Ibid.*, 4
*10 Von Jour Caux, "Hiraki," *Kenchiku Bunka* (May 1987), p. 85

羽深隆雄
掲載建築一覧

湧雲の望楼 P.022
設計：
建築：羽深隆雄・楠工房設計事務所
担当：羽深隆雄、村岡晋平
構造：織本構造設計
担当：村岡久和
電気・機械設備：エフ・ディー・エス
担当：沼田猛

所在地：埼玉県比企郡ときがわ町
主用途：別荘（ゲストハウス）
構造・規模：鉄筋コンクリート造・1階、木造・2階
敷地面積：615.8㎡
建築面積：158.93㎡
延床面積：210.33㎡
竣工：2008年6月

台付欅の家 P.048
設計：
意匠：羽深隆雄・楠工房設計事務所
担当：羽深隆雄、東郷彰博
構造：稲葉建築事務所
機械設備：シグマ設計
電気設備：エス企画設計

所在地：埼玉県川越市
主用途：専用住宅
構造と規模：木造一部鉄骨造・地上2階
敷地面積：182.40㎡
建築面積：90.48㎡
延床面積：168.49㎡
竣工年：1994年9月

仙寿庵 P.068
設計：
建築：羽深隆雄・楠工房設計事務所
担当：羽深隆雄、村上尚彌
構造：織本匠構造設計研究所
機械設備：大地設備設計
電気設備：まちだ設備設計

所在地：群馬県利根郡水上町谷川字西平614
主要用途：日本旅館
構造・規模：RC造一部S造　木造・地下1階、地上3階
敷地面積：25,463㎡
建築面積：2,493㎡
延床面積：3,335㎡
竣工：1997年5月

四季彩一力 P.078
設計：
建築：羽深隆雄・楠工房設計事務所
担当：羽深隆雄、東郷彰博
機械設備：大地設備設計
電気設備：まちだ設備設計

所在地：福島県郡山市熱海町熱海4-161
主要用途：日本旅館
構造・規模：鉄筋コンクリート造・地上5階、塔屋（浴室棟：鉄骨造・平屋）
敷地面積：11,274㎡
建築面積：4,218㎡
延床面積：10,603㎡（増築部分：6,482㎡）
竣工：1994年6月

銀座久兵衛 P.086
別館
設計：
建築：羽深隆雄・楠工房設計事務所
担当：羽深隆雄
機械設備：大地設備設計
電気設備：DEMURA設計

所在地：東京都中央区銀座8-8-20
主要用途：寿司屋
構造・規模：鉄骨鉄筋コンクリート造・地下1階、地上5階、塔屋1階
敷地面積：64.97㎡
建築面積：52.60㎡
延床面積：316.40㎡
竣工年：2006年3月

京王プラザホテル店
設計：
建築：羽深隆雄・楠工房設計事務所
担当：羽深隆雄
電気・機械設備：エフ・ディー・エス
担当：沼田猛

所在地：東京都新宿区西新宿2-2-1 京王プラザホテル 本館7F
主要用途：寿司屋
床面積：99㎡
竣工年：2008年9月

本店（改装）
設計：
建築：羽深隆雄・楠工房設計事務所
担当：羽深隆雄
電気・機械設備：エフ・ディー・エス
担当：沼田猛

所在地：東京都中央区銀座8-7-6
主要用途：寿司屋
工事種別：改装工事
竣工年：2007年9月

会津中央病院 P.104
EAST CENTER
設計：
建築：羽深隆雄・楠工房設計事務所
担当：羽深隆雄、村岡晋平
構造：織本構造設計
担当：村岡久和、荒木洋介
電気・機械設備：エフ・ディー・エス
担当：沼田猛

所在地：福島県会津若松市鶴賀町1-1
主用途：総合病院
構造・規模：PC・PCa造＋一部RC造＋一部S造　基礎免震構造 地上8階建
敷地面積：42,846.16㎡
建築面積：2,907.73㎡（増築部分）
延床面積：14,597.48㎡（増築部分）
竣工：2015年5月

WEST2
設計：
建築：羽深隆雄・楠工房設計事務所
担当：羽深隆雄、渡部廣治
構造：織本構造設計
担当：村岡久和

所在地：福島県会津若松市鶴賀町1-1
主用途：総合病院
構造・規模：PC・PCa造＋一部RC造＋一部S造　基礎免震構造 地上7階建
建築面積：増築1,776.63㎡
延床面積：増築11,367.99㎡
竣工：2009年4月

Takao Habuka
DATA

Wakigumo no Boroh P.022
Architect: Takao Habuka / S.E.N. Architect Associates, Architect in Charge :Takao Habuka, Shinpei Muraoka
Structural engineer: Orimoto Structural Engineers, Hisakazu Muraoka
Mechanical & Erectrical engineer: FDS, Takeshi Numata

Location: Tokigawa city, Saitama
Principal use: Guest house
Structure / Scale: 1st floor / Reinforced concrete, 2nd floor / Wood
Site area: 615.8
Building area: 158.93
Total floor area: 210.33
Completion date: 2008 June

House of Zelkova P.048
Architect: Takao Habuka / S.E.N. Architect Associates, Architect in Charge: Takao Habuka, Akihiro Togo Structure engineer: Takumi Orimoto Structural & Associates, Mechanical engineer: Shiguma Sekkei, Erectrical engineer: Esu kikaku sekkei

Location: Kawagoe city, Saitama
Structure / Scale: Wood, partly steel frame / 2 stories
Site area: 182.40
Building area: 90.48
Total floor area: 168.45
Completion date: 1994 September

Senjuan Hotel P.068
Architect: Takao Habuka / S.E.N. Architect Associates, Architect in Charge: Takao Habuka, Naoya Murakami
Structure engineer: Takumi Orimoto Structural Engineer & Associates, Machine enginner: Daichi Facilities Design

Location: Tanigawa, Minakamimachi, Tone-gun, Gunma
Principal use: Japanese style hotel
Structure / Scale: Reinforced concrete, partly steel frame / 1 basement, 3 stories
Site area: 25,463
Building area: 2,493
Total floor area: 3,335
Completion: 1997 May

Shikisai Ichiriki Hotel P.078
Architect: Takao Habuka / S.E.N. Architect Associates, Architect in Charge: Takao Habuka, Akihiro Togo
Machine engineer: Daichi facilities design, Erectrical engineer: Machida plant engineering

Location: Atami, Koriyama city, Fukushima
Principal use: Japanese style hotel
Structure / Scale: main building - Reinforced concrete /3 stories, West building - Reinforced concrete / 5 stories, Bathroom building - Steel frame
Site area: 11,274
Building area: 4,218
Total floor area: 106,03 (Extention area / 6,482 , Existing / 4,120)
Completion date: 1994 May

Ginza Kyubey P.086
Annex
Architect: Takao Habuka / S.E.N.Architect Associates
Architect in charge: Takao Habuka
Mechanical engineer: Daichi facilities design, Erectrical engineer: Demura Electrical Planning Office

Location: Ginza, Chuo-ku, Tokyo
Principal use: Sushi restaurant
Structure / Scale: Reinforced concrete / 1 basement ,5 stories
Site area: 64.97
Building area: 52.60
Total floor area: 316.40
Completion date: 2006 March

Keio Plaza Hotel Tokyo
Architect: Takao Habuka / S.E.N. Architect Associates
Architect in charge: Takao Habuka Mechanical & Erectrical engineer: FDS, Takeshi Numata

Locarion: Shinjuku-ku, Tokyo
Principal use: Sushi restaurant
Total floor area: 99
Completion date: 2008 September

Main Restaurant (remodeling)
Architect: Takao Habuka / S.E.N. Architect Associates
Architect in charge: Takao Habuka Mechanical & Erectrical engineer: FDS, Takeshi Numata

Location: Ginza, Chuo-ku, Tokyo
Principal use: Sushi restaurant
Completion date: 2005 March

Aidu Chuo Hospital P.104
East Center (phaseⅡ)
Architect: Takao Habuka / S.E.N. Architect Associates,Architect in Charge: Takao Habuka, Shinpei Muraoka
Structural engineers: Orimoto Structural Enginieers, Hisakazu Muraoka, Yosuke Arai
Mechanical & Erectrical engineers: FDS, Takeshi Numata

Location: Aiduwakamatu city, Fukushima
Principal use: General Hospital
Structure / Scale: Reinforced concrete, partly steel frame / 8 stories
Site area: 42,846.16
Building area: 2,907.73
Total floor area: 14,597.48
Completion date: 2015 May

West2 (phaseⅠ)
Architect: Takao Habuka / S.E.N. Architect Associates, Architect in Charge: Takao Habuka, Koji Watabe
Structural engineers: Orimoto Structural Enginieers, Hisakazu Muraoka

Location: Aiduwakamatu city, Fukushima
Principal use: General Hospital
Structure / Scale: Reinforced concrete, partly steel frame / 7 stories
Building area: 1,776.63
Total floor area: 11,367.99
Completion date: 2009 April

梵 寿綱
掲載建築一覧

ある寿舞 P.154
設計：田中俊郎
所在地：東京都世田谷区（現存せず）
主用途：住宅
着工：1959年

インディアナの家 P.156
設計：田中俊郎
所在地：インディアナ州、アメリカ
主用途：住宅
着工：1968年

ある美瑠 P.160
設計：株式会社 梵 設計作務室
所在地：東京都中央区（現存せず）
主用途：事務所ビル
竣工：1967年1月

樹下美人図考 P.162
丹い玉
設計：株式会社 梵 設計作務室
所在地：東京都港区（現存せず）
主用途：商業施設
竣工：1968年

エスト・エスペランサ
設計：株式会社 梵 設計作務室
所在地：東京都港区西麻布2丁目
主用途：旧ケーキ工場
竣工：1969年

ポッゾ・ビアンカ
設計：株式会社 梵 設計作務室
所在地：埼玉県川口市西川口3丁目
主用途：商業ビル
竣工：1970年

プチ・エタン
設計：株式会社 梵 設計作務室
所在地：東京都豊島区池袋3丁目
主用途：集合住宅
竣工：1973年

阿維智 P.168
設計：梵寿綱
所在地：宮城県刈田郡蔵王町遠刈田
主用途：社員保養施設
竣工：1975年9月

秘羅樨 P.174
設計：梵寿綱
所在地：東京都板橋区高島平1丁目
主用途：集合住宅・店舗
竣工：1977年6月

斐醴祈 P.180
設計：梵寿綱
所在地：東京都豊島区南池袋2丁目
主用途：賃貸アパート・複合ビル
竣工：1979年3月

和世陀 P.186
設計：梵寿綱
所在地：東京都新宿区早稲田鶴巻町
主用途：集合住宅・店舗（1階）
構造・規模：6階
竣工：1983年

無量寿舞 P.192
設計：梵寿綱
所在地：東京都東大和市芋窪3丁目
主用途：特別養護老人ホーム
竣工：1985年6月

精霊の館 P.198
設計：梵寿綱
所在地：東京都豊島区（現存せず）
主用途：集合住宅
竣工：1984年

和泉の扉 P.206
設計：梵寿綱
所在地：東京都杉並区和泉1丁目
主用途：集合住宅
竣工：1989年11月

きらめく器 P.210
設計：梵寿綱
所在地：東京都豊島区南池袋2丁目
主用途：店舗・事務所・住宅
竣工：1990年11月

性源寺 P.214
設計：梵寿綱
所在地：福島県いわき市平宁長橋町23
主用途：庫裏客殿
竣工：1992年6月

舞都和亜 P.220
設計：梵寿綱
所在地：東京都杉並区和泉1丁目
主用途：集合住宅
竣工：1992年9月

Von Jour Caux
DATA

Family Home of Esotericism P.154
Architect: Toshiro Tanaka
Location: Setagaya-ku, Tokyo (Not exist)
Principal use: House
Start of construction 1959

Touch of Culture P.156
Architect: Toshiro Tanaka
Location: State of indiana, USA
Principal use: Architect: Toshiro Tanaka
Start of construction 1968

Practice of Mandala P.160
Architect: Brahman Architects Office Co., Ltd.
Location: Chuo-ku, Tokyo (Not exist)
Principal use: Office building
Completion date: 1967 January

Beauty under the Tree P.162
Bola roja
Architect: Brahman Architects Office Co., Ltd.
Location: Minato-ku, Tokyo (Not exist)
Principal use: Commercial facility
Completion date: 1968

Est Esperanza
Architect: Brahman Architects Office Co., Ltd.
Location: Nishi Azabu, Minato-ku, Tokyo
Principal use: before Cake factory
Completion date: 1969

Pozzo Bianca
Architect: Brahman Architects Office Co., Ltd.
Location: Nishi Kawaguchi, Kawaguchi city, Saitama
Principal use: Commercial building
Completion date: 1970

Petit Etang
Architect: Brahman Architects Office Co., Ltd.
Location: Ikebukuro, Toshima-ku, Tokyo
Principal use: Housing complex
Completion date: 1973

Gladiator's Nest P.168
Architect: Von Jour Caux
Location: Zao town, Karita-gun, Miyagi
Principal use: Employees resort facility
Completion date: 1975 September

Hiraki P.174
Architect: Von Jour Caux
Location: Iakashimadaira, Itabashi-ku, Iokyo
Principal use: Housing complex, Shop
Completion date: 1977 June

Condo Hiraki P.180
Architect: Von Jour Caux
Location: Minamiikebukuro, Toshima-ku, Tokyo
Principal use: Rented apartment
Completion date: 1979 March

Waseda el Dorado P.186
Architect: Von Jour Caux
Location: Wasedatsurumaki-cho, Shinjuku-ku, Tokyo
Principal use: Housing complex, Shop (1st floor)
Structure / Scale: 6 stories
Completion date: 1983

Eternal Home P.192
Architect: Von Jour Caux
Location: Imokubo, Higashiyamato city, Tokyo
Principal use: Nursing home
Completion date: 1985 June

Mundi Animus P.198
Architect: Von Jour Caux
Location: Toshima-ku, Tokyo (Not exist)
Principal use: Housing complex
Completion date: 1984

Door to Fountain P.206
Architect: Von Jour Caux
Location: Izumi, Suginami-ku, Tokyo
Principal use: Housing complex
Completion date: 1989 November

Royal Vessel P.210
Architect: Von Jour Caux
Location: Minamiikebukuro, Toshima-ku, Tokyo
Principal use: Shop, Office, Housing
Completion date: 1990 Novembe

Cradle Temple P.214
Architect: Von Jour Caux
Location: Nagahashi town, Aza, Taira, Iwaki city, Fukushima
Principal use: Temple, Hall
Completion date: 1992 June

Trip to Carnival P.220
Architect: Von Jour Caux
Location: Izumi, Suginami-ku, Tokyo
Principal use: Housing complex
Completion date: 1992 September

主な作品

1994年	四季彩一力（日本旅館・福島県磐梯熱海温泉）
1994年	台付欅の家（住宅・埼玉県川越市）
1997年	仙寿庵（日本旅館・群馬県谷川温泉）
1999年	貴祥庵（日本旅館・長野県浅間温泉）
2000年	仙寿庵・料理茶屋（日本旅館・群馬県谷川温泉）
2001年	グランド・ヘリテイジ・ガーデン
2002年	プリスクール水輝（保育園・福島県会津若松市）
2003年	MUSA取手（共同住宅・茨城県取手市）
2005年	大和の湯（温泉施設・千葉県成田市）
2005年	銀座久兵衛 別館（寿司屋・東京都中央区銀座）
2007年	サイプレスリゾート久米島（改装・沖縄県久米島町）
2007年	銀座久兵衛 本店（寿司屋・改装・東京都中央区銀座）
2008年	湧雲の望楼（埼玉県比企郡）
2008年	銀座久兵衛 京王プラザ店 （寿司屋・改装・東京都新宿区）
2009年	会津中央病院 WEST2（福島県会津若松市）
2010年	会津中央病院 WEST1（改装・福島県会津若松市）
2015年	会津中央病院 EAST CENTER（福島県会津若松市）

主な受賞及び発表など

1995年	JCDデザイン賞入選「四季彩一力」
1996年	第16回東北建築賞「四季彩一力」
1998年	1998年日本建築仕上学会・学会賞「仙寿庵」
1998年	日経NEXT PHASE公開セミナー講演
1998年	テクノテル・ホスピタリティ展示招待（ジェノヴァ）
2001年	2000年度日本建築学会北陸建築デザイン賞「貴祥庵」
2004年	第22回福島県建築文化賞「プリスクール水輝」

著書

| 2006年 | 『和風モダン 建築デザイン術
蘇る日本の伝統技法』（六耀社） |

略歴
羽深隆雄

建築家
株式会社 羽深隆雄・栴工房設計事務所
代表取締役

1945年	新潟県上越市生まれ
1975年	栴工房設計事務所設立
1989年10月5日	株式会社 羽深隆雄・ 栴工房設計事務所に改める

株式会社 羽深隆雄・栴工房設計事務所
〒171-0014 東京都豊島区池袋2-59-2-504
TEL : 03-3980-0245
Email : senkobo@pop02.odn.ne.jp
WEB : http://senkobo.co.jp/

Prominent Projects

1994 Shikisai Ichiriki Hotel (Atami, Koriyama city, Fukushima)

1994 House of Zelkova (Kawagoe city, Saitama)

1997 Senjuan Hotel (Tone-gun, Gunma)

1999 Kishoan (Asama Springs, Nagano)

2000 Senjuan Hotel, Restaurant (Tone-gun, Gunma)

2001 Grand Heritage Garden

2002 Preschool Mizuki (Aiduwakamatu city, Fukushima)

2003 MUSA Toride (Toride city, Ibaraki)

2005 YamatonoYu (Narita city, Chiba)

2005 Ginza Kyubey Annex
(Sushi restaurant・Ginza, Chuo-ku, Tokyo)

2007 Cypressresort Kumejima
(Remodeling・Kumejima town, Okinawa)

2007 Ginza Kyubey Main Restaurant
(Sushi restaurant・Remodeling・Ginza, Chuo-ku, Tokyo)

2008 Wakigumo no Boroh (Tokigawa city, Saitama)

2008 Ginza Kyubey Keio Plaza Hotel Tokyo
(Sushi restaurant・Remodeling・Shinjuku-ku, Tokyo)

2009 Aidu Chuo Hospital West2 (Aiduwakamatu city, Fukushima)

2010 Aidu Chuo Hospital West1
(Remodeling・Aiduwakamatu city, Fukushima)

2015 Aidu Chuo Hospital East Center
(Aiduwakamatu city, Fukushima)

Prominent Awards and Presentations

1995 JCD Design Award – for Shikisai Ichiriki Hotel.

1996 16th Tohoku Architecture Award – for Shikisai Ichiriki Hotel.

1998 Annual Japan Architecture Finishing Award –
for Senjuan Hotel.

1998 Nikkei Next Phase Seminar.

1998 Techno-Hospitality Convention,
Genova, Italy.Invitational spesker.

2001 2000 Japan Architecture Society Hokuriku Award –
for Kishoan.

2004 22nd Fukushima Architecture Award – for Preschool Mizuki.

Author

2006 Modern Japanese Style Architecture Refined Technique of
Classic Architecture (Rikuyosha Co.,Ltd.)

Biography
Takao Habuka

Architect
Takao Habuka /
S.E.N. Architect Associates President

1945	Born in Joetsu city, Niigata.
1975	Founded S.E.N. Architect Associates.
1989.10.5	Renamed office to Takao Habuka / S.E.N. Architect Associates.

TAKAO & S.E.N.Architect Associates Inc.
#504, 2-59-2 IKEBUKURO
TOSHIMA-WARD, TOKYO, JAPAN
Phone : +81-3-3980-0245
Email : senkobo@pop02.odn.ne.jp
WEB : http://senkobo.co.jp/

略歴
梵 寿綱

建築家

1934年　東京都生まれ
1962年　アメリカへ留学
1963年　REMINGTON-RAND
　　　　LIBRARY BEAUREUX 勤務
1965年　アメリカとメキシコ周遊を経て帰国
1966年　株式会社 梵 設計作務室設立
1974年　梵寿綱を名乗り、
　　　　梵寿綱とその仲間たちを結成、
　　　　アート・コンプレックス運動を開始

主な作品

1967年　ある美瑠（田中俊郎名義）
1975年　Art ComplexⅠ　阿維智（宮城県）
1977年　Art ComplexⅡ　秘羅橲（東京都板橋区）
1979年　Art ComplexⅢ　斐醴祈（東京都豊島区）
1983年　Art ComplexⅣ　和世陀（東京都新宿区）
1984年　Art ComplcxⅥ　精霊の館（東京都豊島区）
1985年　Art ComplexⅤ　無量寿舞（東京都東大和市）
1989年　Art ComplexⅦ　和泉の扉（東京都杉並区）
1990年　Art ComplexⅧ　きらめく器（東京都豊島区）
1992年　Art ComplexⅨ　性源寺（福島県いわき市）
1992年　Art ComplexⅩ　舞都和亜（東京都杉並区）

＊梵寿綱（田中俊郎）による建築名称は、本人の希望により本書の制作時に
新たに付け直した。そのため、過去の出版物と名称が異なるものがある。一
部文中にて以前の名称を〔　〕内に記した。

Biography
Von Jour Caux

Architect

1934 Born in Tokyo.
1962 Study in the USA.
1963 Work for REMINGTON-RAND
　　　LIBRARY BEAUREUX.
1965 Mexico and USA tour, back to Japan.
1966 Founded Brahman Architects
　　　Office Co., Ltd..
1974 Changed name Von Jour Caux,
　　　To form "Von Jour Caux and his Troupe,"
　　　Started the movement Art Complex.

Prominent Projects

1967 Practice of Mandala (Toshiro Tanaka)
1975 Art Complex Ⅰ　Gladiator's Nest (Miyagi)
1977 Art Complex Ⅱ　Hiraki (Itabashi-ku, Tokyo)
1979 Art Complex Ⅲ　Condo Hiraki (Toshima-ku, Tokyo)
1983 Art Complex Ⅳ　Waseda el Dorado (Shinjuku-ku, Tokyo)
1984 Art Complex Ⅵ　Mundi Animus (Toshima-ku, Tokyo)
1985 Art Complex Ⅴ　Eternal Home (Higashiyamato city,Tokyo)
1989 Art Complex Ⅶ　Door to Fountain (Suginami-ku, Tokyo)
1990 Art Complex Ⅷ　Royal Vessel (Toshima-ku, Tokyo)
1992 Art Complex Ⅸ　Cradle Temple (Iwaki city, Fukushima)
1992 Art Complex Ⅹ　Trip to Carnival (Suginami-ku, Tokyo)

＊The names of works by Von Jour Caux (Toshiro Tanaka) were freshly re-
titled in the compilation of this book, in accordance with his requests. The
previous titles are provided in brackets in some passages.

あとがき

　僕の仕事は、祖国の日本では異端の建築と観られる一方で、
訪日外国人の目には日本でしか見ることができない現代建築と映るようだ。
「The Japan Times Weekly」(1992年8月8日付)に
「Gaudi's Ikebana of cement and steel sets root in Japan
(日本に根付いたガウディ)」と、巻頭4頁で特集紹介され、
以降世間では「日本のガウディ」の異名で馴染まれるようになった。

　シカゴのイリノイエ科大学に留学を志す以前の僕は、
日本の伝統的木造建築の空間構築技術を学んでいて、
その現代建築への再構築を志向していたが、
渡米後に留学校をシカゴ美術館附属芸術大学に代え、
先駆的な美術史を受講し、様式の奥にある意味を学び、
短期間勤めた家庭雑誌社で建築史上の様式が
デザイン情報として敷衍し、庶民住宅の内装にまで
浸透している事情を知り、建築家としての進路に多くの示唆を得た。

　それらの経験を踏まえて、帰国後に大学の建築科講師として、
空間のシステムデザイン講座を立ち上げたが、その第一期生として、
現在の僕の志の後継者で盟友の、羽深隆雄君が学んでいた。
その後僕は、「生命を紡ぎ伝える建築」という旗印として掲げた
インド仏教聖典・ウパニシャドの命題「梵我一如」の「梵」と、
養父が他界したのを期に戒名の「寿綱」を頂き「梵寿綱」を名乗り、
技芸建築運動を開始した。

　そして今ここに、久しく袂を分かっていた羽深隆雄君の
日本建築の魂を現代的に先駆した仕事と、
僕の彷徨の果てに残る軌跡がようやく出版の運びとなった。
この機会を与えてくれた盟友・羽深君に、深甚なる謝意を表する。

梵　寿綱

Epilogue

My home country of Japan viewed my work as nonconformist architecture,
while foreign visitors apparently appreciated such modern architecture found only in Japan.
My work was featured in "Gaudi's Ikebana of cement and steel sets root in Japan,"
which ran on the top four pages of The Japan Times Weekly (Aug 8, 1992).
Since then, my work became known in society as "Gaudi of Japan."

Before deciding to study abroad at the Illinois Institute of Technology,
I studied space construction techniques of traditional Japanese wooden architecture,
for which I endeavored to reconstruct in terms of modern architecture.
After my arrival in the United States, however, my institution of study changed to the
School of the Art Institute of Chicago. I took courses in pioneering art history,
studied the implications to the depths beyond style, and learned how—during brief
employment at a lifestyle magazine firm—styles in architectural history
had infused design information and pervaded the interiors of commonplace housing.
In sum, I gained much perspective for my career as an architect.

Armed with these experiences, I initiated a course on Systematic Design
Programming as a university lecturer upon my return to Japan.
In the first annual class of that course, Takao Habuka, my colleague and
successor in spirit, was a student.

Later, I held up the Indian Buddhist Scripture Upanishad and its proposition
Tat Tvam Asi (Japanese rendering: Von Ga Ichi Nyo) as the mantra to
"architecture that spins and transfers life together." I took "Von" from the proposition
and "Jour Caux" from the posthumous Buddhist name of my foster father,
and launched the Art Complex Movement.

The pioneering contemporary work on the soul of Japanese architecture by
Takao Habuka, from whom I had parted ways for some time, and the surviving
annals of my wanderings far afield have come together for publication in this book.

I express my deepest gratitude to my colleague Habuka-kun
who provided me with this opportunity.

Von Jour Caux, 2017

Praise for the Life
Works of Architects Takao Habuka
with mentor Von Jour Caux

Published 22 February, 2017
First Edition

Edited and Writed
Von Jour Caux, Takao Habuka

Editor
Masae Nazuka (Bijutsu Shuppan-sha, Co., Ltd.)

Assistant Editor
Shinpei Muraoka
(TAKAO HABUKA & S.E.N. Architect Associates Inc.)
Ichiko Enomoto

Cover Design
Hiroshi Ohmizo (Glanz)

Design
Yu Amano (RuffGong DesignStudio)

Photo
Hiroshi Kobayashi (P.011)
Akio Iwanaga (P.153)

Translation
Michael E. Narron
Miyuki Narron
(P.018-057, 068-133)
Von Jour Caux
(P.153-233)

Printing and Bindin
Mitsumura Printing Co., Ltd.

Publisher
Kazuo Nakanishi
Tomoharu Inoue

Published by
Bijutsu Shuppan-sha, Co., Ltd.
B1, La Fuente Daikanyama, 11-1 Sarugaku-cho,
Shibuya-ku, Tokyo 150-0033 JAPAN
+81-3-6809-0673 (editional)
+81-3-6809-0318 (sales)
Transfer: 00110-6-323989
http://www.bijutsu.press

ISBN 978-4-568-60045-2 C0052
Printed in Japan

All rights reserved.

©2017 Bijutsu Shuppan-sha, Co., Ltd.
©2017 Von Jour Caux and Takao Habuka

生命の讃歌
建築家　梵 寿綱＋羽深隆雄

2017年2月22日
初版 第1刷発行

編集・執筆
梵 寿綱、羽深隆雄

編集
名塚雅絵（美術出版社）

編集協力
村岡晋平（羽深隆雄・梅工房設計事務所）
榎本市子

カバーデザイン
大溝 裕（Glanz）

デザイン
天野 優（RuffGong DesignStudio）

撮影
小林浩志（P.011）
岩永明男（P.153）

翻訳
ナロン マイケル
ナロン 美由紀
（P.018-057, 068-133）
梵 寿綱
（P.153-233）

印刷・製本
光村印刷株式会社

発行人
中西一雄
井上智治

発行
株式会社美術出版社
〒150-0033 東京都渋谷区猿楽町11-1
ラ・フェンテ代官山アネックスB1
電話　03-6809-0673（編集）　03-6809-0318（営業）
振替　00110-6-323989
http://www.bijutsu.press

落丁・乱丁の本がございましたら、小社宛にお送りください。
送料小社負担でお取り替えいたします。
本書の全部または一部を無断で複写複製（コピー）することは
著作権上の例外を除き、禁じられています。